virgin film

MARTIAL ARTS

PTJ Rance

First published in Great Britain in 2005
by Virgin Books Ltd
Thames Wharf Studios
Rainville Road
London
W6 9HA

A catalogue record for this book is available from the British Library.

ISBN 0 7535 1086 3

Typeset by TW Typesetting, Plymouth, Devon
Printed and bound in Great Britain by Mackays of Chatham PLC

For my family: Dave, Sheila and Sian;
and my kung fu brothers and sisters

Contents

Acknowledgements

With thanks to: Kirstie Addis and Gareth Fletcher at Virgin Books; Fujian White Crane Kung Fu Chief Instructor Master Dennis Ngo Kah Swee; my kung fu instructor Dave Courtney Jones; Russell Suthern for showing me the White Crane way; Danil Mikhailov for his knowledge of the history of kung fu; Sharmin Ahmed, Adam Horner and Shkar Sharif for allowing me to plunder their DVD collections; everyone at FWC City and Islington for their unrelenting support, enthusiasm and bright ideas; J Clive Matthews for the opportunity and the advice; Ryan Bonder for the contacts; Alex Hogg and Brian Robinson at the British Film Institute; Terence Heng at Shaw Brothers; the staff at the British Film Institute Library for pursuing some very obscure sources; Albert Chen for *Crouching Tiger* and *Volcano High*, among other things; Michael 'Jed' Hills for his faith and his taste in anime; Nick Buglione for editorial consultation services; Ben Letton and the *TMNT*; Phil Adams, Iain Macintosh and Jess Sinclair for putting up with me during the creative process; Dave, Sheila and Sian Rance for always being there; and Shaun Nickless, for everything, forever.

Introduction: Enter the Dragon

There are many reasons for picking up this book. It could be the iconic image of the late Bruce Lee on the cover, or your passion for the early work of the ever-exuberant Jackie Chan. Perhaps you've seen *Crouching Tiger, Hidden Dragon* and want to know where you can get more of Zhang Ziyi somersaulting through the air, sword in hand. You may just have watched *Kung Fu Hustle* and be wondering if there is anything to martial arts films beyond high-octane slapstick, or you might own the entire Yuen Biao back catalogue. Whatever the case, if Jet Li going wild in *Unleashed* or Uma Thurman finally killing Bill marks the beginning or the fulfilment of a love affair with martial movies, then this book is for you. The only criterion for reading it is that you get a kick out of watching action inspired by the fighting arts of Asia, and you're hungry for more.

This book is not intended to be an exhaustive account of every martial arts film ever made. There are far too many, hundreds pouring out of the studios of Hong Kong in the 1970s alone, and the genre is too broad for a book of this size to do them all justice. There are more styles of martial art than there are films examined here. This book is not an encyclopaedia of martial arts movies, although, with the sheer number that exist, such a tome is very useful. One of the best in that category is *Videohound's Dragon: Asian Action and Cult Flicks* by Brian Thomas, which includes plot breakdowns and reviews of hundreds of Asian films released on DVD and video in the last few decades. It does not, however, have a particular focus on martial arts. In contrast, this book traces the development of martial arts films as a genre from their roots in 1920s China to modern Asian productions, the incursion into Hollywood and expansion throughout the world. In doing so, it celebrates both the diversity of the genre and its recurring themes.

The 1960s and 70s saw the production of a tidal wave of martial arts films, spawning a cult which still has a horde of devotees today. The introduction of Chinese language kick flicks to the West was spearheaded by the Hong Kong production houses like Shaw Brothers, American studio Warner Brothers and an actor called Bruce Lee. With the release of *Crouching Tiger,*

Hidden Dragon by US-based Taiwanese director Ang Lee, the cult became mainstream.

Today, with kick flicks from *Hero* to *Rush Hour* performing well in the Western box-office as well as topping the charts in the East, the genre has reached an unprecedented level of popularity. Hollywood has adopted Asian martial arts as its own. The Wachowski Brothers' *The Matrix* made kung fu an essential ingredient of action movies. This book is intended to feed the desire of both long-time fans and new converts to know more about modern chopsocky and martial chivalry films, while placing them within the context of their cult and classic predecessors. Its purpose is to provide a coherent introduction to the vast array of martial arts films out there, making them more accessible to both dabblers and devotees. It is a book for anyone who has thrilled to the sight of Jet Li pirouetting through the air, flinched exquisitely as Tony Jaa destroys an opponent with his elbow or realised that the language barrier presented by *House of Flying Daggers* is no bar to appreciation of the film. Reviewing iconic and seminal martial arts films, it presents their most influential directors and actors, explores the constant themes that run through them and charts their place in the growth of the genre.

The films

Each chapter focuses on a different branch of martial arts films: the early days in China, the Hong Kong boom years, the 'modern Asian classics', Hollywood, the rest of the world, and the appearance of martial arts on the small screen. Following an overview of the sub-section of the genre is a more in-depth analysis of the films that typify it. As only twenty films and television series are covered, some readers may be outraged by the exclusion of their favourite films, or surprised by those that have been selected. But there is method behind the apparent madness. The movies have been chosen, from the vast array of potential subjects, because they fulfil a number of genre-defining criteria.

Imitation is the highest form of flattery, and nowhere is this more true than in the martial arts film industry. Each of the movies covered is the originator of a successful series, has a sequel, or at the very least has spawned a number of copycat releases. Between them they star the biggest names in the business and were made by its most important directors. The films' influence can be seen throughout the development of the genre and they are each representative of a particular aspect of it; through them it is possible to trace many of its key themes. And, for a variety of reasons, they each have a loyal following of fans. Most of them are even pretty good. For their part, the TV programmes reflect the various factors and attributes that have made martial arts successful on the small screen, and each has drawn from and influenced the genre in its own way.

In order to make cross-referencing within the book easier, wherever one of the reviewed films is mentioned elsewhere in the text, it is highlighted in bold. The examination of each film is divided, where appropriate, into the following sections:

CREDITS: Country of origin, date of original release and running time. Listing of production companies, directors, martial arts co-ordinators, producers, writers, cinematographers and composers. Cast list of leading roles, and notable actors and martial artists appearing in smaller or uncredited parts.

EPISODES: For the television series, the title of every episode is listed.

PLOT: A breakdown of the story-line, which may include spoilers: you have been warned.

CASTING: The individual talents, attributes and other film credits of the actors in the lead roles, and how their casting denotes particular types of martial arts films.

MARTIAL ARTS: The styles and systems of martial arts used in the film, whether they are weapons or open-hand based, how authentic the techniques represented are, and the relevance of the particular styles to the nature of the film.

STUNTS AND SPECIAL EFFECTS: An account of the film's most spectacular fight scenes and set piece stunts. Any special effects and enhancement techniques used, or the lack of them, such as wire-fu, animation and computer generated imagery.

DIRECTOR: The role of the director in representing martial arts on screen, their other productions and how they have influenced the development of the genre as a whole.

PRODUCTION: The production techniques that set the film apart, and how they enhance or detract from the overall effect, including camera work, sets, locations, music, costumes and budgets.

TRIVIA: Outtakes, anecdotes, comedy moments and little-known details.

THEMES: One of the things that unite martial arts films and allow them to be grouped as a genre is the consistent themes which run through them. While no film features every theme, each includes several of the following: the tournament; family loyalty; vengeance and revenge; the hopeless student becomes the master; gang warfare; competing schools and styles; Buddhist, Taoist or Confucian morality; spirituality; magic; comedy; nostalgic recollection of ancient ways; traditional values versus the encroachment of modernity; romance; the outsider; national pride; your kung fu is no good!; the student-teacher relationship. Many of these themes have their roots in Asian culture, and martial arts films offer an insight into aspects of, among others, Chinese, Thai, Korean and Japanese traditions.

PLACE WITHIN THE GENRE: The role of the film in the development of the genre as a whole, and where it sits in relation to other movies. Why it is typical of a particular class of martial arts film, and what is unique about it. Comparisons to other films, where its influences have come from and where it is referenced in the rest of the genre.

Summary

Each chapter will end with a critique of the films covered, a review of their importance and a kick-arse action rating. Throughout the chapters there are boxed sections detailing the careers of some of the genre's most famous and influential actors, their films, biographies, trademarks and trivia.

MARTIAL ARTS Introduction: Enter the Dragon

Access to the films

The Asian film industry, and therefore the martial arts genre, is one of the most difficult to research, for a number of reasons. Firstly, during the peak boom years when hundreds of films were being produced, many had a brief cinema release and were then discarded, since it was considered pointless to store them or transfer them to video for commercial sale. Many of the older films have only survived in part, and the preserved prints are often of appalling quality. Since the 1990s, however, Hong Kong Legends and its subsidiary Premier Asia have been buying the rights to distribute classic martial arts movies on video and DVD. They have led the way in remastering previously neglected films, releasing prints with superior image and sound quality, produced at the price of painstaking work. Subtitles have been carefully written to reflect both the words and the meaning of the dialogue, and dubbing is designed to lip-synch. This work has encouraged other production companies to follow suit and has greatly improved the quality of the films on offer.

The recent surge in popularity of Asian martial movies has led to the re-release of many titles which are now available in the West, online and in cult film stores, and even on the shelves of high-street video shops. More obscure titles can be found through Asian distributors, although there is a risk of buying copies without dubbing or subtitling. The most important acquisition for anyone planning to become a kick flick aficionado is a multi-region DVD player.

Names and language

Another factor that makes the genre hard to explore is the language barriers, especially when it comes to names. Every Chinese film has several titles, in both Cantonese and Mandarin, and all of the films released in the West are guaranteed to have appeared under a variety of English names, differing between Europe and North America. In order to capitalise on the subsequent success of actors, titles have been changed for later releases: this is particularly true of any movie involving Bruce Lee. Films released out of chronological order in the West have been retitled to make the earlier productions sound like sequels: *Way of the Dragon*, the Bruce Lee vehicle made before his enormous US hit *Enter the Dragon*, was released in America under the title *Return of the Dragon*, presented as a sequel to feed off the popularity of the more recent film. Actors' names have also been inserted into the titles of their films after they have become more famous. The desire to cash in on big hits has sometimes resulted in totally unrelated films, with entirely different casts and directors, being presented as sequels to earlier movies. Jackie Chan's 1996 outing *First Strike* has been variously titled *Jackie Chan's First Strike* and *Police Story 4*, to link it to the successful detective series. Of course, it is also known as *Police Story 4: Piece of Cake*, *CIA Story*, *Ging Chat Goo Si 4*, *Ji Gaan Daan Yam Mo*, *Jing Cha Gu Shi 4* and *Zhi Jian Dan Ren Wu*, just to make things a bit more confusing.

In an attempt to simplify matters, the films in this book are referred to by their most common English release titles, where they have one, or by their original language title. Even this policy creates some difficulty, as films are commonly released under different names in the UK and the US, distributors translate titles differently, Mandarin language films are made in Hong Kong, Mainland Chinese studios produce Cantonese titles, and Japanese movies are released with Mandarin soundtracks, then dubbed into English. Each film is therefore listed with its alternative titles to assist in their identification.

Translation issues do not affect just the names of films: those of the cast and crew can also have as many as ten variants. Chinese names appear differently in Cantonese and Mandarin, Korean and Japanese names can be written in English with the surname appearing at the beginning, middle or end and still be correct, and when names are translated from Asian characters to Latinate alphabets there are often inconsistencies in the spelling. Added to this, there are two methods of romanising Chinese, the Wade-Giles system and Pinyin. And sometimes the translators just make it up. Actors are the most guilty of multiple name syndrome: screen names, birth names, truncated names and Western names all add to the range of their monikers, along with an injection of creative spelling. Brigitte Lin, androgynous star of camp kung fu classics *The Bride with White Hair* and *Zu: Warriors from the Magic Mountain*, has also been credited as Lin Chiang-Hsia, Lam Ching-Ha, Lin Qing Xia and Venus Lin. The various names actors have been known by are listed in the boxed sections on their careers. Directors and martial arts choreographers are referred to by their most common names, although where this is debatable alternative versions have been noted.

So this is the disclaimer: when it comes to consistency of language use, this book claims none. This is suitably in keeping with the genre as a whole, which refuses to follow any system and uses whatever phrase is most convenient. Mandarin terms are used when they developed in Mainland China, and Cantonese words are applied to Hong Kong-specific phenomena: wuxia pian and gung-fu pian are branches of the same genre, although the terms come from different dialects. Thankfully, the written word circumvents the need to try to pronounce them as well.

Errata

Every effort has been made to ensure that the information in this book is accurate. Bearing in mind that some films no longer exist, remaining records of them have not been translated into English, and movies, cast and crew can be known by multiple permutations of their names, there is a small and uncontrollable margin of error. But then, in a book on a genre filled with continuity errors, incomprehensible plot-lines and subtitles including such classics as 'My kung fu is the bestest in all the martial arts world!', the occasional inconsistency is entirely appropriate.

Dirty Tiger, Crazy Frog: The Martial Arts

This is a book about martial arts films, but it does not cover films on all forms of martial art. In the broadest sense, everything from Greco-Roman wrestling to archery could be described using that tag, so long as the discipline is a fighting form and involves the mastery of set principles and techniques. But face it: films in which the great sumo champions push each other around the ring for hours or anonymous fencers leap back and forth sticking each other with pins are unlikely to inspire and amaze audiences, or become box-office smashes across the world.

The martial arts film genre examined by this book is composed of movies showcasing the high-kicking, fast-punching, sword-slashing Chinese and south-east Asian martial arts. Judo and sumo have no place here. And while anyone can enjoy the spectacle of assailants flying through the air to deliver head-crushing blows, in order to have a true appreciation of the films in this very broad genre and of the martial expertise displayed, it helps to have at least a basic understanding of the different fighting styles. Recognising the origins of skills shown on screen also helps in placing the films within the development of the genre: as with anything, fashions come and go, from the sword-wielding warriors of the early martial chivalry films to today's movies with their balletic displays of modern wushu.

The styles of fighting used by the protagonists in these movies are defined by the talents of the performers, and are also fundamental to many plot-lines. The triumph of one martial school over another is a popular theme, as is conflict between rival gangs bonded by their fighting style. In *Volcano High*, the school is ruled by the sports clubs: the weightlifters, kendo team and karate kids all fight for dominance and the right to be The One. In *Fist of Fury*, the Japanese Bushido School is intent on proving the inferiority of kung fu, as practised by a rival organisation. Mastery of an ancient style, the development of a new one and the superiority of one system over another are all common elements.

The easiest way of differentiating between the Asian martial arts styles – and therefore the films that portray them – is by their country of origin. While an enormous number of kick flicks have come out of the studios of Hong Kong, China and Taiwan, Thailand, Japan and Korea cannot be ignored. Each brings its own fighting systems to the big screen, and nationalistic conflicts are often represented by the contrasting ways in which different nationalities fight. Predictably – and somewhat embarrassingly – the British, armed with their rifles and stiff upper lips, are universally portrayed as bumbling and ineffectual: witness Jet Li's British-bullet-dodging antics in *Once Upon a Time in China* and the inept colonial commander who gets himself kidnapped in *Project A*.

Within each country, too, there are many competing martial systems, with practitioners refining ancient techniques to suit their own needs. This chapter is not an in-depth analysis of the development of Asian fighting styles, but instead offers a brief overview of those you are likely to encounter when delving into the world of martial arts films. The information provided on the different martial arts explains how to tell them apart, highlights classic films that illustrate the highest level of performance in each, and outlines how they developed. Every style is covered in its basic, open-hand form. While most also utilise weapons, these are too many and varied to cover in detail here. In this chapter the reader will discover where all that staff-wielding, nanchuku-swinging, sword-thrusting behaviour comes from.

Kung fu

In the immortal words of the ever-funky Carl Douglas, everybody was kung fu fighting, or so it would seem from the vast catalogue of kung fu films made over the last four decades. The terms 'martial arts film' and 'kung fu film' are virtually interchangeable in many cases, and the latter is commonly, although inaccurately, used to describe the entire genre. The problem arises when you actually try to define it: 'kung fu' is a very general term. Literally, it is the Anglicisation of a Cantonese phrase meaning 'hard work'. This relates to the training and the effort needed to attain any level of skill rather than its practice – as any fan of the chopsocky genre knows, the true artist makes it all look effortless. Perhaps a more accurate translation would be 'patient achievement', the investment of energy ('kung') and time ('fu') to achieve enlightenment. Although whether or not The Bride reached this hallowed state by repeatedly smashing her fist into a board in *Kill Bill Volume 2* is debatable.

The histories of Asian martial arts are generally obscured by the mists of time and legend and are the subject of much debate, but it would probably be fair to say that the majority of them stem from kung fu. Distinctly Chinese martial arts are known to have been practised since the Bronze Age. Surviving historical records focus on weapons training rather than unarmed combat, and differ from the Western martial styles of the time because of their links with Chinese philosophy and medicine. During the last few centuries BC, while European tribes were running around clubbing each other with iron bars, the Chinese were developing the theories of Taoism, the balance of yin and yang and the flow of internal energy or 'chi'. These were used in the practice of fighting styles that harmonised with the opponent, employing breathing techniques and energy flow to produce power.

Although little is known about the origins of Chinese martial arts and specifically kung fu, the later development had a lot to do with monks. The accepted mythology is that in the fifth century AD, the Buddhist prince and monk Bodhidharma, also known as Ta Mo, and as Daruma in Japan, came from India to the Shaolin temple at Songshan – the setting for a hundred kung fu films – and taught the tenets of Zen Buddhism. He also happened to expound a keep-fit doctrine, teaching the feeble monks a series of exercises that strengthened mind and body and assisted their meditation. He himself was so good at meditating that he managed to keep it up for nine years, allegedly staring at a wall until he bored a hole in it. Although there is no proof that Bodhidharma taught fighting techniques, the chi breathing he introduced became the basis for all forms of kung fu and many other martial arts.

Chinese kung fu is divided between northern and southern, and internal and external styles. The differences between them are marked, although many use elements of other styles to complement their basic principles. Northern styles tend to focus on kicking, hence the caricature of the meathead Northern King of Kicks in *Tai Chi Boxer*. In the south, boxing styles are favoured, with emphasis on arm techniques.

One of the best things about kung fu is the outlandish names given to its moves and styles. In 1530 the priest Chueh Yuan rejuvenated the Shaolin martial tradition by creating the five basic animal forms: Dragon for spirit; Tiger to gain tough bones; Leopard to build strength; Crane for sinew; and Snake to develop chi. Animal styles are very popular in kick flicks, for their comedic as well as dramatic properties – Jackie Chan knows them all and demonstrates them in *Wooden Men*. Usually, however, practitioners focus on a single style and take on the characteristics of a given animal. So White Crane involves delicate stepping, wing-like blocks and fish-impaling strikes; Dog style requires a lot of rolling around on the floor; Monkey stylists leap about, in the manner of Donnie Yen in *Iron Monkey*; proponents of Cat style screech and scratch like the crazy Wildcat in *Magnificent Butcher*; and Praying Mantis is composed of the sprung, staccato movements portrayed by Jackie Wu in *Tai Chi Boxer*. Tiger style, while sounding really cool, actually involves some ridiculous gurning and baring of teeth.

The role of the Shaolin Temple in the development of kung fu has led to a number of star turns by the monastery in kung fu films. It was a centre of excellence, where masters came to live and teach for several years, exchanging knowledge and techniques. These masters enriched Shaolin kung fu with new styles, as well as drawing on the skills of the monks, much like the character played by Bruce Lee in *Enter the Dragon*.

The diversity of kung fu techniques increased following the dispersal of the Shaolin monks after the Manchurian invasion of China in 1644. The despotic Ming dynasty was overthrown and the Qing era began, setting the scene for many a kick flick. Revolutionaries hid out in the temples and trained to fight the oppressors. In retaliation, the Qing destroyed the monasteries and the monks fled, taking with them the tenets of kung fu. So it spread among the populace, but in diluted form, and many new styles developed, including the hilarious – and deadly – drunken boxing practised by Jackie Chan in *Drunken Master*. Hundreds exist today, and the most enduring action film stars have mastered several of them.

Kung fu's dark side also stems from this period, when it became inextricably linked with the triads, the Chinese mafia. The resistance organisations set up to undermine the Qing Dynasty, like the eponymous *House of Flying Daggers*, were succoured by the Shaolin Temple and trained in kung fu to increase their chances of defeating the oppressors. They were widespread in southern China, and became very powerful on a local level, protecting but also controlling agriculture and trade, much as the 'Friends' did in Sicily. Under the Japanese during World War II, the triads became powerful crime lords. They are often to be found as the evil influence in martial arts films, such as the Japanese gun-fu movie *Returner*, in which they engage in child smuggling, as well as the usual murder and drug dealing.

The continuous competition between styles in China meant that the proponents of ineffectual ones ended up dead. Defeated masters would lose their students to the victor. The superiority of one style over another is a common theme in kung fu films, and seems particularly popular with Jackie Chan, perhaps because he knows so many. *Young Master* and *Snake and Crane: Arts of Shaolin* both revolve around studying the 'ultimate' style, which then allows the hero to conquer all. In reality, of course, it is not the style but the proficiency of the fighter that makes the difference. It is all about hard work, as shown in the brutal training scenes in traditional kung fu movies, like *36th Chamber of Shaolin*. Sorry, Keanu, but there's no plugging yourself into a computer and them proclaiming 'I know kung fu!' ten minutes later.

T'ai chi

Balancing the dark side of kung fu is the light, the Taoist creation t'ai chi. While the traditional forms of kung fu demonstrated in martial arts films are often hard, external styles, there is a yin to their yang: t'ai chi, the soft style, performed in harmony with an opponent's moves and, when done correctly, the deadliest hand fighting form in existence. By slowly building internal strength, using the whole body as a means of transferring power and turning an enemy's force against them, t'ai chi allows small, light fighters to beat larger opponents. It's not just about old people wearing pyjamas and waving their arms around in parks, as Jet Li effectively proves in *Tai Chi Master*.

Not to be outdone by the Shaolin Buddhists, the Taoist monks adopted kung fu and shaped its development. It is thought that at some point in the fourteenth century the monk Chang San-Feng created the 'soft fist' internal style. Leaving Shaolin, he is said to have become a Taoist hermit on Wudan Mountain (the spiritual home of the warriors from *Crouching Tiger, Hidden Dragon*), abandoning hard kung fu for a softer, more yielding style. Still taught as a fighting form, it was nonetheless slower and more relaxed, focused on internal energy and harmony, and so more in line with Taoist teachings. T'ai chi chuan, 'mind fist', is a direct development of these theories. Chang San-Feng is alleged to have said, 'In every movement, every part of the body must be light and agile and strung together.' This is the foundation of t'ai chi.

Since that time, many internal styles have formed, including sheng-i and bagua. Emphasising stability, with few jumps and kicks, t'ai chi chuan has divided into several 'families'. The most common are Yang, Chen, Wu, Sun and Woo, all of which are derived from the original Chen family style.

Modern wushu

Wushu, the 'art of war', is a term that could be used to describe all martial arts, old and new. In fact, it is a more accurate name than kung fu, which is overused in the West due to the influence of Hong Kong kung fu films released since the 1960s. Today wushu is a very specific performance art form, practised by many of the actors in martial arts films. It was established in Nanjing, China in 1920, and has since become the country's national sport, supported by the government as a means of celebrating Chinese culture. Taught in state schools and dedicated academies, it is one of the fastest growing martial arts in the world.

With its high kicking, flexible moves and emphasis on speed, wushu is the perfect discipline for the martial arts film star, combining traditional skills with the showmanship demanded by modern audiences. Jet Li and Donnie Yen both trained with the Beijing Wushu Team. Since it is more a competitive sport than a fighting art, emphasis is placed on the beauty of movement, flow, and difficulty in set patterns of moves, bare handed or using lightweight versions of traditional weapons. Group routines are carefully choreographed, and the winner is the one with most points, not the one left standing.

The gymnastic feats performed in modern wushu can be traced to the legacy of the Beijing opera that for 200 years has been the height of Chinese cultural expression. As well as singing, dancing and dialogue, the opera includes acrobatic fighting. Some of the greatest martial arts film stars in the world, including Jackie Chan, Sammo Hung and Yuen Biao, trained in the Beijing opera from a very young age, learning skills that were themselves rooted in ancient Chinese martial arts.

Wing chun

Wing chun, the martial style studied by Bruce Lee in Hong Kong, has its origins in the destruction of the Shaolin monastery. According to Lee's teacher, Yip Man, the nun Ng Mui escaped the temple and taught the basics of kung fu to Yim Wing-Chun so that the girl could defend herself against unwanted suitors. Yim then used her skills to help the people against the oppression of the Manchurian government. Wing chun, the basis of the film of the same name starring Michelle Yeoh and Donnie Yen, is an effective street-fighting style which is quick to learn, incorporating the fundamental principles of Chinese martial arts without their inherent complexity.

Karate

While karate can trace its roots back to Bodhidharma and Shaolin, through its basic principles and the history of Okinawa, it is noticeably different from traditional forms of kung fu, and even more so from modern wushu. This has a great deal to do with the nature of its development. A harder, more rigid style, karate grew up in isolation on the island of Okinawa, practised by an oppressed people who were denied other means of defending themselves. In Chinese kick flicks, ironically, it is often the style used by the Japanese oppressors, as in *Fist of Fury* or the Western meatheads in *Enter the Dragon* and *Way of the Dragon*; it is a Chuck Norris speciality.

Before it became part of Japan, Okinawa was an independent island, a refuelling stop on the trade routes between China, Japan, Borneo, Thailand, Indo-China, Malaysia and the Philippines. Consequently the island was exposed to a number of styles of martial arts, which were then combined with its indigenous open-hand fighting techniques. The mixture of geography and history led to this tiny island off the coast of Japan becoming the home of one of the world's most popular martial arts.

In 1429 the rival kingdoms of Okinawa united and, to preserve the peace, weapons were banned. This worked for a couple of centuries, but proved disastrous when the island was invaded in 1609, since the new rulers found the people's lack of weapons very convenient. The Okinawans practised martial arts in secret, often at night: the pyjamas they trained in became the basis for the modern karate uniform, or gi. Known as te, meaning 'hand', their fighting style developed independently in different regions, each with its own emphasis. Shorei-ryu had steady, rooted actions, with synchronised breathing, while Shorin-ryu was a quick, linear style which used natural breathing. Parallels can be drawn between these two styles and hard, external kung fu contrasted with internal t'ai chi.

Universally known as Okinawa-te, these styles were also called tode, or 'Chinese hand'. The character for tode could also be pronounced 'kara', creating the name kara te-jutsu, or 'Chinese hand art'. Modern practitioners changed this to karate-do, using the alternative meaning of kara, 'empty', forming 'way of the empty hand'. This helped to enhance the appeal of karate to the Japanese, who were none too keen on the Chinese association.

Gichin Funakoshi, the father of modern karate, performed the first public demonstration of this secret art in Japan in 1917, impressing both Crown Prince Hirohito and the founder of judo, Dr Jano Kano. With such prestigious backing, the fighting style of the Okinawan farmers and fishermen took hold in Japan. Today, there are four main karate styles in Japan: shotokan, goju-ryu, shito-ryu and wado-ryu.

The way of the samurai

The majority of traditional Japanese martial films are about the code and skills of the samurai warriors. These are not kick flicks – you don't really need to kick your opponents if your plan is to dismember them with a razor-sharp sword – so much as blade-wielding blood-fests. And great fun they are too. The code of the samurai and its bloodthirsty adherents appear in a number of martial arts films, both Japanese and others. The evil Bushido

School master in Bruce Lee's *Fist of Fury* tries to dismember the hero with a katana until Lee manages to disarm him. Being a gent, Lee then throws down his nunchaku and takes him on barehanded. The fictional 'Hanzo sword', the finest made in the samurai style, is the weapon of choice for Uma Thurman's Bride – and anyone else who can get their hands on one – in the *Kill Bill* movies. The skill of the Japanese swordsmen is the defining theme of the *Lone Wolf and Cub* and *Zatôichi* films.

The katana is the ultimate sword. Its manufacturing process ensures the sharpest blade, and it has achieved almost legendary status in the martial arts genre. The men who once wielded these weapons were the bushi (warriors) who became a class in their own right in Japan between the ninth and twelfth centuries, a caste of knight-retainers who gave complete loyalty to their daimyo, the feudal lords whose land they protected.

Rather than swordplay, the first samurai fought with bow and arrow, often from horseback. This was more effective for driving off raiders and rustlers; swords were only used for close combat or beheading captured enemies. Things changed during the battles with the Mongols in the late thirteenth century, when fighting on foot with sword and spear began to take precedence. These are the skills of the samurai we recognise today, with their code of honour, loyalty and bravery: the bushido. Dishonour was unthinkable, and the somewhat painful alternative of seppuku – ritual self-disembowelment – was instituted as a means of saving face. Miyamoto Musashi in the classic text *The Book of Five Rings* says, 'the Way of the warrior is resolute acceptance of death'. So revered were the samurai that they had the right to cut down any commoner who caused them offence.

The sword was the keeper of the samurai's honour: it often had a name, and was regarded as the soul of the warrior. The samurai wore two swords, the wakizashi short sword and the katana, which was always more than 24 inches long. The oldest Asian sword is the Chinese straight sword, the jian, a weapon requiring infinite skill and delicacy of touch. The curved katana is a tougher, sharper weapon, designed for the heat of battle. Newly made blades were tested on the bodies of corpses or extremely unfortunate criminals.

In 1867 the samurai were banned from carrying swords, although many continued to do so, like the hero of *Zatôichi the*

Outlaw, concealed within canes. The samurai lost their position in society when feudalism ended in 1871 and, although they rebelled, they were no match for the national army. Leaderless samurai, or ronin, roamed the land, fighting as mercenaries, and it is these outlaw warriors who most often feature in Japanese heroic bloodshed films, such as the 1954 classic *Seven Samurai*.

Muay thai

Another non-Chinese martial art that will be familiar to even the casual viewer of kick flicks is kickboxing. Muay thai, traditional Thai kickboxing, is the most basically brutal of the Asian martial arts. Developed as a training technique by the ancient Siamese warriors, muay thai has become a physical art form at the heart of Thailand's identity. These days it is an international sport, with fixed rules and format, vying for inclusion in the Olympic Games. But even in its modern, stylised version, the legacy of a more violent time can still be seen.

Known as the 'science of eight limbs', muay thai makes use of fists, elbows, knees and feet, and the fighter wields each as though it were one of the weapons of ancient Siam. So the arms become twin swords, used for defence and attack, the fists jabbing like the tips of spears. The shins act as staffs which block and strike, trained to iron hardness by repeated knocking against walls and posts. The elbows and knees are the battleaxes, swung in an arc to crush and hack. And the feet, striking out at speed, are the arrows and blades. By transforming the body into an arsenal of weapons, the Thais developed a new, viciously offensive fighting style. The use of elbows and knees made it a close-range system that could be employed on the battlefield when all other options were exhausted, ensuring that the Siamese warriors were never unarmed. Even if they lost an arm.

Although muay thai has a long history, entwined with that of the country, it is not easy to trace. After the Burmese sacking of the Thai capital at Ayutthaya, many of the archives were lost, including historical accounts of the development of muay thai. Surviving records come from the Lanna Kingdom in Chiang Mai and from outside observers: these often contradict each other, but all agree on muay thai's usefulness in man-to-man combat on the battlefield.

Interest in muay thai as a sport grew under King Naresan in the 1580s. Every soldier, including the King, trained in it and new techniques evolved. Royalty was largely responsible for the future popularity of the sport: King Prachao Sua, the Tiger King, was so dedicated he fought incognito in local competitions. Contests took place everywhere: in villages, jungle clearings – any open space. No move was illegal: the winner was the last man standing, the fight lasting as long as it took for one to knock the other unconscious. Forearms were bound in rope for protection and power, with raw cotton wrapped around the fists, sometimes stuck with cut glass. The only protection from knee strikes to the groin was a guard made of shell or bark.

In 1929 boxing gloves were introduced as part of a standardisation process that brought muay thai into the ring and confined it to five three-minute rounds. Bouts are still accompanied by traditional music, the pi muay, which may seem oddly distracting to the uninitiated but helps to focus the fighters. Before each bout, the opponents perform the ram muay, a ritual dance which reflects the original, formalised spirit of muay thai. The contrast between old-style muay thai and modern competitions is starkly presented in *Kickboxer*, where the American 'World' Kickboxing Champion travels to Thailand to take on their best and is quickly taught a paralysing lesson in how it is really done. Later in the film, Jean-Claude Van Damme is challenged to fight in 'the old way', with rope-bound knuckles dipped in resin and ground glass.

In traditional training schools, the students swear an oath before they begin: 'I will look after myself so that I am clean, strong and behave with honesty. I will not bully the weaker. We will love one another, be united, and help one another wherever possible. I will do good deeds beneficial to others, and be loyal to the nation. I will avoid any case of disorder.' They are then free to beat the hell out of each other. But even in martial arts films, where muay thai is often used to represent the hardest, least elegant of fighting styles, there is a sense of honour and decency. So the disciple monk Ting in *Ong-Bak* refuses to use his deadly skills against others, until they force him to do so.

Tae kwon do

Korea's answer to muay thai, tae kwon do claims a 2,000-year history. It has been known as soobak, soobakhee, soobyuk, takkyeon, beekaksool, soobyukta and kwonbub, but every variation has the same roots. Its premise is that everyone has the natural instinct to protect themselves when attacked, and that this can be developed through training. It looks like people kicking each other. A lot. Many martial arts stars, notably Tony Jaa and Donnie Yen, have trained in tae kwon do to increase their kicking ability. Although punching, especially with the back of the fists, is part of tae kwon do training, the key moves are front and side kicks, often striking with the heel. The emphasis is on simplicity and versatility through the use of basic moves.

Evidence of the origins of tae kwon do has been found in the early kingdoms of Korea. Royal tombs house murals depicting the basic patterns and sparring stances of Soobakhee. Historians have dated the paintings from 3 AD to 427 AD, creating an argument for tae kwon do being the oldest formalised open-hand martial art in the world, preceding the development of Shaolin kung fu.

Further development of the martial art took place in the Silla kingdom, with its youth military system, the 'Hwa Rang Do'. It is on their martial training that tae kwon do is based. The Hwarang or 'Flower Knights', trained by the monk Won Kwang Bupsa, were responsible for a host of military victories. (Hwarang is also the name of the high-kicking Korean fighter in the video game *Tekken*.)

Under the Lee Dynasty (1392–1910), tae kwon do became the people's martial art. Its principles are recorded in the textbook *Mooyae Doba Tongjee*, which includes detailed diagrams and scientific explanations of the development of the style. This manual is mirrored in **One-Armed Swordsman**, in which the hero learns a unique fighting style from an ancient text. With the end of the Lee dynasty and the Japanese occupation, tae kwon do went underground, but it has experienced a resurgence in the last fifty years.

Hapkido

Korea has spawned another martial art that is popular in the movies: hapkido. A relatively modern style, it combines the force-redirection techniques of aikido and jujitsu, the joint locks and throws of kung fu and the kicks of tae kwon do. It also includes long and short stick techniques. Originally taught by Korean Buddhist monks, hapkido faded away with the introduction of Confucianism to the country. It re-emerged in the early twentieth century under the influence of Yong Sool Choi. One of his most promising students was Ji Han-Jae, who went on to star in a number of Hong Kong films.

Having impressed Bruce Lee when they met in 1972, Ji coached him in hapkido before starring as one of his adversaries in the fight scenes shot for *Game of Death*. Ji went on to appear with Sammo Hung in *Hapkido*, a film later renamed *Lady Kung Fu*, much to the disgust of the style's proponents. Indeed, they were also insulted by the speed with which Bruce Lee defeats Ji in *Game of Death*. Hapkido is the subject of much disagreement, as its lack of history has resulted in the development of a number of competing spin-off styles, with several masters claiming to follow the true way. This pattern reflects the path of development of many martial arts, as practitioners take what they can from traditional styles then add their own twist. The most extreme example of this is arguably Bruce Lee and the creation of jeet kune do.

Jeet kune do

Although he began his martial training in wing chun, Bruce Lee studied many different martial disciplines throughout his life, including muay thai, judo, jujitsu and several forms of kung fu, taking from each the elements that he felt to be most effective. In his own words, his intention was to 'absorb what is useful and reject that which is useless'. The result was jeet kune do, the 'way of no way', which proved to be devastating when practised by its creator. Although this martial art is still taught by the people who trained and studied with Lee, it can be argued that it is such a personal way of fighting it can be neither taught nor learned, only developed through an understanding of the human body and the way it is used in martial arts.

It is also unlikely that anyone will ever be as good at it as Lee was, given that he created jeet kune do out of his own knowledge and training, from many different strands of martial lore. By its

very nature, jeet kune do contains no patterns or forms to guide
the student, and requires that all formulaic moves be discarded.
Perhaps the best filmic record of jeet kune do is contained in the
fight scenes produced for *Game of Death*, shortly before Lee's
demise, although a fair representation of the style can be seen in
Way of the Dragon.

Once Upon a Time in China: The Beginnings of Martial Arts Films

Whatever route you take through the development of martial arts films, there is no question about where to begin: Mainland China in the 1920s. The Chinese film industry was founded in Shanghai in 1917, and it turned quite naturally to wuxia literature to supply stories for its silent films. Dating from the ninth century, these popular tales of martial chivalry draw on Chinese mythology, chronicling the adventures of heroic knights who travel the land righting wrongs. Set in an undefined period in China's distant past, they involve magic, swordplay, outlawry and lots of flying. Serialised stories were printed in newspapers from the nineteenth century onwards, and the well-known tales were dramatised in Chinese opera, the actors using martial acrobatics to enhance their performances.

The key elements of these stories are martial arts – wu – and the valiant knight-errant – the xia. Across their pages, heroes and villains battle for control and martial power. China's troubled history under a series of corrupt political regimes, rife with assassination and intrigue, had undermined the people's faith in the rule of law and made them look elsewhere for protection. The xia heroes, both male and female, came to represent justice, dealing out vengeance for wrongs done to the people from their position outside the system.

The most common motivation is revenge, grounded in the Confucian teachings of obligation to family and teacher. Following some great wrong done to their elders, the child or student takes matters into their own hands, using violence as the foil for vengeance. The xia are set apart from society by their willingness to become outcast, and use force to achieve their ends: individuals in a communal society. They flout authority and treat social superiors with contempt. Such egalitarian ideals were almost unheard of in traditional Chinese society.

The world through which the xia travel is the jianghu, a term originally used during the Ming dynasty to describe the place where hermits live. It came to represent a parallel universe – the underworld, and the world of martial arts – dominance of which is the theme of many wuxia tales. The literal translation of the jianghu is 'river-lake', an environment filled with secret societies and bandits. These underground organisations are often crucial in story-lines, like the one in *House of Flying Daggers*. If the wuxia have allegiance to anything, it is to these confederations of outlaws who provide support and shelter to the people in time of hardship, as well as physical protection against tyrannical landlords. In contrast to mainstream culture, these societies accept women as equals, and many hold high rank within them.

The modern wuxia literature on which the early martial arts films are based began during the Ming and Qing dynasties and was incredibly forthright in its criticism of government. In the 1920s, silent films were made portraying warriors with superhuman powers, using basic special effects to create the fantasy elements. Bolts of chi and mythical creatures were created by drawing or scratching directly on to the film. *Burning of the Red Lotus Monastery*, made in 1928, is one of the first great wuxia pian – martial chivalry films – and a template for those that came after. Based on the book *The Legend of the Strange Hero* by Xiang Kairen, it includes essential elements that came to define the genre, such as heroes striking assailants down with their 'palm power' and then flying across the screen by means of rather obvious wire-work.

The Swordswoman of Huangjiang (1930), one of the earliest surviving examples of wuxia pian, albeit missing its beginning and end, also reflects the popularity of female leads, which is almost unique to the genre. This trend arose in part from the structure of Chinese society in the early twentieth century. Until the introduction of silent films, the main form of popular entertainment had been the theatre, specifically Chinese opera. Women were forbidden from appearing in the opera, which itself included many elements of Shaolin kung fu, taught to actors by monks as a means of preserving their skills in the face of Manchurian oppression. Female roles were played by men, and these male performers held a venerated position in the social hierarchy: note the attitude of the stuck-up opera players in *Once Upon a Time in China*.

Film was considered an inferior medium, and China's actors refused to lower themselves to performing in something that took far less skill and training than traditional opera. So the roles fell to

women, including those of male characters. The Chinese audience
was so used to seeing men in female roles at the theatre that it
readily accepted the reverse approach. Consequently the part of
the woman in male drag became an enduring feature of the genre
even after the introduction of male actors. And so the first martial
arts action movie star was a woman – Xu Qing-Fan, the lead in
Swordswoman of Huangjiang. She plays the typical heroic knight,
travelling the country with her brother and vanquishing
evil-doers. She is also, incidentally, the grandmother of Sammo
Hung, acclaimed stuntman, actor and director of Hong Kong
kung fu cinema from the 1970s onwards.

The violence and magic portrayed in the wuxia pian were
considered contradictory to Confucian ideals, and the Chinese
government restricted film production in the 1930s. With the
coming of sound, a law was passed stating that all soundtracks
had to be recorded in Mandarin, the predominant dialect of the
country. Cantonese-speaking filmmakers began to emigrate to
Hong Kong, where there were fewer restrictions. During World
War II Chinese film production halted, and in 1949 the coming of
Communism drove many of the remaining filmmakers to the
British colony.

The 1950s saw a resurgence in the production of martial arts
films. In the 50s and 60s, wuxia pian flourished, and many special
effects and stunt techniques still used today were developed during
this period, such as thin wires, harnesses, trampolines, speeded-up
action sequences and reverse shots. Directors adopted some of the
stylistic elements of Chinese opera, which would later allow
opera-trained performers such as Jackie Chan and Sammo Hung
to defect from this fading art form to the burgeoning film
industry. The strict moral codes of the opera can still be seen
reflected in many movie plot-lines.

At the forefront of the Hong Kong film industry in the 50s and
60s were the Cathay Film Company and the behemoth that is
Shaw Brothers Studio. In 1924, Runme and Run Run Shaw set up
the Unique Productions film company in Shanghai. They later
moved to Singapore where they founded Shaw Brothers as an
organisation to screen the films they were making in China. In
1958, Run Run Shaw expanded the company into Hong Kong,
and the rest is film history. The Shaws invested unprecedented
budgets in high production values, enormous sets and

international distribution. They built an entire 'film city' at Clearwater Bay in Kowloon, miles from anywhere, that contained recording studios, a film lab, sets and a huge wardrobe department: everything that was required to produce the enormous number of films being churned out by the studio. By 1966, they were releasing 40 per year.

In the 1960s, new literary influences helped to develop the characters of the xia further, making them flawed, complex and more prone to human emotion. Subtle imagery and framing became more important, especially in the work of the director King Hu – for example 1966's *Come Drink With Me* – in which more complex choreography and sophisticated art direction heightened the visual spectacle.

Meanwhile, a group of directors spearheaded by Chang Cheh were introducing a bloodier, more violent style. Influenced by Japanese period dramas, which portrayed a more realistic type of sword fighting, the Hong Kong film industry began to focus on martial arts skill, achieved through arduous training, rather than on the endowment of magic powers through an ancient weapon or secret manuscript. It was at this point that the modern kung fu film – gung-fu pian – came into being, distinguishable from the wuxia pian by the recurrent pattern of common people achieving great things through hard work and practice, then beating the hell out of their enemies.

These films include little or no magic, and hand styles take precedence over elaborate swordplay. Action directors moved to the fore, handling first the choreography of the fight scenes and eventually, in the case of Yuen Woo-Ping among others, taking over the director's role. Set against more realistic, contemporary backdrops, often in the early Chinese Republic, gung-fu pian celebrate the southern heroes of Shaolin. Although a unique creation of Hong Kong – even the name gung-fu is a Cantonese phrase – these films had greater international appeal than the traditional, more culturally specific and formulaic wuxia pian. Kung fu films spread through Mainland China and then the rest of the world. From the 1960s onwards, Sir Run Run Shaw and his directors oversaw and dominated a golden era of Hong Kong martial arts films.

The Story of Wong Fei Hung, Part 1

(aka *Huang Feihong Chuan, Shangji, The True Story of Wong Fei Hung: Whiplash Snuffs the Candle Flame*)

Hong Kong, 1949, 72 minutes

Production Company: Yongyao
Director: Wu Pang
Martial arts director: Leung Wing-Hang
Producer: Cheung Tsok-Hong
Screenplay: Ng Yat-Siu
Based on the story by: Chu Yu-Chai

CAST: Kwan Tak-Hing (*Wong Fei Hung*), Tso Tat-Wah (*Leung Foon*): Sek Kin, Lee Lan, Tse Chi-Wai, Yuen Siu Tin, Lau Cham, Lau Hoi Saan

PLOT: *The Story of Wong Fei Hung* – which was released as two films, a few days apart – tells the tale of a legendary Chinese hero who taught martial arts in Canton. The audience is introduced to his awesome martial prowess as he performs a lengthy, intricate and technically correct lion dance. The sifu of the Authentic Shaolin Boxing School, Wong Fei Hung accepts a new student, Leung Foon, into his academy. In true heroic style, Fei Hung is then called upon to save a damsel in distress, who has been captured by the standard evil goon. Wounded on his righteous mission, the ascetic warrior is rescued by a seductive courtesan, who takes a shine to him. Although she tries all of her many feminine wiles on the kung fu master – much to his evident alarm – he manages to repel her advances. Meanwhile, Wong's erstwhile student Foon is running amok, and another bad guy has cropped up in need of defeat. This opponent comes in the form of a rival sifu, and the film climaxes with the confrontation between the two masters, during which Wong snuffs out a pair of candles with the tip of a steel whip. *The Story of Wong Fei Hung, Part 1* ends on a cliff-hanger, and audiences at the time had to wait two days to see

Part 2, released with an alacrity that would make fans of *Kill Bill Volume 1* seethe.

CASTING: Kwan Tak-Hing redefined the way martial arts roles were performed. A popular veteran of the Chinese opera, he was a skilled acrobat and fighter, and brought a realism to the role that was previously unseen in wuxia pian. For many, Kwan is synonymous with the historic character of Wong Fei Hung, hardly surprising when you consider that he played the part in 77 *Wong Fei Hung* films, as well as reprising the role in a number of Hong Kong kick flicks, making cameo appearances as Wong in *The Skyhawk* (1974), *Magnificent Butcher* (1979), *The Magnificent Kick* (1980) and for the final time in *Dreadnaught* in 1981. In fact, as far as the on-screen legend of the historic martial artist, healer and teacher is concerned, Kwan Tak-Hing *is* Wong Fei Hung. His own life even mirrored the great man's later years, in that he opened a pharmacy and taught kung fu. Perhaps his chi was stronger, though – he outlived Wong by 14 years, dying at the age of 91.

Kwan Tak-Hing is perfect in the role, but he almost didn't get it. Established matinee idol Wu Chu-Fan was originally cast, despite his lack of martial ability. Kwan eventually secured the part because of his knowledge of the lion dance, pole fighting and hung-kuen, all arts practised by the real Wong. He was proud of displaying authentic martial arts on screen, even mimicking Wong's trademark moves in his quest to perfect his portrayal of the great man. Kwan was the forerunner of martial artists who became actors, rather than actors who mimicked martial artists. In his own unique style, he was the grandfather of Bruce Lee and Jet Li. He was already a star in his own right, having earned the epithet Patriotic Entertainer for touring with his opera troupe behind enemy lines to entertain Chinese soldiers during World War II. The final endorsement came from Wong Fei Hung's widow, who thought Kwan the ideal choice to play her husband. He was honoured to be chosen, and even as his fame grew he never tried to exploit his position as the 'true' Wong Fei Hung.

In an interview with TVB in 1989, Kwan outlined how seriously he took the part, and how he felt Wong Fei Hung should be portrayed as a man of substance. 'I don't play him simply. Each time I do a film, I would pay my respects . . . supplicating to

Master Wong, and vow[ing] to do my best with the film.' He made over 90 pictures and asked to be paid only $4,000 for each. One could argue that Wong Fei Hung gained even greater substance by being played by Kwan Tak-Hing.

Hard as it may be to imagine anyone else in the role, several other actors have attempted it with some success. In Tsui Hark's epic *Once Upon a Time in China* series, Jet Li tackles the master's political years, playing Wong as the implacable martial artist using his skills to defend his country's rights. (Zhao Wen-Zhou took on the role for Part 4 before Jet Li returned for *Once Upon a Time in China and America*.) Jackie Chan made Wong's teenage years his own in *Drunken Master* and *Drunken Master 2*, although he was far from adolescent when he made the latter in 1994. Gordon Liu added his interpretation to the mix in *Challenge of the Masters*, and Jimmy Wang Yu gave Wong a darker, more brooding aspect. The role has even been played by a girl: wushu champion Angie Tseng appeared as the ten-year-old Wong in *Iron Monkey*. It is homage to Kwan Tak-Hing, however, that none of them tried to play Wong Fei Hung in his later years, a part perfectly interpreted by the original actor.

Despite director Wu Pang's desire to create a real kung fu movie, a non-martial artist was chosen for the role of Wong's ill-disciplined disciple, Leung Foon. Tso Tat-Wah was a popular actor at the time and helped to raise public interest in the film. His role does not require exemplary martial arts, and his fame was probably more beneficial to the success of the film than superior fighting abilities would have been.

The villain of the piece, the evil sifu, is played by Sek Kin, who became almost as loved by audiences as Kwan for repeatedly being defeated by Wong Fei Hung, repenting his crimes and reforming. Despite multiple appearances in *Wong Fei Hung* films, his most famous role, certainly in the West, is that of Han, the one-handed Dr No character (complete with cat) in Bruce Lee's *Enter the Dragon*. He was clearly so well suited to playing the bad guy in *The Story of Wong Fei Hung* that he was typecast forever.

MARTIAL ARTS: In *The Story of Wong Fei Hung, Part 1*, the martial arts are the defining feature of the movie, and set it apart from other early films in the genre. That is not to say that they were not central to the classic wuxia pian; the fighting abilities of the heroic swordsmen and women and quests to find the ultimate technique had always been major themes in the plots of traditional films. But with the *Wong Fei Hung* series the martial styles used were, for the first time, real.

Many of the martial features that came to define the genre can be found in this ground-breaking film. In the words of its star, Kwan Tak-Hing, 'Before, everything was swordplay and magic!' The roots of formulaic fight choreography and set pieces can be identified, including the displays of weapons skill and, most notably, the all-the-bad-guys-in-the-room-simultaneously-rush-the-hero scenario, which is found in nearly every kick flick ever made.

Nonetheless, the fighting in the film falls a little flat. Many of the martial displays are shot in documentary style, with a single camera, such as the opening lion dance. The flow of the story is brought to a sluggish halt on a number of occasions as the actors showcase traditional kung fu forms: the staff pattern performed by one of Wong Fei Hung's students, while very worthy, verges on tedium. The fight scenes feel staged and forced – they break out in much the same way as hardened revolutionaries suddenly break into song in the musical version of *Les Misérables*. The fights are frenetic, preventing the viewer from appreciating the talent of the performers and the level of skill involved, and, despite the film's stab at authenticity, feel somewhat whimsical. Most of the fighting is with weapons, although among the standard swords and staffs we are treated to a butterfly knife display. Little fundamental kung fu is apparent. Despite the filmmakers' best intentions, it proved impossible to break away entirely from the style of fighting of their fantastical predecessors. It has to be recognised that extended sequences and stilted action were the only available means of demonstrating authentic fighting skills, and this way of presenting kung fu to the audience fails to do it justice. To demonstrate how the martial art should really be performed would have involved massive exaggeration, moving further away from the film's original concept by dragging the fighting into farce.

In general, compared to modern films, the kung fu shown in this movie isn't actually very good. Lacking the techniques that would later be used to make traditional martial arts look flashy and exciting, *The Story of Wong Fei Hung, Part 1* only manages to make them appear basic and direct. Of course, in many ways this is more realistic – why expend an enormous amount of energy leaping around and kicking your opponents when you can dispatch them with a single technique? Except that it looks good on the big screen.

But despite the generally pedestrian pace of the fighting, there are some gems in the film. Wong Fei Hung charges, Errol Flynn-style, up a staircase, then shuns the use of a weapon, preferring to defeat his enemies with his bare hands. Using a number of kicks and even 'pushing hands' – the fundamental principle of t'ai chi that allows the fighter to harmonise with an opponent in order to overcome them – Master Wong triumphs in a scene shot in slow motion and accompanied by a Tchaikovsky piano concerto. It is this sequence, above all, that fulfils director Wu Pang's desire to create a real martial arts movie.

The original Wong Fei Hung was famed for his hung-kuen kung fu abilities. His personal techniques included the Vanquishing Fist, Iron Wire Fist, Five Forms Fist and, most famously, the Shadowless Kick, while his skill in the Southern style lion dance – that incredible acrobatic performance undertaken while supporting an elaborate (and heavy) lion's head – earned him the epithet 'King of Lions'.

Later episodes in the series make a far better job of the portrayal of kung fu as an exciting and dramatic fighting style. Changes in the location and scenery of the arena in which Master Wong defeats the bad guys help to keep the battle scenes fresh and interesting, as does the use of comedy devices in which the folk hero fights with a gorilla or, on occasion, dresses as a cockerel during a dragon dance (this fancy-dress battle was reprised by Jet Li as Wong Fei Hung in *Last Hero in China*). A host of kung fu styles are showcased throughout the series, which also helps to add variety, resulting in such classics as *How Wong Fei Hung Pitted a Lion Against the Unicorn* and *Wong Fei Hung Meeting the Heroes with the Tiger Paw*. Master Wong is required to contend with everything from Mantis style to Crane Claw, via the excruciating Genital Crushing Fist. He also has to deal with opponents wielding such terrifying weapons as the Soul Severing Spear. He handles it all with aplomb.

The fight scenes in *The Story of Wong Fei Hung, Part 1* should be lauded for what they are trying to do and judged by the standards of the day. They may not look that impressive to anyone who has feasted on the spectacular feats of modern kick flicks, but without these beginnings, *Project A* and *Fist of Fury* could never have been made.

STUNTS AND SPECIAL EFFECTS: *The Story of Wong Fei Hung, Part 1* is unique in the genre for its lack of stunts. This is real kung fu, performed by real martial artists, standing on their own two feet. Jackie Chan may perform his own stunts, at risk to life and limb, but they are still that: stunts set up with the safety of the actors in mind. The fight scenes in this film are less dramatic, but they are completely authentic. Director Wu Pang deliberately refrained from post-production special effects, and the film is the better for it.

DIRECTOR: Wu Pang can be said to be directly responsible for the advent of the serious martial arts movie. Although it was not until the late 60s that this branch of the genre really took off, *The Story of Wong Fei Hung, Part 1* represents the beginning of an entirely new style of Chinese filmmaking. Along with scriptwriter Ng Yat-Siu, Wu is responsible for the launch of a series that became a major part of Cantonese film production and almost a sub-genre in its own right.

It is no exaggeration to say that Wu is the father of modern kung fu films. As a director, he had been raised with an ethic of strict realism, a principle from which he refused to be parted. The very idea of the fantasy-oriented wuxia pian was anathema to the director, and he was determined to make a martial arts film that was devoid of flying fighters, magic swords and the ubiquitous knights-errant. He deserves to be celebrated simply for this stance and for his constant adherence to it. While palm power and feuding clans make for entertaining viewing, the *Wong Fei Hung* films allowed for a real appreciation of kung fu, astounding in its own right.

It was personal conviction that encouraged Wu to pursue the authentic approach, but it was talent that enabled him to turn it into a marketing tool. It was a risk for any production company to fund a film that disregarded so many conventions of current fashion, in favour of a gritty realism that was potentially less enthralling. But Wu was already half way to success when he hit upon the idea of using a real folk hero as the star of the film. It was an ingredient that appealed to the cinema going public and became part of a recipe for success, central to later films that portrayed real martial artists from a particular period of Chinese history. The financial success of the idea is illustrated by its myriad sequels, and by the enduring popularity of the character.

PRODUCTION: Viewed in the light of modern production techniques, *The Story of Wong Fei Hung, Part 1* is basic, poorly structured and, frankly, cheap. Shot in black and white, the flimsy cardboard sets and overblown, operatic acting give the film the appearance of a tacky TV serial. The direction is limited to either documentary-style frankness or filmed theatre. With no precedent to learn from, Wu Pang had yet to figure out how to make authentic martial arts work on screen without the flashiness of magic special effects to enhance them. The director should not be condemned for this, however, as the genre did not manage to represent this type of fighting effectively until the 1960s; the film is a product of its time.

The simplicity of style actually serves to enhance the film's position as a less fantastical form of wuxia pian. In both approach and financing *The Story of Wong Fei Hung, Part 1* is pure Hong Kong: the funding came in part from local martial artists as well as from production company Yongyao.

TRIVIA: *Wong Fei Hung* folklore has it that the idea for the movie and the subsequent mammoth series came to director Wu Pang while reading a newspaper on a ferry in Hong Kong Harbour. The newspaper's serialisation of a novel on the life of Master Wong was the genesis of one of the most enduring stories in film history. The Hong Kong martial arts schools – many of which were run by students of the original Wong – were so enthusiastic about the film that they not only acted as consultants but also helped to pay for it. Many of the schools' students appeared in the film as Wong's disciples, while Beijing opera actors were brought in to help perform the acrobatics. In later episodes of the series, Wong Fei Hung's widow, Mo Kwei Lan, herself a dragon dancer and martial performer of some note, was a regular guest star.

THEMES: As is to be expected of a film that influenced so many others, the identifiable themes in *The Story of Wong Fei Hung, Part 1* reappear throughout the genre. The most obvious is the inclusion of real-life figures from Chinese history to ground the story-line in the real world, a device used to differentiate the gung-fu pian from the more fantastical wuxia. Although Wong Fei Hung is the most frequently portrayed character in Asian motion picture history, little is known about the great man's real life, but in some ways it is less important than the myth that now surrounds him. Indeed, the lack of research undertaken into his past suggests that the Chinese people would rather not view their hero as anything so base as human.

What *is* recorded of his real life is legendary enough, and has provided the inspiration for dozens of kick flicks. Born in Canton Province in 1847, Fei Hung was the son of Wong Kai-Ying, one of the Ten Tigers of Canton, a local band of heroes bound by a strict honour code. In spite of his martial prowess, Wong Senior (who turns up in *Once Upon a Time in China 3* as well as *Drunken Master*) allegedly refused to teach his son, fearing that he would become involved in fights and get hurt. Had it not been for Fei Hung's determination to learn, the history of martial arts films might have turned out very differently.

Turning to his father's sifu, Ah Choy, to instruct him, Wong Fei Hung excelled in kung fu, and began demonstrating on the streets to earn money. He was later appointed martial arts instructor to the Guangzhou Civilian Militia and to the 5th Regiment of the Cantonese Army. His association with ranking officers led to involvement with politics and, when the people of Fujian Province rose up against the government, calling for a new democratic state, it was Wong Fei Hung they wanted as their Commander-in-Chief. The rising was crushed, and Wong fled to Canton. There he established the Bo Chi Lam clinic and kept his head down. Married several times, the last time to the teenage Mok Kwei Lan, he died at the age of 77 in 1924.

Wu Pang fixed *The Story of Wong Fei Hung, Part 1* to a specific moment in Chinese history. The director's altruistic nature was not only responsible for the development of realism in the genre, but also for his creation of a movie designed to respond to the needs of disenfranchised Chinese. He was determined to use the medium of film to make a statement about the social ills prevalent in Hong Kong, and offer the audience an alternative view of both themselves and their country, one that they could take comfort in. The year of the film's release, 1949, saw China embroiled in civil war, with the Communists poised on the brink of victory. Hong Kong, the final outpost for those fleeing from the Red regime, had become an overcrowded melting pot of people, British colonial culture all but eclipsing that of the local and immigrant Chinese. There was little concern for their traditional life, and its structure and mores were rapidly disintegrating.

By reviving and reinventing the legend of Wong Fei Hung, Wu gave Chinese viewers a reason to be proud of their heritage. The martial arts shown on screen were not to be revered simply for their efficiency but for their place in the country's social and political history. Kung fu was uniquely Chinese, something they could cling to in the sea of confusion created by the pressures of Hong Kong's international society. The film celebrates the spiritual side of kung fu and its roots in Buddhist and Confucian ethics. Violence is portrayed as a last resort, to which Master Wong is reluctant to turn. For the sake of drama and excitement, he is always forced to use his skills in the end, but his reticence sent an important message about the need for restraint and for finding other solutions to social frustrations.

The film celebrates traditional martial forms, and concentrates on the aim of students to become masters by studying hard under the best teachers. The sifu-student relationship is an omnipresent theme in later kung fu films, due to the nature of the discipline. You can't learn kung fu from a book, you must be taught by a master. Although martial manuals are common in the genre, it is their translation by a skilled practitioner that is crucial, as with the Wudan text stolen and misused by Jade Fox in *Crouching Tiger, Hidden Dragon*. Those who wanted to excel would dedicate their lives to serving and learning from their teacher, as the troublesome Leung Foon does in *The Story of Wong Fei Hung, Part 1*. The teaching scenes in this film are the basis of the near-compulsory training sequences in the kung fu movies that followed.

Wong Fei Hung is represented as a virtuous father figure, providing moral guidance for his students and supporting the poor, the weak and the dispossessed. This was to become a classic theme. The wayward student, characterised by Leung Foon, is a popular role in the genre: at first they fail, then they are forced to attend to their teacher. A veritable paragon, Wong reprimands his disciples for brawling and using their skills to get even, lecturing on the benefits of remaining aloof. Unlike the traditional wuxia pian, vengeance is not an important motivation driving the characters of *The Story of Wong Fei Hung, Part 1*. Instead, Master Wong is seen stoically rescuing his hapless students and any damsels that happen to be in distress. While his disciples might wish for retribution to be brought down upon their tormentors, their master uses violence only when necessary. Because the student-master relationship is a constant theme, conflict between different schools of martial arts is never far from the narrative. Wong's students naturally believe in the superiority of their style which, in the later films in the series, their master is required to demonstrate.

Wu Pang tried to educate his audience, not just about morality but about their national heritage. Hence the extended scenes detailing folk culture and fighting styles. In that way the film disseminated and, to an extent, revived southern Chinese culture among both the Hong Kong residents and Chinese expats overseas. Similarly, nostalgia for a golden age in China – which the movie reveals to have existed in recent memory – replaced the need for magic and special effects. This is good, clean, down to earth, bone-breaking, traditional Chinese fun. Confucian morality is also a clear theme, used to celebrate the glories of Eastern culture and make the viewers feel better about their society.

PLACE WITHIN THE GENRE: This film is a first. The first in the authentic kung fu sub-genre, and therefore the first gung-fu pian. The first of a series that totalled nearly eighty episodes. And the first movie to feature the legendary martial arts instructor, healer and political hero Wong Fei Hung.

In the 1940s both the Chinese film industry and interest in authentic martial arts were in decline, squeezed on all sides by the encroachment of Western culture. The film industry did little to change this situation, relying on supernatural story-lines set in China's distant past, until *The Story of Wong Fei Hung, Part 1* created an entirely new type of martial arts movie. This story of a nationalistic crusader, defending his people with his bare hands, fighting against injustice and corruption, resonated deeply in Hong Kong.

Long before the new wave kung fu films directed by the likes of Chang Cheh and Wei Lo developed, the *Wong Fei Hung* series had created the foundations for the formulaic chopsocky movie. In its revolutionary use of martial arts on screen and its lack of magical special effects, it can be seen as a precursor of the Jackie Chan movies of the late 70s in which the star performed all of his own stunts. More recently, this mantle has fallen upon the Thai offering *Ong-Bak*, in which Tony Jaa's acrobatics are made even more impressive by the audience's knowledge that no CGI is involved. As the character of Wong Fei Hung provided an example and guidance to his disciples, so *The Story of Wong Fei Hung, Part 1* created the mould for the cinematic portrayal of kung fu in which later films would be cast.

Despite their tendency to become dated, the *Wong Fei Hung* films have never been abandoned. Many were broadcast on television, in the manner of British Bond movies, and continue to be today. Kwan even returned to the role in the 80s for a TV series. Several generations of Chinese filmmakers have grown up on a diet of these movies, working on as well as watching them, and it would be impossible to overestimate the effect of the series, and of its initial episode, on the development of kung fu films. The industry's repeated return to the character of Wong Fei Hung, in all his incarnations, is a reflection of how deeply the original films are rooted in its consciousness. For some critics, the moral stance, authentic martial arts and altruistic character of the film make *The Story of Wong Fei Hung, Part 1* the first in a series that represents the best of Hong Kong martial cinema.

Heroic Ones: Kwan Tak-Hing

- AKA: Kuan Te-Hsing.
- Not to be confused with: Wong Fei Hung.
- Martial style: Kung fu, old-style.
- Born: 1905 in Guangdong, China.
- Died: 28 June 1996 in Hong Kong, from pancreatic cancer.
- Biography: At 13, the man who was to become synonymous with the character of legendary kung fu hero and bonesetter Wong Fei Hung joined a circus troupe in Singapore. Having learned his trade, in 1932 he scored a bit-part in the USA-filmed movie *Sentimental Song of Companions' Tide*. He

returned to Hong Kong for political reasons and joined the anti-Japanese movement. There he won his first leading role in *Song of the Yesterday* (clearly he had a thing about singing). During World War II Kwan toured the US, raising funds for China. In 1947 he was selected for the role of Wong Fei Hung because of his knowledge of kung fu, and the rest is history – over 75 films worth of history. Allegedly, when he met the widow of the real Wong, who died in 1924, she told him that he looked just like her late husband. Before Jet Li took on the role in the *Once Upon a Time in China* series, most filmgoers would have been certain that Wong Fei Hung looked exactly like Kwan Tak-Hing. In all he appeared in almost a hundred films about Wong, even playing the long-suffering master in Sammo Hung's *Magnificent Butcher*, as well as starring in a TV series about the great man. He made more than 130 films altogether, the last in 1994, two years before his death. The most bizarrely titled is probably *How Wong Fei Hung Used an Iron Fowl Against the Eagle*, although *How Wong Fei Hung Vanquished the Bully on the Red Opera Float* has to get a look-in.

- Best kick flicks: *The Story of Wong Fei Hung, Part 1* (1949) et al, *Magnificent Butcher* (1979).
- Trivia: Kwan was awarded an MBE in 1983.
- Where are they now: Dead, but not forgotten.

Dragon Gate Inn

(aka *Dragon Inn, Longmen Kezhan*)

Taiwan, 1967, 111 minutes

Production company: Union Film Company
Director: King Hu [Hu Jianquan, Hu Jiang-Chuen, Hu Jin Quan]
Martial arts co-ordinator: Han Ying-Chieh
Producer: Sha Jung-Feng
Associate producer: Chang Chiu-Yin
Screenplay: King Hu
Director of photography: Hua Hui-Ying
Music: Chou Lan-Ping

CAST: Shangkuan Ling Feng (*Chu Huei*), Shih Chun (*Hsiao Shao-Tzu*), Pai Ying (*Eunuch Tsao Shao-Chin*), Tsao Chien (*Innkeeper Wu Hei-An*), Sieh Han (*Chu Chi*), Miao Tien (*Pi Hsiao-Tang*), Han Ying-Chieh (*Mao Tsung-Hsien*), Kao Fei (*Army*

Commander), Wen Tien (*Tou La*), Hsu Feng (*Yu Hsin*), Chi Wei (*Yu Kuang*), Yu Chi-I (*Yu Chien*)

PLOT: A martial arts film set in a pub: what could be more appealing to a British audience? But the Dragon Gate Inn isn't your usual local. Patrons risk poisoning, booby traps and impalement, even if all they came in for was a quiet cup of rice wine. Set in 1457, *Dragon Gate Inn* is an old-style martial chivalry period drama, a rip-roaring tale of honour, betrayal, cross-dressing, castration and men convicted of crimes they didn't commit.

The story unfolds against the backdrop of the Ming Dynasty, corrupted and controlled by the powerful court eunuchs who terrorise government officials and populace alike. The eunuchs are pulling all the strings in the Imperial Guard, running the Dong Chang (Eastern Group) secret police and generally making life very difficult for anyone who opposes them. One such is Minister of War Yu, leader of the now impotent army. To punish him for challenging their power, the eunuchs find a convenient crime to frame Yu with – the aiding of foreigners – and promptly cut his head off. His family is sent into exile from Beijing to the frontier town of Dragon Gate.

But the Yus' troubles are only just beginning. Chief Eunuch Tsao cannot bear the thought of Minister Yu's children living on and honouring his memory, and plots to have them assassinated on their journey. They survive, however, largely thanks to the intervention of the Chu 'brothers', who appear from nowhere in the nick of time. The journey to Dragon Gate continues, but Tsao learns of their survival and sends the Dong Chang to lie in wait for them at the local inn.

The Dong Chang, under the command of First Captain Pi Hsiao-Tang and Second Captain Mao Tsung-Hsien, take over the inn, ready to ambush the Yus when they arrive. To secure their position, they wipe out the local militia, which is billeted at the inn, and most of the other customers. Wandering hero Hsiao Shao-Tzu arrives to visit the innkeeper, Wu Hei-An, and refuses to play the game. Insisting on waiting for the absent Wu, Hsiao is forced to survive three assassination attempts by the Dong Chang – who really don't like company – which include poisoning and more straightforward violence. Using what are clearly exceptional martial skills, he survives, earning the respect of Captain Pi.

Innkeeper Wu returns, closely followed by a storm and the mysterious Chus, one of whom is clearly a woman in unconvincing drag, although the other characters are apparently incapable of seeing through her disguise. Hsiao saves the Chus from poisoning and then these disparate characters meet up, along with the innkeeper, to discuss how they will defend the Yu family. It becomes apparent that all were loyal followers of Minister Yu, and are intent upon revering his memory and protecting his children. Innkeeper Wu is the former General Wu Ning, a soldier loyal to the Emperor. Chu Huei reveals that she is really a girl, or rather a highly skilled female warrior. The heroic knights embark upon a game of cat-and-mouse with the Dong Chang, each of them looking for a weakness in the other's martial arts.

The Yus arrive and the patriots slip out of the inn to meet them. Battle commences as they have to fight their way back in. A series of indecisive skirmishes results in the wounding of both the Chus and the death of Second Captain Mao. The rebels are joined by the commander of the slaughtered garrison and two Tartars, Tou La and his younger brother. The Tartars have defected from the Dong Chang, which they had been forced to join, very much against their will – they didn't take very kindly to being press-ganged and then castrated to reduce their desire to go AWOL. The Tou brothers were also loyal to Minister Yu, and are delighted to have a cause to fight for against their oppressors.

Exasperated at their agents' inability to finish off their targets, Chief Eunuch Tsao and Colonel Gui of the Imperial Army arrive to take charge. Or rather, Tsao does. When Gui attempts to assert his authority, Tsao decapitates him – his favoured solution to the irritating problem of challenges to his authority. He cannot deal with the freedom fighters in a similar way, however, as they have snuck off, leaving the inn filled with booby traps. Unhindered by this cunning ruse, Captain Pi gives chase, ambushing the patriots on the road. Chu Huei and the Tartars defeat him when fighting breaks out in earnest, and Pi is killed. Realising that if you want something done right you have to do it yourself, Tsao blockades the rebels at a strategic pass and demands a meeting with Hsiao. Hsiao agrees, taunting the eunuch about his lack of virility. Greatly annoyed, Tsao, who considers himself invincible, is incited to a battle to the death. Unable to beat the eunuch alone, Hsiao is joined by Chu, Wu and the Tartar boys. On the brink of his own death, Tou La manages to decapitate Tsao, just revenge for his enforced castration. The Yu family is then escorted to safety by Hsiao.

CASTING: *Dragon Gate Inn* is a wuxia pian in the best historic tradition, encompassing all the required elements including the evil master, itinerant heroes and strong female character battling it out with the men, albeit in drag. Shangkuan Ling Feng, who plays Chu Huei, went on to make a career for herself in such roles, and is ideally suited to this one. The Brigitte Lin of her day, she is one of the elite group of female actors, including Cheng Pei-Pei and Michelle Yeoh, who defined the martial films of their era. Her apparent androgyny, though it may not be immediately apparent to audiences unfamiliar with the clothes and hairstyles of Ming Dynasty China, led to similar roles in films such as *Back Alley Princes*. *Dragon Gate Inn*, for better or worse, left Shangkuan typecast as tomboy.

The film was also a starting point for a number of director King Hu's core stable of actors. Pai Ying, Han Ying-Chieh and Hsu Feng all make appearances here, in preparation for their outing in Hu's 1970 follow-up *A Touch of Zen*. The choice of actors to play the villains in *Dragon Gate Inn* was almost more important than casting the fey heroes, who drift into the story as it suits them. In contrast, the bad guys arrive with a bang, presented during the film's introductory sequence in all their evil glory. The varying abilities of the eunuch sect define the fight scenes, as the patriots make their way through the enemy ranks, defeating increasingly competent fighters at each stage. Pai Ying, as Head Eunuch Tsao Shao-Chin, displays a convincing mix of autocratic arrogance and deep-seated feelings of inadequacy about his 'half-man' status.

Next in line in the hierarchy of evil is Miao Tien in the role of First Captain Pi Hsiao-Tang, the very personification of aesthetic villainy. Played with intelligence and intensity, the character is the most admirable of the trio of corrupt officials. Miao went on to appear in *Rebels of the Neon God* and *The River*, directed by Tsai Ming-Liang.

Han Ying-Chieh has an early outing in the bad guy role in *Dragon Gate Inn*. The film's action director, he was no mean martial artist and was so convincing as the ruthless and brilliant fighter Second Captain Mao Tsung-Hsien that he was upgraded to villain-in-chief in *A Touch of Zen*. Han famously played the eponymous character in *The Big Boss* opposite Bruce Lee, becoming one of the most name-checked über-villains in kick flick history.

MARTIAL ARTS: One of the first of the new wave wuxia pian made in the 1960s, following the conception of this sub-genre with King Hu's *Come Drink With Me*, *Dragon Gate Inn* imitates the martial style of its root films: there are a lot of swords in it. But the movie adds another dimension to the traditional duelling seen in its predecessors. As well as having a firm grasp of their Chinese straight swords, these knights-errant can turn their martial abilities to deflecting poison, marking the addition of internal kung fu to the more traditional external styles in the new wave films.

Action choreographer Han Ying-Chieh successfully combines the use of realistic fighting techniques with superhuman abilities. The authenticity is underlined by the painstaking recreation of historic costumes, which must have been equally painful to fight in. The slick, complex action scenes owe a great debt to the acrobatic stagecraft of the Beijing opera with their heavy emphasis on wushu moves. Now accepted as a standard means of creating dramatic, thrilling fight sequences, at the time combining opera and film was a daring innovation in an essentially traditional Chinese action movie which could trace its beginnings back to 1928.

The genesis of these energetic, lavish action effects can be seen in King Hu's earlier outing, the Shaw Brothers production *Come Drink With Me*, which Han Ying-Chieh also choreographed. The style was further developed in his later films. In addition to the new forms of fighting with which they express themselves, the characters are endowed with their own particular strengths. The admirable Hsiao is a scholar with lightning-fast martial abilities: at one point he pauses while eating his dinner to grip a flying dagger in his chopsticks, at another he catches an arrow in a wine jug, which he uses to fling the missile straight back at the archer. Clearly this is a man who likes to play with his food. Former General Wu Ning plans everything in terms of military strategy while, in comparison, Chu Chi is fiery and impulsive, with no rein over his temper. The ultimate fighter, against whom the heroes must unite in order to triumph, is Eunuch Tsao. Skilled in the arts of chi gung – the creation of strength through manipulation of internal energy – and weightlessness, his strikes can cause violent internal bleeding and he is almost unbeatable.

The battle scenarios in *Dragon Gate Inn* introduce several devices that have been used throughout the development of the wuxia pian. The hectic, unceasing battle between Chu Huei and Mao Tsung-Hsien, which flits from ground level to rooftops, is referenced in the fight between Yu Shu Lien and Yu Jen in *Crouching Tiger, Hidden Dragon*, made almost a quarter of a century later. Likewise, Chu and Mao clash beneath a hail of arrows, which come almost as thick and fast as those deflected by Nameless and Flying Snow in Zhang Yimou's *Hero*.

STUNTS AND SPECIAL EFFECTS: As you would expect of a movie firmly rooted in the wuxia tradition, *Dragon Gate Inn* is built around elements of magic and mystical powers that need somehow to be represented on screen. While King Hu avoids fire-spouting palms in favour of intricate swordplay, flying wire-work is fully in evidence. The lack of overblown special effects serves to support the film's position as a period drama: it is set in the real world, and so its characters and their abilities must be real – or, at least, mostly believable.

DIRECTOR: King Hu (1931–1997), is responsible for prolonging the life of the wuxia pian in the face of the assault made on it by a gritty new style of martial film. As a leading light among the new wave directors, he revamped the genre to make it more appealing to 1960s audiences, gaining new fans while ensuring he didn't alienate the old. By taking some of the popular elements used in the hardcore, brutal kung fu films being made by Chang Cheh and his ilk, and combining them with the artistry of the original wuxia pian, Hu created a format that went on to be used by successive generations of directors, including Tsui Hark and Ang Lee.

Hu made his first films for the Shaw Brothers Studio. Having achieved some success co-directing *The Love Eternal* and *The Story of Sue San* with Li Hanxiang in 1963 and 1964 respectively, he took sole charge of the reins for *Sons of the Good Earth*. His breakthrough came with the 1966 hit *Come Drink With Me*, in which many of the themes of his later films make their first appearance, including the perpetual dominance of the female lead. It was this film that catapulted the twenty-year-old Cheng Pei-Pei to stardom. No martial artist, she has Hu to thank for her meteoric rise in martial arts films: 'He saw my eyes and said that they were more like those of a kung fu man to him. I had a zestful body and so he said to me that he thought I could be a very good martial arts lady.' Hu was convinced that Cheng had the screen presence to play a woman warrior and taught the actress how to carry off the heroic chivalry parts that she went on to make her own.

Come Drink With Me was Hu's first wuxia pian, a genre that he came to dominate. Despite the film's popularity, the director decided he no longer wanted to come drink with Run Run Shaw, and walked out of his contract with the studio. He only escaped because he had originally been contracted, in the 50s, to work as an actor, so was within his rights in directing films elsewhere. He agreed to act in two more films to fulfil his contract, on the condition that the scripts were right, and promptly moved to Taiwan.

Producer Sha Jung-Feng enticed Hu to become involved in his new venture, Union Film Company, and their first project was *Dragon Gate Inn*. It is doubtful whether either man realised the impact that the movie would have. Filmed in the mountainous interior of Taiwan, *Dragon Gate Inn* set a box-office record for a Chinese film in that country. But you don't cross the big daddy of Hong Kong movies and get off lightly: Run Run Shaw was in no mood to make life easy for Hu. He refused to sanction the release of the film until after that of *Golden Swallow*, the supposed sequel to *Come Drink With Me*, directed by Hu's rival Chang Cheh. Hu got the last laugh, however, because *Dragon Gate Inn* was lapped up by audiences in Hong Kong and ultimately out-grossed *The Sound of Music*.

Within *Dragon Gate Inn* you can see the outline of the majority of Hu's later films, but he should not be seen as a director with only one idea. Given the context of his filmic education, it is understandable that he consistently returned to established themes. In the historic culture of China – in its opera, literature and music – originality was not seen as a virtue in itself. Hu's films reflect his own moral and intellectual position, influenced by Chan

Buddhism and Chinese aesthetics. He felt it was wrong to laud the violent, arbitrary behaviour of those who considered themselves above the law, and he shaped his films as moralistic cautionary tales. He was not entirely immune to outside influence, and has stated that his decision to focus on the Dong Chang, the secret militia ruled by a despotic leader, was based on the popularity of the James Bond films of the early 60s.

PRODUCTION: Made by an infant production company far removed from the bounty of the Hong Kong film industry, *Dragon Gate Inn* was not blessed with a lavish budget. Hu no longer had access to the sets, props and extras on tap at Shaw Brothers, and had to make do with what he could source locally. What he discovered was the sweeping landscape of Taiwan, and his imaginative use of the island's scenery as the backdrop for this monumental period drama ensures that the film is every bit as impressive as the more elaborately produced *Come Drink With Me*.

In many ways, the sheer variety and availability of locations to be found in Taiwan defined the tone of Hu's new wave wuxia. The scenes are more richly coloured and the framing more imaginative. The limitations of the Hong Kong studios, and their predilection for filming on set in Clearwater Bay, made many of their films look strikingly similar. Here was something completely different, the director's early career in Hong Kong as an artistic consultant influencing his intensely visual style.

Freed from the claustrophobia of the studio, Hu was more liberal with his production techniques. His usual flowing camera work is interrupted by a series of rapid edits, punctuating the action. Although the camera focuses on the movement in a scene, it has been remarked that 'the flow of individual shots sometimes encompasses as many as three "monumental" or emblematic compositions glimpsed in passing'. This novel structure is developed in Hu's later work, but has its foundations in *Dragon Gate Inn*.

One innovative device used in the film is the opening sequence, when the trio of evil agents are introduced by a narrator. The voiceover denounces their corruption of the court, and describes the execution of Yu as unwarranted. As the narrator speaks, the credits are shown on a series of scrolls, and the viewer is left to wonder if the writer is also the unknown narrator. The bad guys may be vilified from the outset, but at least the audience knows who they are: when it comes to introductions, the heroes hardly get a look-in. The patriots have to be identified as they appear throughout the film, and their motives, initially at least, can only be guessed at.

The strict hierarchy of fighting skills possessed by the protagonists and their opponents is emphasised by the use of traditional opera music, which was deep-rooted in the Chinese consciousness of the time, representing cultural order and social position. The flowing, liquid movement of Han's fight scenes is perfectly balanced by the syncopated, percussive clash of the soundtrack, leaving the audience in no doubt who is in the right and who should die.

TRIVIA: The scrolls on which the opening credits of *Dragon Gate Inn* appear are in King Hu's own distinctive calligraphy. The final scroll, which the unknown scholar is seen beginning to roll up, includes Hu's credit as director and writer. Raymond Lee's remake of the film in 1992 paid it such direct homage that he didn't even bother to change the name. In some releases, however, it is referred to as *New Dragon Gate Inn*.

THEMES: When dissecting its story-line, on one level it would be easy to see *Dragon Gate Inn* as a seamless continuation of the traditional wuxia pian idiom. All the necessary devices are there, most obviously the righteous rebels, standing outside society, who take on the cause of justice in the face of social and political evil, represented by the corrupt eunuchs. They right wrongs with the blades of their swords and an unwavering sense of decency. They are loners, but are intent upon avenging their fallen leader, all having at one time been loyal to Yu. The patriots fight a series of villains, from the low-ranking grunts who are dispatched with ease, up through the orders of increasing martial skill until they face the ultimate challenge. This plot format existed long before Hu began directing, and can be seen in many of the films that come after, from *36th Chamber of Shaolin* to *Game of Death*.

But the characters are far more complex than that, and so is the film. They conceal their identities and motivations from each other, despite their close proximity. This concept, even down to women in drag, reaches as far back as Ming Dynasty fiction, and continues to appear throughout the genre, notably in the modern martial classics. In *Crouching Tiger, Hidden Dragon*, Jen disguises herself as a man and goes off to seek excitement in the outside world. She too ends up at an inn, and succeeds in destroying it during the ensuing fight. Li Mu Bai and Yu Shu Lien spend an enormous amount of time together without revealing their true feelings for each other, and Jade Fox, the vitriolic murderer of Li's master, lurks in their midst. Similarly, the entire plot of *Hero* is based on the ability of Nameless to hide his true identity and motives, while in *House of Flying Daggers* no one is really who they seem. Secret societies infiltrate the police force, policemen pretend to be mercenaries, blind girls can really see and no one is totally sure whether anyone really loves them.

Hu's flight to Taiwan awakened his political beliefs and, while he was too cautious to make any transparent statements in the film, it is possible to interpret it as an expression of his distaste for the Chinese government. The aftermath of the Cultural Revolution was in full effect, and it is easy to draw parallels between the unjust beheading of Minister Yu, and the exile of his family, and the arbitrary attacks on individuals in Chairman Mao's China. Perhaps the fate of Eunuch Tsao is in some ways a cautionary tale, aimed at the Great Helmsman.

In its apparent political stance, *Dragon Gate Inn* is not far removed from its predecessors and their commentary on the evils of corruption in the Ming and Qing Dynasties, their moral standpoints and their creation of folk heroes who would avenge society's wrongs. Where it does differ, however, is in the extent to which it explores the theme of sexuality: this was the 60s, after all. While cross-dressing and eunuchs were common enough in the genre, *Dragon Gate Inn* was the first film of its kind to include a wealth of sexual imagery and cite characters' sexuality as motivation for their actions. The twisted head eunuch, frequently used in the genre to represent the evils of corrupt government with no reference to his lack of manhood, is in this case defined by his asexuality. When taunted by the warrior-scholar Hsiao about his mutilation and lack of sexual prowess, Tsao is infuriated and chops down a disturbingly phallic tree before launching himself into battle. In the end, the eunuch loses his head to the Tartar boy whom he unmanned, a final symbolic castration which renders him fatally impotent.

PLACE WITHIN THE GENRE: *Come Drink With Me* was King Hu's first wuxia outing, and effectively set the standard for all Chinese action films that came after. Shades of the movie can be seen in *Crouching Tiger, Hidden Dragon*, as well as a ghost from the past in the form of kung fu diva Cheng Pei-Pei. It was in *Come Drink With Me* that the depiction of the righteous commoner fighting for justice first took root. The film's cinematography has the beauty and delicacy of a Chinese watercolour, and its themes include poetic romance between men and women, which became common in King Hu's work. But despite the seminal nature of Hu's first wuxia pian, *Dragon Gate Inn* was the project on which he had the creative scope to make the film he wanted to make. Freed from the confines of Hong Kong, it was a sweeping epic that took the best of all its predecessors and channelled them in a new, dynamic direction. The film set fictional characters in an actual period in China's past, and took unprecedented care in researching and rendering historic detail. Where *The Story of Wong Fei Hung, Part 1* abandoned the precepts of the wuxia pian to retell the story of a real hero living in recent times, *Dragon Gate Inn* brought the genre into the real world in a time and place that suited its story-line.

The open landscapes of Taiwan allowed Hu to experiment with a visual beauty lacking in the competing genre of kung fu films, the gung-fu pian. Whereas they were simple and straightforward in appearance, Hu used every artifice to make his films as visually complex as possible. The rolling deserts and swaying forests of *Crouching Tiger, Hidden Dragon* and the decisive colour-coding of *Hero* owe a great debt to Hu's vision. Time and again the motifs of *Dragon Gate Inn* are repeated in the genre, underlining the film's profound influence.

In depicting the martial arts, Hu made a stark departure from the norm. Working with Han Ying-Chieh, he created a mixture of fantasy swordplay, traditional kung fu and Beijing opera acrobatics that shaped fight scenes in the martial arts genre for the next three decades. The development of computer generated special effects technology and the increased skill of martial actors have only enhanced his original genius.

While romance is largely ignored and the characters in the film who retain full possession of their genitals never get the chance to exploit this advantage, it still makes a brave attempt at introducing the subject of sexuality to the genre. The scene in which Tou La and his brother's unfortunate physical state is revealed is among the most moving in the film, and merely to examine castration as an issue makes this film unique for its time.

Heroic Ones: Gordon Liu

- AKA: Gordon Liu Chia-hui, Gordon Lau, Gordon Li, Lau Kar-Fei, Lau Ga-Fei, Lau Ga-Fai, Lau Ka-Fai, Liu Chia-Hui, Liu Gu Hiu, Ka Fei Lau, Ka-Fai Lau.
- Nickname: Master Killer.
- Not to be confused with: Sonny Chiba.
- Martial style: Hung gar kung fu, usually as performed by a bald-headed monk.
- Born: 1955 in Guangdong, China.
- Biography: The adopted brother of martial arts director Liu Chia-Liang, Gordon Liu learned traditional kung fu from an early age and later used his skills to become a stuntman and martial arts instructor in the movies. His first acting hit came in 1974 with Chang Cheh's *Shaolin Martial Arts*, and he appeared in several of the director's classic kung fu films. His real break, and the film for which he is most famous in the West, was his brother's 1978 masterpiece *36th Chamber of Shaolin*, from which he got his nickname 'Master Killer', and which established him as a hero of the genre. Making the role of the kung fu monk his own, Liu was the star of 70s Hong Kong cinema, but he struggled in the 80s with the growing popularity of comedy and gun-battle films. The resurrection of the genre in the 1990s led to his rehabilitation, which was completed by his dual casting as the vitriolic, eyeball-snatching kung fu instructor Pai Mei and yakuza hard-man Johnny Mo in Quentin Tarantino's *Kill Bill* films.
- Best kick flicks: *36th Chamber of Shaolin* (1978), *Heroes of the East* (1978), *Last Hero in China* (1993).
- Trivia: As a mark of respect to his instructor, Liu Cham, he took on the name Liu Chia-Hui.
- Where are they now: Although acting roles are now limited, Liu can still be seen on Taiwanese and Hong Kong television and manages his own film production company.

One-Armed Swordsman

(aka Dubi Dao)

Hong Kong, 1967, 111 minutes

Production Company: Shaw Brothers
Director: Chang Cheh [Zhang Cheh]
Martial arts directors: Tong Kai, Liu Chia-Liang [Lau Kar-Leung]
Producer: Runme Shaw
Screenplay: Ngai Hing, Chang Cheh
Directors of photography: Yuan Zengshan, Guan Hanle
Music: Wang Fu-Ling

CAST: Jimmy Wang Yu (*Fang Gang*), Tien Feng (*Qi Ru-Feng*), Pan Yingzi (*Qi Pei*), Chiao Chiao (*Xiao Man*), Huang Zongxun (*Wei*), Chen Yen-Yen (*Mrs Qi*), Liu Chia-Liang (*Ba Sheung*), Tong Dik (*Smiling Tiger Cheng*), Yang Zhiquing (*Long-Armed Devil*), Ku Feng (*Fang Cheng*), Tong Kai (*Killer*): Zhang Beishan, Cheng Lei, Chao Hsiung, Hung Liu, Chang Pei-Shan, Fan Mei Sheng, Wong Kwong Yue, Gai Yuen, Ho Lee-Yan, Cliff Hok, Yang Yee-Kwan, Yuen Cheng-Yan, Yuen Woo-Ping, Mars, Chow Siu Loi, Chan Chuen, Chai No

PLOT: The hero of the piece, Fang Gang, is the adopted son of a great swordmaster, Qi Ru-Feng. The master is also rich and famous, the relevance of which will soon be revealed. The film opens with an assault on Qi's school, from which the master is saved, at great personal cost, by his servant, Fang Cheng, who dies in the process. To honour his saviour, Master Qi raises Fang's orphaned son as his own, and is quite pleased he did when the lad turns out to be a promising martial artist. Meanwhile, Qi's spoiled and petulant daughter, Pei, has her eye on Fang Junior. What's a girl to do when handsome young men insist on standing around chopping wood with their shirts off?

Despite this flirtatious female attention, Fang Gang is not happy. The other students taunt him for his low birth, resenting the presence of a commoner at a school which they consider should only be for the privileged rich. Deciding to run away to avoid causing trouble for his master, Fang is accosted on the road by some fellow students, among them the jilted Qi Pei. During the disagreement that follows, Pei slashes at Gang who, unprepared, fails to defend himself. Incredibly, she manages to cut off his right arm. Pouring blood, Fang Gang staggers to a bridge and promptly falls over the edge, dropping on to the boat of farm girl Xiao Man. While Master Qi is lamenting his death in the river, Fang Gang is being nursed to health by Xiao Man. Predictably, the two fall in love.

Equally predictably, Xiao Man has her own story of woe and orphanhood. Her father was part of the world of martial arts and was killed, leaving her alone. Naturally, she is none too keen on her new love returning to that world. But Fang has other ideas. Hearing that his master is again under attack, he returns to defend him. Failing, he comes back to Xiao Man, who admits that her father left her his secret martial arts manual when he died. The tome has unfortunately been burnt, but, conveniently, the surviving pages propound a unique form of left-handed short sword fighting. Fang Gang learns the art by spending a lot of time on his own in the forest.

Meanwhile, his enemies have developed a cunning, and somewhat unsporting, sword locking technique, which allows them to disable the broadswords used by the Qi School fighters. What they don't know, of course, is that Fang fights with the broken end of his father's sword, which is immune to their ploy. Thank Buddha for dead fathers' dubious heirlooms.

Master Qi's birthday is rapidly approaching and his enemies, led by Long-Armed Devil, are plotting to destroy him at the happy event. As Qi's students journey there, they are picked off one by one. Fang learns of the plot and has a quick bout of inner turmoil while he decides whether to save his sifu or honour his promise to Xiao Man to leave all that martial stuff behind and settle down as a farmer. Fortunately for the sake of a dramatic finale, loyalty to his teacher wins, and he heads off to meet his enemies and exact his revenge.

CASTING: Jimmy Wang Yu was the ideal choice to play the one-armed loner, ostracised from society. It clearly suited him, as he went on to make a career out of being the Chinese James Dean. The most exciting thing in the film by far, Wang Yu broods magnificently. Although not a martial artist by training – his physical talents lay in swimming and water polo – he nonetheless captured the audience's imagination as the outcast who returns to defend the one man who was kind to him. His casting revived the trend, which had slipped out of fashion following the *Wong Fei Hung* films, of employing actors instead of martial artists in the genre's lead roles. This practice has continued over the years, with mixed success, although it certainly bore fruit in the outstanding performance of Chow Yun-Fat as the Wudan warrior Li Mu Bai in *Crouching Tiger, Hidden Dragon*.

Jimmy Wang Yu brings more to the film than the ability to fake kung fu – his posturing and teenage angst are almost enough to carry it on their own. His first major role was as the lead in the lumpen *Tiger Boy* in 1964, also directed by Chang Cheh, but it didn't hinder his career. He did well in a number of Shaw Brothers productions, becoming a popular star by the time he was offered the lead in *One-Armed Swordsman*. Developing a degree of theatrical martial skill, Wang Yu raised playing the heroic loner into an art form, with a good line in agonising deaths and an even better one in one-armed fighting. His last major contribution to the industry was as yet another warrior challenged in the limb department in 1977's *One-Armed Chivalry Fights Against One-Armed Chivalry*. He failed in all his attempts to make a buddy movie, and would never have suited the sifu-disciple themed films that were later made by Liu Chia-Liang and Yuen Woo-Ping, both of whom, incidentally, appear in *One-Armed Swordsman*.

Other one-armed exploits for Wang Yu include *Return of the One-Armed Swordsman*, *One-Armed Boxer*, the imaginatively titled *One-Armed Swordsmen* and the Japanese-made *Zatôichi and the One-Armed Swordsman*. One can only assume he became very proficient with his left hand. Clearly suffering from some kind of masochistic complex, Wang Yu's films all end with the hero maimed, drenched in blood or, better yet, dead.

MARTIAL ARTS: Although Jimmy Wang Yu was not a martial artist, there are plenty of actors in the film who are, including the two action choreographers, Tong Kai and Liu Chia-Liang. The fighting style in 1960s gung-fu pian, among which *One-Armed Swordsman* is a defining production, is more brutal than that of the wuxia pian and is based on real martial skill. The trend for action directors to appear in the fights as well as choreograph them became firmly established at this point. Other notable kick-merchants who get an outing alongside the one-armed hero are Yuen Woo-Ping and the enigmatically named Mars.

In the staging of its fight scenes, *One-Armed Swordsman* sparked a revolution by pitting different fighting styles against one another. The emphasis on a warrior's training and struggle to achieve mastery is an early development of this popular theme, showing a greater appreciation of the difficulties in gaining martial arts skills. No magic scroll is going to make up for not putting in the hours. But the film does not complete the theme: there is no representation of the master-student relationship that would come to dominate later kung fu movies. When Liu Chia-Liang and Yuen Woo-Ping sat in the director's chair, the 'You killed my master! Now you must die!' plot-line became almost statutory. But Jimmy Wang Yu, the brooding loner, did not fit this mould. His were martial arts achieved through stoic determination, sweating alone in a forest, with the assistance of a few cunning special effects. For the One-Armed Swordsman, attitude is infinitely more important than aptitude.

Perhaps because of the star's lack of martial knowledge (he manages to get his arm cut off by a stroppy teenager wildly waving a sword about, after all), there is a heavy reliance on gimmicks. With the clamping sword used by the bandits to disable the Qi broadswords, Chang Cheh harks back to the unique, individual weapons of early wuxia. In many ways, the emphasis on the weapons used has more parallels with Japanese samurai films, in which the soul of the samurai resides in his sword. In Chinese swordplay, the weapon should be a physical extension of the fighter's own power. In this respect, *One-Armed Swordsman* misinterprets kung fu philosophy, a theme that would play a central role in later films in the genre.

Still, it all looks pretty good. The fight at the roadside tea stall has inspired a hundred combat scenarios. On its own terms, the sequence also pays tribute to the teahouse brawl in *Come Drink With Me*. Facing off against the bandits, Jimmy Wang Yu attacks them with a mesmerising display of brute force that remained unmatched until the arrival of Bruce Lee in the 1970s. Some of the early fight scenes are overly simple and fail to mask Wang Yu's inadequacies (although the champion swimmer has some bulging biceps behind his sword strokes), but during the course of the movie the action becomes both more convincing and more exciting. Filmed with vitality, the 'hyper-real' battles between characters who, although they are unable to fly, are just a little bit more than human, are satisfyingly forceful, as Fang launches himself head-first at his opponents.

STUNTS AND SPECIAL EFFECTS: The nature of this film as an original gung-fu pian requires that the fighting be enhanced with a minimum of special effects. While the actors are helped on their way by the occasional trampoline or wire lift, there is no full-on, gravity-defying wire-work, no fancy acrobatics, just a lot of good, honest, kick-arse action. Don't expect flashes of lightning and palpable bolts of chi flying from sword tips to decimate enemies. The fighting is basic and straightforward, often failing to exploit the talents of the highly skilled martial artists in the cast.

DIRECTOR: Chang Cheh (1923–2002), who drew so many blood baths, and whose influence can be seen down the years until it comes to graphic fruition in Quentin Tarantino's *Kill Bill* films, was Shaw Brothers' favourite son. He made *One-Armed Swordsman* into a franchise, reprising the character with *Return of the One-Armed Swordsman*, starring Jimmy Wang Yu again, and *New One-Armed Swordsman* with David Chiang in the title role.

The Godfather of Hong Kong action flicks began his film career writing screenplays in Shanghai. He was already a director when he moved to Hong Kong in 1957, having made films in Taiwan. He joined Shaw Brothers in 1962 and, finding the necessary support for the kind of films he wanted to make, went on to direct some of the best known kung fu movies of all time, among them *Golden Swallow*, *Vengeance* and, of course, *One-Armed Swordsman*. Chang lorded it over the Hong Kong film industry in the 1960s and 70s. His achievements were only matched by those of King Hu, and his popularity only threatened by Bruce Lee.

Chang's influence on the invention of a new, more hardcore type of kick flick is undeniable. The director himself claimed to have utterly changed the focus of wuxia pian, abandoning central female characters for a more masculine style of violence: he is comparable to the Italian director Sergio Leone in his creation of dramatic brutality. Chang raised the star value of male actors, including Wang Yu, to a new level, and the rest of the industry followed. He paved the way for Bruce Lee, Sammo Hung and Gordon Liu to take the leading roles in kung fu films, relegating his female characters to helpless damsels or abandoned lovers. He also mentored director John Woo, his assistant director on *Blood Brothers*, who would go on to make some of the most violent films in Hong Kong history. In the 1980s, Woo spawned gun-fu, martial arts with bullets, filled with hard-bitten male anti-heroes like Chow Yun-Fat in *A Better Tomorrow*. In fact, that film and *The Killer* have been described by Woo as 'wuxia in modern drag'. 'To me the gangster films are just like Chinese swordplay pictures. To me Chow Yun-Fat holding a gun is just like Wang Yu holding a sword.'

Of his first wuxia, *Young Dragons*, Woo says, 'There are many shadows of Chang Cheh in it.' Conclusive evidence of Chang Cheh's influence on his protegé is Woo's 1979 costume drama *Last Hurrah for Chivalry*, a nostalgic and cynical diatribe on the loss of the value system of the knights-errant in their search for justice. The director created what he describes as a 'grim sense of a fog of amorality settling over the jianghu', which the few remaining swordsmen can do nothing to reverse. The film contains many of the elements seen in Chang's productions, and takes his preoccupation with alienation to the extreme, where the virtuous xia are seen as relics, outcasts in their own world. John Woo has said of Chang Cheh that he forever 'changed the techniques and the level of skill in the Hong Kong action film' and was 'a pioneer of martial arts films'.

PRODUCTION: The surviving prints of *One-Armed Swordsman* are very dark, making it hard to appreciate the quality of the production. Shot in widescreen, the entire frame is used to encompass the action, so it's best not to sit too close. The story pounds along, and the film's lively camera work complements it well. Chang Cheh openly acknowledged the influence of director Arthur Penn in his use of slow motion and unusual choice of focus: on the blade of a sword rather than the man who holds it, for example. Penn's 1967 gangster movie *Bonnie and Clyde* provides the most obvious comparison with Chang's work. The death scene at the end of the American film is recreated in the

Chinese director's *Golden Swallow*, the unofficial sequel to *Come Drink With Me*, only with swords instead of guns.

In direct contrast to King Hu's detailed introduction of his evil protagonists at the start of *Dragon Gate Inn*, Chang raises suspense levels by showing Fang Gang's nemesis, Long-Armed Devil, from the back throughout the entire movie. Only in the final scenes is the tyrant revealed in all his villainy.

Although much of the action, especially the fighting, appears staid and plodding due to the limited capabilities of the 1960s Hong Kong film industry, Chang nevertheless created some special moments, making the most of the tools at his disposal. The teahouse fight scene is lit in glorious golden sunshine, with a handheld camera achieving extreme angles to create the impression of space in a cramped area. Moments such as this have allowed *One-Armed Swordsman* to endure as a classic despite the primitive quality of its production.

TRIVIA: Scriptwriter Ngai Hong wrote over 400 screenplays in the course of his fifty-year career. Not only did he pen the majority of films made by Chang Cheh, he went on to write the classic Bruce Lee vehicles *The Big Boss* and *Fist of Fury*. When Tsui Hark remade *One-Armed Swordsman* as *The Blade* in 1995, he felt that the concept of a highly skilled martial hero losing his arm to an inferior female was too implausible, and changed the plot to have the hero relieved of his limb by bandits from whom he has just rescued his master's daughter. Interestingly, the film also abandons Tsui's trademark magical flying, and leaves his heroes to rely on their own – very apparent – physical abilities. Other knockoffs of the original include *One-Armed Swordswoman*, which can only have inspired Chang's disgust, given his attempts to downgrade the role of women in the genre.

THEMES: Unsurprisingly, one of the major themes of this late-60s film is teenage angst and alienation. Jimmy Wang Yu might as well be Marlon Brando or Jimmy Dean, all brooding looks and feelings of being misunderstood. Parallels can easily be drawn between *One-Armed Swordsman* and *Rebel Without a Cause*. Wang Yu's character is rejected by his classmates at the Qi Kung Fu School and mutilated by his master's daughter for rejecting her advances. Even his new girlfriend doesn't seem to understand that martial arts are his life and, frankly, just a bit more exciting than being a farmer. The loss of his arm is the ultimate symbol of Fang Gang's exile from the world he grew up in. In China, left-handedness has long been considered undesirable. By having his hero relieved of his right arm, Chang Cheh ensures that he must struggle both for acceptance by society and to learn to fight again, in spite of his handicap.

The imagery of the film enhances the sense that Fang is an outcast. He wears plain, homespun clothes, in direct contrast to the fine apparel of his richer fellows. These students, who scorn him while he completes his chores, are also outcasts in a way: instead of being taught by their wealthy martial artist fathers, they are packed off to be raised by Qi Ru-Feng at the kung fu equivalent of Eton. Qi's daughter Pei is also rejected, spurned by Fang Gang, although it's hard to feel sorry for someone who cuts off her would-be lover's arm because he doesn't fancy her. Ultimately, however, it is Xiao Han who suffers most. Born to the world of martial arts, she is kept from it by her mother after her father is killed, and doesn't even know her real family name. Fatherless, she hates the world that took him from her, yet nurses her lover back to health so that he can return to it. Sacrificing her own happiness, she gives Gang her father's kung fu manual, which he died defending, allowing her new love to learn the forgotten left-handed style.

Essentially, this is as much a character drama as a standard chopsocky movie, and the director's attention to detail in his protagonists' development raises *One-Armed Swordsman* to a higher plane than many of the films that followed in its wake. Even in Chang's sequel, *Return of the One-Armed Swordsman*, the plot and characters are far sketchier, although the theme of alienation persists. The greatest martial artists in the world are held hostage and their sons instructed to sever and deliver their own right arms in order to get their fathers back. In cutting off their limbs, the sons face irreversible banishment from the society of swordsmen. In the sequel, Fang Gang himself has reached the point of being utterly disillusioned with the martial world, and spends most of his time mooching around in a moody fashion.

The common element of a student's unwavering loyalty to his master is strongly felt throughout the original film. Fang takes devotion to a new level to save the man who raised him, but the

film does not show the development of their relationship –
something that is central to many other martial arts films, from
The Story of Wong Fei Hung, Part 1 to *The Karate Kid* – avoiding
sifu-student training scenes in favour of Fang Gang studying alone.
There is no real closeness between the two men, but this just
makes Fang Gang's determined faithfulness stand out all the more.

The theme of one clan fighting another for dominance and the
right to say their kung fu is best is evident in all of the *One-Armed
Swordsman* films, as it has been since the very beginnings of
wuxia. With Fang Gang, Jimmy Wang Yu creates the ultimate
anti-hero, engaged in the quest for revenge and rehabilitation.
Think of The Bride in *Kill Bill*, seeking redress for having had her
life ripped away from her. This is a classic plot device in kung fu
films: Chang Cheh's *Vengeance* is named for its protagonist's
main motivation.

Pursuing revenge with a newly learned skill, such as left-handed
knife fighting, is another staple of the genre, as is the unfulfilled
desire to leave the martial world or someone else's desire for the
hero to do so. Just as Xiao Man in *One-Armed Swordsman* lost
her father in a kung fu fight, so Butterfly in *Butterfly and Sword*
lost hers and allows herself to be fooled into believing that her
secret agent husband is a common merchant. In *Tai Chi Boxer*,
Jackie's father, the renowned master, tries to leave the martial
clan for the good of his son, but is repeatedly pulled back by
people wanting to challenge him to prove they are better.
Naturally, he finds this exasperating, but obliges by throwing
them into nearby trees.

Romance is also much in evidence in *One-Armed Swordsman*,
although not in the poetic form seen in the films of King Hu.
Unrequited or doomed, it provides motivation for the characters,
and in the case of Fang Gang, is both the cause of his alienation
and his means of return. The chronic overacting of Chiao Chiao
as she rushes off in tears every time Gang waves a sword in the air
is also typical of the genre, generated from its beginnings in opera
dramatics. Women are lucky to get a look-in in this film; in most
of Chang Cheh's work they are incidental or an unavoidable
annoyance, and he focuses instead on the relationships between
men. A common emphasis in gung-fu pian, it can also be seen in
the male-bonding, buddy-movie style of the Hong Kong gangster
films that grew out of them.

PLACE WITHIN THE GENRE: *One-Armed Swordsman* is often seen as the moment when traditional wuxia pian morphed into the modern kung fu film. Indeed, it has even been referred to as 'the most significant wuxia in Hong Kong film history'. Poised between the old and the new, it draws on elements from *Come Drink With Me*, the *Wong Fei Hung* series and many of the martial arts movies of the 1950s and early 60s, while maintaining an idiom all its own. With its swordplay and costumes rooted in the wuxia genre, and many of what would become typical kick flick devices already in evidence, the film hangs between the two, bridging the gap – although its feet are firmly planted on the side of the modern movie.

It was also monumentally successful, the first film in Hong Kong history to gross $1million at the box-office. It appealed both to a generation of teenagers who felt alienated from traditional society and to their elders who had been forced to leave behind life in China for the colonial outpost and could draw parallels between themselves and the exiled swordsman. That Tsui Hark (*Once Upon a Time in China*) chose to remake the film is a testament to its impact – although, as he was also producer on a remake of *Dragon Gate Inn*, Tsui clearly recognises the attributes of both branches of martial film.

One-Armed Swordsman wouldn't be the film it is if it didn't draw on outside influences. Chang Cheh looked beyond the boundaries of the Hong Kong and Chinese film industries and found inspiration in the cinema of Japan. At the time, Shaw Brothers was losing business to Japanese productions, and had decided to wrest back its market share by exploiting some of its rival's most popular features. It is fitting, when you consider that the movie proved to be as influential as *Seven Samurai* in the sheer number of films that can be traced back to it, that *One-Armed Swordsman* bears some resemblance to bushido films. The bloody battles, the lone swordsman and the emphasis on the types of weapons used all recall Japanese films. The favour was returned when Jimmy Wang Yu introduced a Chinese influence to the classic Japanese *Zatôichi* series, appearing as the eponymous disadvantaged warrior in *Zatôichi Meets the One-Armed Swordsman* in 1971. Once again he is cast as the outsider, this time in a strange land, having fled his home for undisclosed reasons. The resulting clash of cultures and comedy moments of misunderstood words are sadly somewhat lost in the all-English subtitles.

Today's viewers, used to non-stop action, slick editing and high production values, may find *One-Armed Swordsman* less exciting than its place in the genre, and its general conception, would suggest. The poor quality of the surviving prints doesn't help, either. But even if the fight scenes seem slow, the romance over-acted and the motivation of the main characters frankly questionable, there are moments of genius throughout that remind the viewer just how important this film was in the founding of the modern martial arts movie.

Heroic Ones: Jimmy Wang Yu

- **AKA:** Wang Yu, Jimmy Wang, Wang Yue, Wang Zheng-Quan, Wong Yu-Lung, Yue Wang.
- **Birth name:** Wang Yu.
- **Martial style:** Chinese straight sword, although not originly trained as a martial artist. Known for playing warriors somewhat lacking in the limb department.
- **Born:** 28 March 1944 in Wuxi, Jiangsu Province, China.
- **Biography:** Athletic, charismatic and brutal, Wang Yu reclaimed the martial arts film genre from the women who had dominated it through the 50s, creating a new and more violent hero in *One-Armed Swordsman*. By starring in what was to become a turning point in the development of the wuxia pian, Wang Yu became the premier martial arts star in southeast Asia, and remained so until a young man by the name of Bruce Lee hit the big screen. Signing with Shaw Brothers Studios in 1963, he became, through his physical and acting abilities, the golden boy of Hong Kong cinema, and ensured the position of the Shaws as the pre-eminent force in the industry. Taken on as a leading man by director Chang Cheh to star in his early heroic bloodshed films, Wang Yu became synonymous with the character of the warrior who has his arm chopped off by a vindictive female and has to learn a new style of fighting. *One-Armed Swordsman* was a massive hit in Hong Kong and its success was quickly followed by *Golden Swallow*. Various *Swordsman* sequels were subsequently made, but Wang Yu left Shaw Brothers in the 70s to direct and produce his own films. Few were popular, and rumours of links with the triads as well as a murder charge in Taiwan didn't help. The later decades of his career failed to match the prolific output of the 60s and 70s.
- **Best kick flicks:** *One-Armed Swordsman* (1967), *Golden Swallow* (1968), *36th Chamber of Shaolin* (1978).

- Trivia: Wang Yu is a former Hong Kong Swimming Champion, a feat he presumably achieved with both arms.
- Where are they now: Jimmy Wang Yu was last publicly seen attending the funeral of his mentor Chang Cheh in 2002. He was included in footage from *Savage Killers* in *Kung Pow: Enter the Fist* (2002).

Summary

These films represent three very distant points on the map of the martial genre's development. Nonetheless, it would be impossible to separate them when plotting the course of its growth, just as it would be impossible to sever a major artery and expect blood to continue nourishing the brain. *The Story of Wong Fei Hung, Part 1* is best viewed in the context of its time; unless they have a marked preference for the silent movies of the 1920s, this film will leave modern viewers in search of kick flick action cold. It is notable for its pioneering role in allowing wuxia to move beyond mystic flying and for gilding the legend of Wong Fei Hung, but is not a movie that martial arts film fans would choose to watch again and again – which is just as well, as it is almost impossible to get hold of.

Dragon Gate Inn suffers less in comparison with modern action films, although people are far more likely to have seen the remake than the original. This is a great shame, as the earlier film showcases the many fine qualities of King Hu's films, providing a feast for the senses as well as adrenalin pumping action. Naturally, it holds an important place in the continuing expansion of the wuxia pian, but, on a less highbrow level, you just can't go wrong with a film set in an inn full of booby traps.

What *One-Armed Swordsman* may lack in aesthetic quality, it makes up for in bloody carnage. This is a film for the lover of classic samurai movies, complete with spurting blood, severed limbs and fantastically gratuitous violence. The real beginning of the gung-fu pian – it might be hard to see the connection between Jimmy Wang Yu's baleful hero and the cheeky chappie played by Jackie Chan in the 1980s, but you cannot have one without the other – this is where kung fu action was given its head. Enjoy it for the gore and Wang Yu showing what happens when you give a misunderstood adolescent a sword and the skills to use it.

Rumble in Hong Kong: The Golden Age of Kick Flicks

Events of the early 1970s changed the face of martial arts films forever. In the decades that followed, Hong Kong became the powerhouse of Asian filmmaking, and its main currency was kick flicks. Movies that had been made for a largely domestic market began to find a passionate audience across the globe and gained a cult following. In the wake of the innovators of the 60s came a new breed of directors who took the genre to another level, and with them came the martial arts action superstars who could rise to the demands placed upon them to be both flamboyant fighters and convincing actors.

Recognising the appeal of the genre, in the 1970s Shaw Brothers focused increasingly on the production of kung fu films, costume dramas and sword-fighting epics, and in the most successful cases combining all three. The studio began to co-produce movies with Western film companies, whose interest in the genre was burgeoning, giving the studio access to larger budgets than the genre had previously commanded. This, combined with American and European technologies, allowed for a better quality of production and a wider international audience.

But Run Run Shaw also sensed bad omens in the West. He looked to America and saw the growing popularity of television. Fearing that the draw of films shown in cinemas would wane as more and more people enjoyed on-screen entertainment at home, he diversified, cutting down film production and founding TVB, Hong Kong's first terrestrial commercial TV station, in 1973. This move opened up the film industry to other, smaller production companies, including Golden Harvest, set up by Raymond Chow, Leonard Ho and Leung Feng in 1970. Having previously worked for Shaw Brothers, Chow wanted to continue in movies, which he still felt had massive potential. Golden Harvest became largely responsible for the successful penetration of the international market, for two very powerful reasons.

The first was the vision of its founders. Producing four films in their first year, starting with *The Invincible Eight,* directed by Lo Wei, they expressly intended to reach a wider audience, including overseas viewers. Early on they made a *Zatôichi* film as a co-production with the Japanese, showing a desire to expand and utilise the resources of foreign organisations.

The second reason was an American-born Hong Kong actor by the name of Bruce Lee. Signed by Golden Harvest in 1971, Lee made only four complete films in his adult career, but he remains the most famous martial artist ever, and arguably one of the most recognisable actors in the world. Only Jackie Chan comes close in terms of fame – and only after a career spanning 35 years – and no one in the industry is comparable in terms of fighting ability. Lee's charisma, devastating martial talent and command of English opened up new markets for Asian kick flicks and raised the bar in terms of style, content and realism. While his first films, *The Big Boss* and *Fist of Fury*, are notable mainly for Lee's characteristic fighting style – shirt off, bouncing on his toes, kicking with the power of a demolition ball – and his menacing, camera-pleasing looks, it was **Enter the Dragon** that made him an international icon. Not his best film – it was restricted by the requirements of its US financiers, Warner Brothers, and directed by a man who knew little about martial arts and less about how to make the most of his star – this is still the best-known film in the history of the genre. It represents the power of Hong Kong movies to take on the rest of the world, the willingness of Western studios to back kick flicks and the culmination of Lee's career as an actor.

Then in 1973 Lee died, and the martial arts film industry almost collapsed. His early death has, of course, only added to his fame. Even more so than Jimmy Wang Yu, whose star he eclipsed, Lee can be compared to James Dean: both died before their time, leaving behind a few masterpieces that illustrate their potential and an image that is instantly recognisable. Lee's effect on the industry, however, has been far greater than Dean's.

Desperately seeking a replacement for their lost star, the Hong Kong film industry's eyes lit upon Jackie Chan. Cathay cast him in a number of kung fu movies (directed by Lo Wei, who made Bruce Lee's first two films), including the blatantly derivative *New Fist of Fury*, but they failed to force him into the Lee mould – Chan just could not pull off the smouldering looks and muscle flexing – and martial arts films seemed destined to languish in a plethora of bad Bruce Lee impersonations. But Jackie Chan had other ideas. Funded by Golden Harvest and supported by his Chinese opera school classmates Sammo Hung, Yuen Biao and action director Yuen Woo-Ping, Chan took breathtaking acrobatic martial moves and mixed them with comedy. The results were works of genius, and tremendously successful in the Asian market. Comedy and kung fu were the perfect mix, giving the audience the chance to enjoy action films without being painfully reminded of Bruce Lee. From 1979's *Snake in the Eagle's Shadow* to the opera brothers' smash *Project A* in 1983, the wu da pian (fight films involving martial arts and bone-crushing stunts) were the model that almost everyone in the industry followed. Traditional martial arts were given the operatic treatment, with the likes of Chan, Hung and Yuen somersaulting and back-flipping their way to fame.

The resurgence of the genre has another man to thank, however. Alongside the slapstick of the wu da pian, the kung fu films – gung-fu pian – were also developing. Spearheaded by director Liu Chia-Liang (otherwise known as Lau Kar-Leung), real kung fu was finally getting the treatment it deserved, and the legend of Shaolin was born. A proponent of hung gar kung fu, Liu can trace his martial lineage back through Wong Fei Hung to Zhi Shan, a monk from the Shaolin Temple who escaped the Manchurian suppression and taught kung fu to the people. Having worked as action director on a number of kung fu films, including *One-Armed Swordsman*, Liu came to the role of director wanting to show what the trained martial artist could really achieve, and where their skills originated. Largely abandoning wire-work, and refusing to follow in the footsteps of the wu da pian's crazy stunts, he displayed his genius in choreographing stunning fight sequences to showcase the talents of his actors. Among these movies, *36th Chamber of Shaolin* is his masterpiece. Directors such as Cheng Yan-Yim and Xiao Long followed in his wake, keeping the spirit of Chang Cheh's earlier films alive.

In the 1980s, Hong Kong was the centre of south-east Asian cinema. Of the four 'economic dragons', Singapore, South Korea, Taiwan and Hong Kong, only the last had a movie industry that reflected its overall social and financial development. This was due in part to the continuing popularity of cinema in the face of competition from television, despite the fears of Run Run Shaw. The freedom of expression possible in Hong Kong, with its more liberal government and less restrictive censorship, also helped to support the film industry. Owing to British influence in the colony, its filmmaking incorporated both international and traditional Chinese elements, and managed to balance the absorption of Western influences by the Chinese with their desire to hang on to their cultural roots.

But despite this success, there was also a sense of approaching crisis. The British had agreed to hand over the colony to the Chinese government in 1997, and the predominant feeling in the film industry was that it was living on borrowed time. To an extent this drove the filmmakers to greater heights: success was one way of guaranteeing that they would be left alone to get on with it. Hong Kong citizens were examining their identity, and the plot-lines of films now reflected this trend. The structure of the industry changed too. Smaller production houses took over from the big studios. In the mid-80s, Shaw Brothers stopped producing films in Hong Kong, focusing its efforts on TVB. A new generation of filmmakers arose to take on the challenges of a new era. Unlike their predecessors of the 60s and early 70s, who had mostly been born in Mainland China, the new school were bred in Hong Kong and raised in television studios and on Western film lots.

This era saw a shift from period dramas set in the good (or bad) old days of China and Hong Kong to contemporary settings. The landscapes of the jianghu and early colonial settlements gave way to urban scenes. Dean Shek and Karl Maka's company Cinema City did it with *Aces Go Places* in 1982, Sammo Hung followed suit with the *Lucky Stars* series and Jackie Chan was hot on their heels with his *Police Story* films. Even director Tsui Hark, who had begun his career with *Butterfly Murders*, set in historic China, and would later go on to revive period drama, tried his hand at modern comedy. The industry moved away from the traditional and created cinema that belonged to contemporary Hong Kong, with great success. Nostalgia for the old days was restricted to the history of Hong Kong, exemplified by **Project A**, and Canton patriots abounded. China was portrayed in the light of its relationship with Hong Kong and costume epics disappeared for the rest of the decade.

But the 1990s saw the comeback of traditional wuxia pian. Recognising that reunification with China was inevitable, some filmmakers tried to soften the blow, among them Tsui Hark with his epic *Once Upon a Time in China* series. In Jet Li he found the perfect star – a champion of modern wushu who combined traditional martial arts with the ability to put on a great performance. The resurgence of the genre in the 1990s even drew Shaw Brothers out of hibernation, and in 1995 the studio began sporadically producing films again.

Still the international market had not been breached. Jackie Chan's US outings *The Big Brawl* and *The Protector*, released in 1980, had gone nowhere, and Hong Kong cinema was largely restricted to art houses around the world. But the genre survived from the death of Bruce Lee to the mid-1990s because of the loyalty of audiences at home, in cult followings throughout the world and by constantly reinventing itself. Responding to political, social and technical change, martial arts stayed at the forefront of Asian cinema.

Enter the Dragon

Hong Kong/USA, 1973, 102 minutes

Production companies: Warner Brothers, Golden Harvest,
Concord Productions
Director: Robert Clouse
Fight sequences staged by: Bruce Lee
Producers: Fred Weintraub, Paul Heller
Associate producer: Raymond Chow
Music: Lalo Schifrin

CAST: Bruce Lee (*Lee*), John Saxon (*Roper*), Jim Kelly (*Williams*), Shih Kien [Sek Kin] (*Han*), Ahna Capri (*Tania*), Bob Wall (*Oharra*), Angela Mao Ying (*Lee Su-Lin*), Betty Chung (*Mei-Ling*), Geoffrey Weeks (*Braithwaite*), Yang Sze (*Bolo*), Peter Archer (*Parsons*): Lam Ching Ying, Chuck Norris, Sammo Hung, Mykelti Williamson, Jackie Chan, Steve Sanders

PLOT: Lee is training at the Shaolin Temple when the Abbot tells him how one of their former monks and martial arts students, Han, has turned to the dark side of kung fu. He is using his skills for personal gain, and doesn't care whom he harms along the way

– against the temple's teaching. The monk introduces Lee to Braithwaite, a very British member of an undisclosed intelligence agency which sells its information to international governments. Braithwaite convinces Lee that he must enter Han's martial arts tournament to find out more about his opium- and people-smuggling operations. Han, who lives in an island fortress, will not allow guns anywhere near him, so Lee's martial skills should come in handy, as well as giving him a reason to be on the island. There is already a female operative there, Mei-Ling, with whom Lee must attempt to rendezvous.

As the competitors gather in Hong Kong to be escorted to Han's island, a series of flashbacks illustrates their motivation. As well as being in the employ of the British intelligence agency, punishing Han for desecrating the ways of Shaolin and generally being against prostitution and drug smuggling, Lee is provided with a further incentive by a visit to his father. During Han's last tournament, three years previously, Lee Senior and his daughter, Su-Lin, were in Hong Kong. Su-Lin was molested by some of Han's men, including evil henchman Oharra, resulting in her father slashing Oharra's face and Su-Lin being forced to flee. Despite demonstrating some fine martial skills, Su-Lin is run to ground and, rather than be raped by Oharra, commits suicide with a sheet of broken glass. Lee is then seen at his mother's and sister's graves, apologising for the violence he is planning to commit to revenge Su-Lin's death.

Then it is Roper's turn. The compulsive gambler and con man is up to his neck in debt to the mob. He fights off the mafia goons on a golf course with some unexpected karate but, having only $67 in the bank, is forced to accept Han's challenge in the hope of winning the prize money, or at least some wagers. Williams, a member of an all-black karate dojo, is on the run after beating two racist policemen and stealing their car. Already on his way to the tournament when he was accosted, he is now forced to seek sanctuary there.

On the boat to Han's island, Roper and Williams greet each other as old 'Nam buddies, and Lee demonstrates to the Kiwi contestant, Parsons, the art of fighting without fighting. Reaching their destination, all the contestants are invited to a lavish party, with entertainments including sumo wrestling, acrobatics and a choose-your-own-seafood tank. Their host arrives, heralded by a gong and escorted by a host of lovely women, who prove that they are also deadly by throwing darts into apples. Among them is Mei-Ling. Later that night, further entertainment is on offer in the form of women on tap. Lee requests Mei-Ling, who reveals that she is trapped on the island and has been unable to leave the palace to find out what is going on. She does know, however, that women keep disappearing from the place.

At the tournament, Roper and Williams con the spectators out of their money and show that they are competent fighters. Lee takes revenge on Oharra for the death of Su Lin, breaking his neck. At night, Lee dons a black cat suit and jumps out the window to have a look around. As well as beating up a couple of goons, he finds Han's underground chambers, which house his prisons and opium-processing plant. Williams also chooses to take a wander, is spotted by the guards and in turn notices Lee returning to his room.

The following day at the tournament, Han punishes his guards for letting his guests wander around at night, having Bolo kill them and then checking to see if any of the contestants are shocked. Summoning Williams, he accuses him of being a spy. Williams denies it, pointing out that all he cares about is winning and looking good. In return Han kills him, bludgeoning him to death with an iron hand. Han then goes after Roper, threatening to guillotine his own cat before revealing the details of his drug and slavery business and offering Roper the post of factor in America. Roper, while having nothing against drugs and prostitution per se, draws the line when he realises that Han has killed his friend Williams, who no longer looks good, beaten to a bloody pulp and suspended over a vat of acid.

While snooping around that night, Lee narrowly avoids being bitten by a cobra and radios for help. The radio sets off an alarm and he is forced to fight for his life, using a range of weapons wrested from the guards he defeats, before being trapped in a steel-walled well. The following day, Lee and Roper are matched against each other, neither knowing what the other has been through. Refusing to fight someone he has nothing against (and who is very, very good), Roper instead takes on the mighty Bolo, narrowly defeating him before joining Lee to beat off the combined might of Han's martial army. Mei-Ling, meanwhile, has released all the prisoners, who join the fray. Lee goes after

Han, who attacks him with various artificial hands before leading him into a hall of mirrors. Heeding his teacher's advice to shatter illusions, Lee smashes the mirrors to find the real Han, tells him that he has dishonoured Lee's family and his temple and kicks him on to a spear. An exhausted Lee and Roper give each other the thumbs up before the British cavalry arrives. Finally.

CASTING: It is a little-known fact that Bruce Lee was an actor before he was a martial artist. Following in his father's footsteps, he appeared in eighteen Chinese language films before he was as many years old. *Enter the Dragon* was conceived to showcase Lee's talents, and no one else could have played his part. It is a shame that there is not more martial action – there is almost too much plot and not enough of Lee doing what he is best at, as if the filmmakers didn't quite realise why people would be going to see the movie.

As for the acting, it is not how well Bruce Lee plays the part but how well the part fits him. Having rewritten half the script, Lee finally got the character he had always wanted to play, mixing his philosophy of martial arts with demonstrations of his awesome skills. Refusing to be swayed by the desires and influences of others, the fictional Lee remains aloof, involving himself only when he deems it necessary, and then on his own terms. The causes of family and honour are his motivation, and in some ways all of Lee's previous roles can be seen as leading up to this point.

Bruce Lee had a gung-ho attitude and intense charisma that ideally suited this first US venture into Hong Kong territory. Warner Brothers had cautiously waited to see the popularity of the genre grow before they invested money in it, and they chose their star with equal care. Had it not been for Lee's ability to be all things to all people, mixing Chinese culture with the kind of individualism Americans demanded from their film stars, it is unlikely that a US-funded martial arts film would have been made as early as 1973. It didn't hurt that he was good-looking and amazingly toned, and was happy to remove his shirt and flex his muscles at the slightest provocation.

In spite of all this, Warner Brothers was still not comfortable with the idea of an Asian leading man, or at least believed its audiences wouldn't be. In the US cinema trailers, Lee is either credited third, after Saxon and Kelly (who was even less well known than Lee), or jointly with Saxon. Trying to make *Enter the Dragon* representational, yet fearing that the viewers wouldn't be able to identify with an Asian male lead, the studio ended up creating a series of trailers that bear little relation to the story-line. Proving the doubters wrong, the instant success of *Enter the Dragon*, and the performance of its real leading man, made Lee an international superstar and had film producers desperate to cast him. They were to be disappointed: Lee had died six days before the film was released.

When filling the parts for *Enter the Dragon*, Warner Brothers' criteria seem to be based on the martial arts honours won by the cast. Jim Kelly, who plays Williams, was not an actor, and this was his first film. Before that, he was busy winning the title of International Middleweight Karate Champion. Bob Wall, cast as the scarred henchman Oharra, was a Professional Karate Champion, while Yan Tse, the implacable Bolo, was Shokotan Champion of Asia. Angela Mao Lin as Su-Lin, whose martial displays are sadly limited to the fight scene preceding her death early in the film, was another titled competitor; an opera performer who discovered her flexibility was well suited to martial arts, she was Black Belt Hapkido Champion of Okinawa.

Even John Saxon, known more as a B-movie Hollywood actor than anything else, possessed a black belt in karate. And if his kicks seem a little ungainly, and don't quite reach head height, perhaps the blame should rest with his tight grey flares rather than his lack of flexibility – 70s fashions were very bad for martial arts.

Sek Kin does a fine, if stereotyped, turn as the evil Dr No character Han. Well used to playing the bad guy from his adventures opposite Kwan Tak-Hing in the *Wong Fei Hung* films, he is right at home in the moustachioed, cat-stroking role. It is impossible to fully appreciate his acting, however, as his voice is dubbed throughout.

The rest of the cast is made up of some of the best stuntmen and martial artists in Hong Kong. And some very ropy extras. Sammo Hung, who gets a cameo in the opening sequence, made sure that all his little opera brothers got in on the action, including Jackie Chan, Yuen Biao and Yuen Wah. Having appeared in the movie as an extra, Sammo was called back to film the opening scene. Already working on another project, he was none too pleased and, the story goes, challenged Lee to show him what he'd got. He was on his back in a second, and has since said that Bruce Lee was the fastest man he has ever seen. A cynical observer might comment that Hung was chosen for the opening fight, in which the two men appear stripped to their very short shorts, because of the contrast between his rotund form and the wiry Lee.

MARTIAL ARTS: Opening with a sparring round at the Shaolin Temple between Lee and Sammo Hung, the film quickly covers both the physical side of kung fu – and how good Lee is at it – and its spiritual aspects, in discussions with the head monk and one of Lee's pupils. The choreography of the fights in *Enter the Dragon* is clearly the work of Bruce Lee. Slickly performed, the blows are convincing and well-timed for the camera. More tellingly, the hero doesn't get a scratch on him until the final fight with Han, where he gets rather a lot – but only for aesthetic purposes and to allow him to do his blood-tasting routine, first seen in *The Big Boss*. Generally speaking, the good guys, when they're not trying to fix the betting, win with ease and the bad guys break a lot of bones. Although it might take the shine off the man's legend, it would almost be refreshing to see Lee take a knock or two occasionally.

But perhaps that would be asking too much. The fights are designed to fit the plot and, if they are over too quickly, it is perhaps the fault of director Robert Clouse rather than Lee. Maybe the American, who had never directed this type of film before, didn't realise that a kick flick is about the quality of the kicking and not about how quickly each fight reaches its conclusion; and that if the hero gets knocked down, it means he can return with all the more fury to exact his revenge. In general, the fighting lacks heroism, a vital part of the wuxia mould. The film puts style before technique, as in the training sequence on Han's island, which includes some very dodgy stance-work and bad punching. But it looks good from above, with hundreds of white-suited men striking and blocking in unison.

When Lee has more chance – meaning more opponents – to show off his skill, he executes some classic moves. Fighting the guards in an underground cavern, he makes his way through a series of weapons from his feet via a long staff, then two short ones, to his favoured nanchuku. From the time when he was shot disarming the Japanese master in *Fist of Fury* to when he performed this scene, he had become so fast with the weapons that the film had to be slowed down so their movement could be followed. On close observation, it is noticeable that Lee doesn't blink much during the sequence. The different styles used by the fighters at the tournament also make for interesting viewing, while the ability of former monk Han to beat the much younger Williams is a comment on the superiority of Shaolin kung fu, as well as the advantages of clubbing someone with a concealed iron hand.

Enter the Dragon was Bruce Lee's chance to follow his dream of disseminating his individual form of combat. Although he is apparently an instructor at a Shaolin Temple (why no shaved head?), the philosophy he expounds to his young student is that of his own way of no way, jeet kune do. The famous 'finger pointing at the moon' quote, in which he explains that if you concentrate on the finger you will miss 'all the heavenly glory', was at the heart of his martial beliefs, as was his demand that his student express himself through his moves. Lee held that it is restrictive to follow one particular style, and that ultimately it is better not to resort to violence. When Parsons challenges him to prove his ability, he demonstrates 'fighting without fighting' by tricking him into a boat which is then dragged behind the junk, disabling his opponent without laying a finger on him. But ultimately, in trying to appeal to a critical, highly vocal Asian audience educated in how martial arts should look on-screen, as well as international viewers who expected a bit more plot with their action, *Enter the Dragon* doesn't quite succeed in satisfying either.

STUNTS AND SPECIAL EFFECTS: Interestingly, while this film is all about Bruce and the way he moves, it shows his character performing stunts that he himself could not. A brilliant fighter, Lee was no acrobat, and his flips and leaps are the work of the Chinese opera trained Yuen Wah. The majority of the stunts arise out of people trying not to get hurt by Lee. The film was made in Hong Kong with local stuntmen and far fewer safety precautions were taken than Warner Brothers would probably have liked. This applied also to the props, which include both snakes and glass bottles.

One stunt that went wrong could have wrecked the whole venture when it caused damage to its most valuable commodity.

During his confrontation with Oharra, Lee is attacked by the big man, who is wielding two broken bottles. He kicks them out of Bob Wall's grip, but at first Wall did not let go soon enough, causing Lee to cut a tendon in his hand. Filming was halted for several days, Lee had stitches and Wall was walking on eggshells for the rest of the shoot.

DIRECTOR: Robert Clouse (1928–1997) has come in for a lot of criticism over the years for his handling of *Enter the Dragon*, and rightly so. His experience with martial arts filming was non-existent, and in *Enter the Dragon* it shows. One can only assume that he understood neither the rules of the genre nor the culture that begot them. It is probably better not to think about what *Enter the Dragon* could have been in the hands of another director. Warner Brothers insisted on Clouse, and it was holding the purse strings.

But while the director may not have done much for the film, it certainly did a lot for him. Clouse went on to make several martial arts action films, including Jackie Chan's US flop *The Big Brawl* and, more notably, the *China O'Brien* movies starring Cynthia Rothrock, on which he was also scriptwriter. In 1978, Clouse was credited as the director on *Game of Death*, the film that was to be Bruce Lee's defining moment, bringing together everything he wanted in a movie as an actor, writer and martial artist. Had Lee lived, he would no doubt have directed the film himself. It does Clouse no credit to be associated with it – Lee only completed the fight sequences before his death, putting the project on hold while he made *Enter the Dragon*, and the rest of the film is cobbled together using body doubles and old footage. Clouse also penned a biography of Bruce Lee, securing his place in the ranks of those who profited from the actor's iconic status after his death.

PRODUCTION: Anyone seeing *Enter the Dragon* for the first time may be disappointed by how dated it looks. This is one disadvantage of the new trend for Hong Kong action flicks to use contemporary settings that have since become dated: the 70s motifs are dominant throughout. It is also the result of shoddy production values. While it must have saved Warner Brothers money to film in Hong Kong with a local crew, the budget allocated to the film was minimal compared to what big studios were investing in major films at the time. Added to the budget restrictions was the obstacle of having to pass instructions through as many as five translators to overcome the language barriers between the Americans and speakers of various Chinese dialects. While some Hong Kong movies have achieved cult status precisely because of their low budgets, obvious wire-work and appalling dubbing, the poor quality of *Enter the Dragon* undermines the film.

Although it set out to be, and in some ways is, a very cool movie, there is no excuse for what has been called the 'stylistic shoddiness of slow motion camera work, clumsy editing and derivative set design'. The dissolves into flashbacks are laughable. Even the scene that should have been the most visually stimulating, Han's opening night party, falls strangely flat. The tumblers are lacklustre, the sumo wrestlers unconvincing and there just isn't enough food. When everyone freezes on Han's entrance and continues where they left off as he departs, it looks more like a poorly executed gimmick than the arresting disorientation it ought to have been.

One idea that does work is the showdown in the mirror room, although, given that it is borrowed from Orson Welles' *Lady from Shanghai*, perhaps this should come as no surprise. It took 8,000 mirrors to create the hidden maze, and a great deal of planning to make sure that no cameras, crew or lighting were reflected in any of them.

TRIVIA: The original script for the film was entitled *Blood and Steel*, which sounds more like a Jean-Claude Van Damme movie than a Hong Kong martial arts film. *Enter the Dragon* is still one of Warner Brothers' top ten grossing films of all time, more than 30 years after it was made. It has taken more than $200 million worldwide, having been produced for just $850,000. By comparison, *The Godfather*, released in the same year, cost $17 million and has grossed approximately $88 million.

Bruce Lee's widow, Linda Lee Cadwell, has revealed that while the final cut of the cobra scenes has Bruce casually stuffing the snake into a bag and later holding it down with his foot, during an earlier take the irate serpent managed to bite the actor. Fortunately, it had already had its venom removed. Frequently challenged on set by stuntmen and extras, Lee only took one –

very persistent and equally foolish – man up on it. After constant goading, he felt that in order to save face, prove that he was not a 'paper tiger', and continue to have the stuntmen following his direction, he would have to fight. In the best of humour, Lee toyed with his opponent briefly before flattening him, and was not asked to prove himself again for the duration of filming.

THEMES: In *The Big Boss* Lee swears that he will sacrifice his own life to avenge those of his murdered cousins. In *Fist of Fury* he defends the honour of his martial arts school in memory of his poisoned master, as well as fighting for the rights of the Chinese under Japanese occupation. In *Enter the Dragon* he kills Oharra for messing with his sister, and shows Han that you can't disrespect the Shaolin temple and get away with it. While the film misses the point when it comes to martial arts movies, it does at least give the hero a cause to fight for. The addition of the James Bond-style spy plot is unnecessary in the context of Hong Kong action films – insult to family and temple would have been enough to set Lee after Han, and these are the two factors he cites before killing his enemy. But Warner Brothers felt additional motivation was needed to appeal to an international audience; filial loyalty clearly wasn't enough.

National and cultural identity were themes Lee had touched on in earlier films, but they are almost crowbarred into *Enter the Dragon*. So we have Saxon as the all-American hero (somewhat lacking in morals, but there is a point beyond which he will not go), Jim Kelly in the African-American corner (following hot on the heels of the Civil Rights Movement) and Lee satisfying the Asian audience. Or not. In many ways the Chinese roots of the film are ignored. The Hong Kong setting is irrelevant – Han's island could be anywhere. With the exception of Lee, the Chinese are represented either as kung fu automata, Buddhist monks or Han's Fu Man-Chu style villain. Williams says 'Man, you come right out the pages of a comic book', and with Han uttering lines like 'We forge our bodies in the fire of our will', the karate champion has a point.

On the plus side, *Enter the Dragon* does include that staple of kick flicks, the tournament. Rooted in the 'my kung fu is better than your kung fu' plot-line, the theme of proving who's the man and winning the prize money/woman/mastery of the jianghu is repeated again and again, particularly in Western interpretations of the genre. The tournament is the focus of *The Karate Kid*, and Jean-Claude Van Damme made it his own in *Bloodsport*. It is reassuring to find it even here, in this strange bastardisation of the genre.

PLACE WITHIN THE GENRE: Love it or hate it – and some will do both – there is no escaping the fact that *Enter the Dragon* is the most famous martial arts film of all time. The death of its star before its release did nothing to prevent it earning iconic status, but the fact that it was the first kick flick made for an international market is what really achieved that result. As the first taste of the genre that most people in the West had ever had, *Enter the Dragon* served an important purpose, opening their minds to a new world of Asian action movies.

It made a lot of money for Warner Brothers, but the film also elevated Golden Harvest, the company that co-produced it, to pole position among the studios in Hong Kong, undermining the dominance of Shaw Brothers for the first time in twenty years. *Enter the Dragon* made Bruce Lee the most bankable star in the world, allowing the industry to keep on making money out of his name for decades. People who impersonated him became stars, and the film was a passport to fame for many of those who appeared in it.

Once again, the Hong Kong film industry had reinvented itself, this time by combining forces with Hollywood and opening itself up to a world audience. The success of *Enter the Dragon* became the success of the whole genre, sparking international interest in martial arts and breathing new life into south-east Asian filmmaking. The impact of this movie, some three decades after its release, cannot be overstated.

Heroic Ones: Bruce Lee

- **AKA: Little Dragon Lee, Lee Sui Lung, Yam Lee, Li Xiaolong, Lee Xiaolong, Xiaolong Li, Siu-Lung Lee.**
- **Birth name: Lee Jun Fan Yuen Kam.**
- **Nickname: Little Dragon.**

- Not to be confused with: Bruce Li, Bruce Le, Bruce Lo, Bruce Lai, Bluce Ree, Dragon Lee, Jason Scott Lee or Brandon Lee, all of whom have imitated him at one time or another.
- Martial style: Jeet kune do, the way of no way, or, in his own words, 'a smooth, rhythmic expression of smashing the guy before he hits you, with any method available'.
- Born: 27 November 1940 in San Francisco, California, USA.
- Died: 20 July 1973 in Hong Kong, reportedly of cerebral oedema.
- Biography: Bruce Lee is the most famous, and in many people's eyes the greatest, martial arts movie star of all time. Yet he completed only four films before he died at the age of 32, robbing the world of his dynamic presence and what should have been his definitive martial arts movie, a completed *Game of Death*. In many ways, Lee's untimely end has added to his legend. Like a kung fu Elvis, he reached iconic status in the years following his demise, the films he starred in being recognised as classics of their time. Dying at the peak of fame is the next best thing to immortality, and has left the oft-asked question 'Who would win a fight between Bruce Lee and . . .' unanswerable. There is no way of knowing if his career would have continued on its meteoric rise – it is only possible to judge it on its impressive, if meagre, beginnings. One thing can be said with certainty: Bruce Lee is largely responsible for the introduction of the martial arts film to a Western audience, and for the enduring popularity of the genre from the early 70s to the present day. Born in the US while his father, Cantonese opera singer Lee Hoi Cheun, was working in the country, 'Bruce' Lee Jun Fan was entitled to American citizenship, a fact that would later dictate his path through life. When he was one, his family returned to Kowloon, Hong Kong, where he began to play child parts in local films. Beaten up by a street gang when he was about thirteen, Lee took up wing chun training with Yip Man, the only formal martial arts instruction he would ever receive. So dedicated was he that he would sometimes wait outside the class for the other students, tell them the sifu wasn't coming that day, then enjoy a session of personal tuition with the great man. Famed throughout the world for his martial arts, the brooding hard-man of kung fu was also (a less well-known fact) a cha-cha dancer and winner of a Hong Kong dance championship. When he became involved in trouble on the streets of Hong Kong, his parents sent him to the US to take up his American citizenship, and on the boat over he made extra cash by giving cha-cha lessons to the first-class passengers. At the age of nineteen Lee arrived in San Francisco and waited tables before moving to Seattle to study philosophy. In 1963 he met Linda Emery, his future wife, and opened his first Jun Fan Kung Fu school. Competing in national tournaments, he came to the notice of TV producer William Dozier (via his hair stylist). Lee was cast as Kato in the series *The Green Hornet*, which, while not overwhelmingly popular, introduced Lee to an American audience. And they loved him. By this

time Lee had three martial arts schools and was training the likes of James Coburn and Steve McQueen, who wanted to add an element of realism to their tough-guy images. Throughout his years in the US, Lee studied other forms of martial arts, including karate and tae kwon do, and began to develop his own style of fighting. Jeet kune do combines elements of all fighting forms, effectively applying whichever technique is most appropriate to the situation. Refusing to be limited by the boundaries of one traditional style, Lee decided to use them all as it suited him. In his view, all human bodies were essentially the same, so any real fighting principle could work for anybody. Of course the fact that he was incredibly fit, athletic, flexible, fast and strong helped too. Cameo TV roles in the States led to stardom in Hong Kong, and Raymond Chow's Golden Harvest studios were keen to cash in. Lee was offered the starring role in the Lo Wei-directed film *The Big Boss*. It cost little to make, was shot in Thailand, and made a fortune in the cinemas of Hong Kong. *Fist of Fury* quickly followed, with Lee smouldering as the rebellious kung fu student whose quick temper and devastating fighting skills bring about the destruction of his school. Box-office records were also destroyed. Lee set up his own production company, Concord, through which he wrote, directed and starred in his next movie, *Way of the Dragon*. With its climactic fight scene between Lee and Chuck Norris in the Roman Coliseum, it is less famous but a far better film than the one that came next. Hollywood wanted a piece of the martial arts pie, and they got it with *Enter the Dragon*. The best-known kick flick of all time, Bruce Lee's last complete movie benefited from the publicity lavished upon it by Warner Brothers and, morbidly, the death of its star. Having finished shooting in Hong Kong, Lee died in controversial circumstances after taking a headache pill. The verdict was cerebral oedema caused by an allergic reaction, but conspiracy theories live on. Some 20,000 people came to pay their respects and view Bruce Lee's coffin, and millions have since mourned his loss – not least because of the travesty of exploitation that followed his death: rehashed films including Bruce Lee outtakes and actors with masks held before their faces, an appalling version of *Game of Death* – the project that would have been Lee's ultimate movie and for which he had filmed only the fight scenes – and documentaries about the star's life. Few are worth watching. As a tribute to the man, his martial arts and the charisma that created a legend, the films he finished during his life are the only legacy required.

- Best kick flicks: *The Big Boss* (1971), *Fist of Fury* (1972), *Way of the Dragon* (1972).
- Trivia: Bruce Lee Jun Fan Yuen Kam was born in the Year of the Dragon, at the Hour of the Dragon. Lee's maternal grandfather was German. His son, Brandon Lee, also died young, on the set of *The Crow* in 1994.
- Where are they now: The legend lives on.

36th Chamber of Shaolin

(aka *Shaolin Dapeng Dashi*, *Shao Lin San Shi Liu Fang*, *The Thirty-Sixth Chamber*, *The 36th Chamber of Shaolin*, *Master Killer*, *Disciples of Master Killer*, *Shaolin Master Killer*)

Hong Kong, 1978, 111 minutes

Production company: Shaw Brothers
Director: Liu Chia-Liang [Lau Kar-Leung]
Martial arts directors: Liu Chia-Liang, Wilson Tong Wai-Shing
Producers: Mona Fong Yat-Wah, Run Run Shaw
Screenplay: I Kuang, Eric Tsang Chi-Wai
Director of photography: Huang Yueh-Tai

CAST: Gordon Liu Chia Hui (*Liu Yu-Te/Monk San Te*), Wang Yu (*Boss Wang*), Henry Yu Ying (*Hung Sze-Kwan*), Wai Wang (*Teacher Ho*), Lo Lieh (*General Tien Ta*), Lau Kar-Wing (*General Yin*), Hon Gwok-Choi (*Lin Zhen*), Wilson Tong Wai-Shing (*Tang San-Yao*), Wa Lun (*Liu Yu-Te's friend*), Kok Lee-Yan (*Abbot*), Chan Shen (*Monk*), Simon Yuen Siu-Tin (*Monk*), Chan Si-Gaai (*Teacher Ho's Assistant*), Casanova Wong (*Sa Ka Fa*)

PLOT: This film is based on the true story of a monk who taught kung fu to the people of China. The Tartars (otherwise known as the Manchurians or the Qing/Ching dynasty) have invaded. If you feel a sense of déja vu it is because this period of Chinese history is very popular in martial arts films, providing a convenient and ubiquitous enemy that audiences can unite in hating. The high-handed Tartars are oppressing everyone in sight and persecuting 'rebels' – Hans who aren't that keen on having their country stolen, even if the previous Ming Dynasty did do a good line in corruption. When the story opens, General Yin is discussing with patriot Teacher Ho his plan to kill the tyrant General Tien Ta. His attempt to do so results in a spectacular sword fight and his execution. Cut to Teacher Ho's schoolroom, where he gives a quick lesson in patriotism to his students, including Liu Yu-Te. The students later see the body of General Yin, and Yu-Te comes to the unpleasant attention of Lord Tang San-Yao, General Tien's second in command. Narrowly escaping arrest, Yu-Te decides it's time to stand up for what is right and goes with his friends to Teacher Ho to offer their services to the resistance.

Hitting upon the less than foolproof plan of smuggling documents in his fishmonger father's produce, Yu-Te is forced to flee when they are discovered. His friends and teacher are killed, and he decides that the only way he can take revenge for their deaths is by learning kung fu at the Shaolin Monastery before returning to get the bad guys. Injured by Tang's men, he finally makes it to the temple, getting in through the gates with the help of a friendly innkeeper (a fixture in the genre) who hides him in the monks' groceries. Discovering him unconscious, the monks heal him and then try to send him on his way. Displaying characteristic determination (he has just limped all the way to Shaolin on one leg), Yu-Te begs to be allowed to stay. Against the advice of his monks, the Abbot agrees, and Yu-Te becomes San Te, the first adult layman ever to enter the monastery.

After a year of sweeping floors, San Te mentions that he really came to learn kung fu and discovers that all he had to do was ask. In order to master the techniques and disciplines of the art, he must complete the challenges in each of 35 chambers. Always ambitious, he elects to try the hardest first, and is utterly baffled by the Buddhist mantras he hears within. Not one to give up (he really is a very tenacious young man), San Te starts from the beginning, learning an important lesson about foundation training. He then proceeds through the various chambers in record speed, practising day and night. After conditioning his arms, wrists, legs, eyes and head in various painful ways, he moves on to weapons training. As each level is achieved, he is promoted within the monastery, the Abbot pointing out that, with all the troubles going on in the outside world, they might be in need of someone ambitious with a talent for violence.

When he passes the final test, San Te is offered the chance to become the head of any chamber of his choice. The Justice Officer (whose voice of dissension has been heard throughout) suggests that before San Te is awarded such an honour, he should have to beat him in a fight. San Te tries every trick he can think of, but the

Justice Officer and his butterfly knives prove too good for him time and again. Finally, training in the traditional bamboo forest, he strikes upon the idea of a jointed staff, becoming the first person to develop the triple-hafted weapon. He defeats the Justice Officer and proclaims that he wishes to become head of a 36th chamber, one that teaches kung fu to commoners, so that they can defend themselves against the Manchu. The Abbot refuses, pointing out that the temple does not involve itself in worldly affairs. San Te won't take no for an answer, and as a 'punishment' for his presumption is sent out into the world to collect alms, seven years after leaving it: the perfect opportunity to recruit likely lads to join his chamber.

He has matters to attend to first, however. Seeking his family, he discovers that they have been killed. Going to the cemetery to pray for them, he discovers Lord Tang about to deal with some rebels who are burying their executed fellows. When the rebels prove unable to defeat the Manchu (they have no kung fu, remember), San Te steps in. Defeating Tang, he allows his friend to strike the final blow, then agrees to teach him kung fu. Gathering other disciples by demonstrating his martial skill, San Te forms a plan to deal with General Tien, involving Miller Six and a lot of rice flour. He entices the General to follow him to the requisite showdown on a mountain top, where the final confrontation ensues, in which the three-part staff comes into its own and San Te becomes the first Buddhist monk to beat a man to death with a stick. The film closes with him presiding over his newly created 36th chamber.

CAST: Director Liu Chia-Liang cast his stepbrother in the role that would make him a star. It would also forever typecast him as the martial monk. He shaved his hair off for the role (in fact, his brother shaved it for him), and stayed bald throughout his acting career. Given that this is, on the surface, a standard gung-fu pian, all that should really be required of the leading man is a proficiency in kung fu. What makes the film anything but standard is Gordon Liu Chia Hui's ability to act as well as fight. Every stage in his character's development, from naïve student to dogged disciple to masterful monk, is convincing. He wins the viewer's admiration and affection, and the film is enthralling not because we wonder whether he will succeed in his quest – this is a typical film in that sense – but because we are captivated by how he gets there. One reason why Liu was cast as a Shaolin monk in so many of his subsequent roles was that he was so believable in this one. Physically, he is no match for the likes of Bruce Lee – his diminutive frame doesn't boast the same rippling muscles – but in many ways this is more in keeping with the role of the everyday guy who succeeds through determination rather than talent. His youthful features will melt the heart of the most hardened gore-fest fan.

The director cast his real brother in the film too. Lau Kar-Wing shows that his father didn't teach kung fu to only two of his sons, as he takes on the evil Tang in the role of rebel general Yin. It is a shame that he is killed so early in the movie, but a treat to see him nonetheless. Another notable actor who doesn't get nearly enough screen time in this or almost any other film is his opponent, Wilson Tong Wai-Shing. One of the better martial artists of his generation, he never made the big time.

Lo Lieh does a great job as the arrogant Manchu General Tien, laughing evilly but not hammily, sporting a great moustache and being so confident of his martial ability that he charges off after a trained Shaolin monk without any of his soldiers to help him. Clearly he didn't realise just how long the monk had been waiting to get together with him.

MARTIAL ARTS: From the minute *36th Chamber of Shaolin* opens, there can be no doubt that this is a film dedicated to martial arts. The audience is assailed by the spectacle of Gordon Liu going through his paces with weighted training rings on his arms. The kung fu in this film is about as realistic as you are likely to see. Apart from a couple of wires here and there, the action is utterly convincing, which is exactly what you would expect from Liu Chia-Liang. In this film the dedicated martial artist and filmmaker's creativity was finally allowed free rein: *36th Chamber of Shaolin* is the ultimate training film, and started a new trend in the genre, showing how hard work, discipline and self-effacement are the roads to kung fu mastery and enlightenment. In doing so, Liu squeezes every ounce of martial talent out of his gifted stepbrother.

The last and most difficult chamber is the one in which Buddhist philosophy is taught and finally understood, showing that, despite all the physical challenges that must be faced, kung fu is an internal journey and requires the disciple to overcome mental and emotional foibles. This film was the first to really show how hard it is to learn Shaolin kung fu and the spiritual journey that had to be made.

The physical side of the training gets extensive coverage too, including a physics lesson from an old monk about the properties of water and how to walk on it. The detail with which San Te's journey is narrated is fascinating, and serves to make the final fight scenes infinitely more satisfying as the viewer identifies each of the skills the monk has learned as he brings them into play. It borders on the cheesy, but even the flash of light in his eyes is thrilling.

Director Liu chose his historic period well. In spite of their insistence that worldly affairs were the concern of others, after the Manchu conquest the Shaolin Temples began to place greater emphasis on the skills of armed combat, teaching fighting with staffs, spears, swords and knives. They were also known to harbour Ming nobles and rebels who wanted to resurrect the old dynasty. Eventually, fearing rebellion, the Qing Dynasty ordered the temples burned down. The result, however, was that the surviving monks went into hiding, and began to teach outsiders the martial arts that had for so long been the province of the monasteries. Set in the early days of Manchu rule, *36th Chamber of Shaolin* includes a number of prescient moments, when the Abbot and San Te predict the way the world will turn. On a less highbrow level, setting his film in this era also allowed Liu to showcase a lot of weapons fighting, which is always fun.

STUNTS AND SPECIAL EFFECTS: Gordon Liu leaping on to a floating log while holding one foot in the air is clearly done with the assistance of wires – not that you can see them, but no man has calves that strong. Apart from this, however, there is little outside interference. The idea was to show what the human body can achieve, not create a magical fantasy, and the lack of effects, albeit within tightly choreographed fight scenes, emphasises this.

Similarly, Liu Chia-Liang does not resort to the kind of crowd-pleasing stunts that Yuen Woo-Ping began to make popular around this time. No one throws themselves off buildings or across abysses. But then, they don't need to: the authenticity of the action speaks for itself.

DIRECTOR: And so to the man himself. This film could not have been made by any other director. Schooled in the early gung-fu pian, Liu Chia-Liang brought to the genre a unique perspective on martial arts in the movies. His father Liu Chim, was a highly respected actor who was also skilled in hung gar kung fu. Liu Chim's sifu was Law Sai-Wing, a disciple of Wong Fei Hung, and from the age of seven his son studied in his school. Joining the Hong Kong film industry when he was a teenager, Liu Chia-Liang became a stuntman and then action director on various 50s and 60s kick flicks, several times appearing with, and even fighting, his father.

A dedicated martial artist, he was the fight choreographer for *The Jade Bow* with Tong Kai, before the two moved to Shaw Brothers. He worked on Chang Cheh's *One-Armed Swordsman* and became the dominant martial arts director of the 1970s. Having served his time, Liu began to make the films he really wanted to, focusing on the spiritual aspects of kung fu as well as the inherent violence. During his work with Chang Cheh at Shaw Brothers, Liu began his love affair with the history of the Shaolin Temple and its great masters. Together they made *Shaolin Martial Arts*, *Five Shaolin Masters* and *Shaolin Temple* in the mid-70s. After creative differences with Chang erupted, Liu began directing, beginning with *Spiritual Boxer* in 1975. He mentored several rising stars, including his stepbrother and Alexander Fu Sheng, a talented actor and martial artist who tragically died during the shooting of Liu's last Shaw Brothers movie, *The 8 Diagram Pole Fighter*.

Showing that he could also see the lighter side of martial arts – indeed comedy frequently punctuates his films – Liu and his brother went on to make *Return to the 36th Chamber*. A crazy parody of the original, this film plays with the conventions that the director had spent so many years establishing. Gordon Liu plays a bumbling commoner who learns kung fu at Shaolin through menial tasks, only discovering on his return home that he has become a brilliant fighter. While it contains all the elements of a kung fu film, *Return to the 36th Chamber* shows that Liu was not hung up on making the same movie over and over again, despite the success of his previous efforts. Along with Sammo Hung, he helped to usher in the kung fu comedy of the 1980s. Liu even went on to work with Jackie Chan on the long awaited sequel *Drunken Master 2*, but the two men's styles were incompatible, and Liu left before the film was finished. He is still credited as the director. Having stepped away from the world of films, he was joyously welcomed back when he made *Drunken Monkey* for the Shaw Brothers in 2002.

PRODUCTION: As if the realism of the training sequences wasn't enough to entice and engage, the camera work makes them sparkle. A section of the film that, with the wrong director, could have become tedious filler material – a death knell for a movie in which the training stages take up the majority of the running time – is actually its best feature. Sending his cinematographer into the pond to film the walking on water scene, or reversing up the narrow stone walkway in front of Gordon Liu while he carries buckets filled with water at arm's length, Liu finds the angle to make every shot seem fresh and the action real. The audience feels as though it is in the temple, suffering San Te's trials with him.

In the chamber of the eyes, the giant sticks of incense are shown at such close range that the viewer can almost sense the heat and flinches when San Te burns his face. As he follows the rapidly swinging lamp with his eyes, it is apparent that the film has not been speeded up, for the smoke continues to rise at a steady rate. The only fantastical element is the flash of light that appears in San Te's eye as he gains the power to follow the fastest movement without turning his head, along with the sci-fi noise that accompanies it. Liu can be forgiven these indulgences because of the brilliance of the fight during which he revisits them.

TRIVIA: Presumably to increase sales among a bloodthirsty audience, the American release of *36th Chamber of Shaolin* was renamed *Master Killer*. There can be no other reason: even as a hardcore kung fu monk, San Te kills only one person, hardly qualifying him as a master of the art. Also, it is a very odd title for a film that is essentially based on the philosophy of Buddhist sages who literally wouldn't hurt a fly. (Although, as San Te points out late in the film, they are not averse to rooting out evil.) More aptly, director Liu Chia-Liang is so knowledgeable about his martial art that he is known as 'The Dictionary of Kung Fu'.

THEMES: Part of a proud lineage of kung fu films based on the deeds of legendary, or historic figures, *36th Chamber of Shaolin* is one of the classic movies that tell the tale of how kung fu came to the people. It says that anyone can learn kung fu, and lauds the triumph of hard work over adversity. As with many of Liu's films, it looks at the spiritual side of the martial art as well as the fatal results.

36th Chamber of Shaolin was part of a new breed of martial arts film that abandoned the need for romance and relationships in favour of exploring the roots of martial arts. Unsurprisingly, at the forefront of this movement was Chang Cheh. With this film, however, Liu took the theme to new heights. As Gordon Liu says, 'At that time, no one had yet shot a film about monks. No one would shoot a film about monks. Usually they would shoot martial arts hero films with heroic guys and great heroes.' The lack of a love story would have been an insurmountable problem for most Hong Kong directors in the 1970s – although it should be noted that Jackie Chan has always tried to avoid them – and you just can't have a love story involving monks. Not real monks, anyway.

And so Liu created a love story of the soul. 'What did we finally shoot?' asks Gordon Liu. 'The story of the spirit. The kung fu moves and the perseverance of the monks.' Says his stepbrother, 'I wanted to shoot a film about kung fu. Kung fu is not about fighting.' Rather it is about using the entire human body, each part in unison with the rest, resulting in the extended training sequences that became standard for the gung-fu pian that came after. When it comes to kung fu, Liu's influential film shows that Shaolin really is the original and best. Firmly rooted in the history of the martial art, the final scene of *36th Chamber of Shaolin* shows San Te teaching his new disciples – real characters, many of whom became famed martial artists and whose students still make movies in Hong Kong.

Liu Chia-Liang's films often focus on friendship and strong communities, rather than the tragic, bloody deaths that end most of Chang Cheh's martial offerings. Yu-Te is part of a school, a family and a village society. He is driven to revenge when all of these are destroyed. Liu also included strong roles for women in many of his films, although not in *36th Chamber of Shaolin*: only Liu Yu-Te's mother and Teacher Ho's assistant have speaking roles, and they only appear at the beginning of the film. There are no attentive maidens who will heal Yu-Te and then conveniently fall in love with him. Rather, the monks slap a bit of vegetation on his leg and then try to kick him out of the temple.

PLACE WITHIN THE GENRE: This is the ultimate martial arts film, made by martial artists, about martial arts. Fortunately, it's not just for martial artists. Anyone can enjoy this glorious insight into the ways of the Shaolin Temple and how one man brought its teachings to the people. Even the uninitiated will leave the film as embryonic fans of the genre – if they don't, they haven't got a soul. Homage to the fighting monks of the Shaolin Temple, this is a traditional kung fu movie that gives so much more. Films that concentrate on the hero's training have become a sub-genre in their own right, and this is the finest example. Chang Cheh's early attempts at Shaolin training are worthy but cannot match Liu Chia-Liang's labour of love. The kung fu shines with style and grace, and there is thought behind every move. The Lius cannot have guessed the impact the film would have, but it is only right that it has proved to be one of the most enduring productions in the genre, given the amount of effort the brothers put into its creation.

Shaw Brothers' number one hit of 1978 (an impressive feat, given how many films they produced each year), *36th Chamber of Shaolin* won the Best Martial Arts Award at the 24th Asian Film Festival. Released as part of a package of eight Shaw Brothers films shown at Cannes, including *Spiritual Boxer Part 2* – which also starred Gordon Liu and was directed by Liu Chia-Liang – *36th Chamber of Shaolin* was described by a company executive as 'the best kung fu film being shown at present'.

This seminal movie retains an important place in the history of the martial arts genre, and also in the history of the dissemination of kung fu, the events of which it narrates. The real San Te taught, among others, Hung Shi Kuan and Fong Sai Yuk. Both men were later portrayed by Jet Li, in *The New Legend of Shaolin* and *The Legend of Fong Sai Yuk* respectively. These films, and many others, would never have been produced had it not been for Liu Chia-Liang's vision in making *36th Chamber of Shaolin*.

Heroic Ones: Jackie Chan

- **AKA:** Jacky Chan, Chan Yuen-Lung, Chan Yuan Lung, Chan Kong-Sang, Long Cheng, Lung Chen, Wellson Chin, Yuan Lung Chan, Yuen-Lung Chan, Chen Lung, Sung Lung.
- **Birth name:** Chan Kong Sung.
- **Nicknames:** Yuen Lo, Sing Lung, Big Nose.
- **Not to be confused with:** Anyone, although it's not very likely is it?
- **Martial style:** Acrobatic, comedic, slapstick, death-defying kung fu.
- **Born:** 7 April 1954 in Hong Kong.
- **Biography:** The most famous, recognisable and popular, and probably the richest martial arts star alive, Jackie Chan is undeniably a legend in his own lifetime: as different from that other great icon of the genre, Bruce Lee, as a blunderbuss is from a semi-automatic. Chan has no one to live up to, having created and then dominated his own style of filmmaking for over 25 years. He learned his trade, like many top Hong Kong stuntmen and actors, at the China Drama Academy opera school, to which he was apprenticed by his parents at the age of six. One of the stars of the school, Chan was offered the role of stunt player in a small film and decided that, with the popularity of opera fading, this was how he would make his name. In fact, his name came from the film *Master with Cracked Fingers*, in which he played the part of Jackie Chan, and it stuck. After the death of Bruce Lee, the hunt was on for an actor to fill his trademark black slippers, and director Lo Wei thought he had found his man in Chan. Then an up-and-coming stuntman and action director, known for taking high risks to get spectacular results, Chan certainly had the moves to play the part. In fact it is Chan, doubling for the evil Japanese karate instructor, who is kicked through a wall by Bruce Lee in the finale of *Fist of Fury*, a stunt which momentarily knocked him unconscious. Lo's *New Fist of Fury* followed directly on from the original and cast Chan as the rebellious successor to Lee's character, Chen. He could not carry it off, however, managing to thump himself while swinging Lee's trademark nunchuku. Several flops followed, and it was only when Chan started playing it for laughs that audiences began to warm to him. Realising he could not – and did not want to – live in Lee's shadow or take his place, Chan instead combined comedy and action, with lasting success. In his directorial debut, *The Young Master* (1980), he plays the hapless Dragon, who must overcome his failings to save the honour of his school. Cue fighting in a skirt and with a fan, and being pursued by a deranged Yuen Biao. Drawing directly from the work of Harold Lloyd, Buster Keaton and the silent slapstick of the 1920s, Chan has combined comedy with breathtaking martial arts to create some of the most successful films in Hong Kong history. He famously performs nearly all of his stunts himself, resulting in toe-curling out-takes at the end of his films

(always sit through the credits, or risk missing the best bits) and the fact that he cannot get insurance to cover his own action scenes. To this day he has a hole in his head where a piece of skull was removed after he fell on it. Having recently broken into Hollywood with the *Rush Hour* and *Shanghai Noon* films, he can justifiably be called the biggest movie star in the world. You'll laugh at him until it hurts – but never to his face, or it really will hurt.

- Best kick flicks: *Drunken Master* (1979), *Project A* (1983), *Police Story* (1985), *Armour of God* (1986), *Rumble in the Bronx* (1995).
- Trivia: Chan Kong Sung, Jackie's birth name, means 'Born in Hong Kong'. In 1976 he had plastic surgery on his eyelids to make them appear more Western: *Shaolin Wooden Men* is the last film in which he appears pre-surgery. Chan was awarded an MBE in 1989.
- Where are they now: Still breaking bones. Chan has recently finished work on *Rush Hour 3* and *Joe's Last Chance* is in production.

Project A

(aka *A Gai Waak, A Ji Hua, Jackie Chan's Project A, Pirate Patrol*)

Hong Kong, 1983, 101 minutes

Production Company: Golden Harvest
Directors: Jackie Chan, Sammo Hung (uncredited)
Action director: Jackie Chan
Written by: Edward Tang, Jackie Chan
Cinematography: Cheung Yiu-Chu
Music: Michael Lai

CAST: Jackie Chan (*Dragon Ma*), Sammo Hung (*Fei*), Yuen Biao (*Inspector Tsu*), Dick Wei (*San-Po*), Mars (*Jaws*), Wu Long Cheung (*Hoover Club Bouncer*), Kwan Hoi-Shan (*Captain Chi*), Wan Fat (*Thug*), Lau Hak Suen (*Admiral*), Wu Ma (*Mah-jong Player*), Isabella Wong (*Winnie*), Benny Lai (*Coast Guard*), Yim Chan Tang (*Pirate*), Chris Lee (*Pirate*): Tai Bo, Wong Man Ting, Lai-Chu Ng, To Siu-Ming, Yun Kin Chow, Ho Kai Law, Wong Wai, Lee Hoi-Sang, John Chang

PLOT: It is Hong Kong at the turn of the (last) century, and the willing but incapable coast guards are having trouble apprehending a gang of pirates, led by the fearsomely tattooed San-Po, who are plaguing the shipping in the area. The coast guards are at odds with the police force, who think them ill-disciplined and useless, while the coast guards taunt the police for doing nothing but blow their whistles. Action opens on a council of war, with the British Secretary of Security demanding that the Admiral stop the pesky pirates. With new ships recently built, the Admiral is sure the coast guard will succeed, although Police Chief Chi seems less than convinced. Cut to coast guard Sergeant Dragon Ma, sent to requisition more ammunition from Captain Chi, who attempts to humiliate Ma before discovering that the joke is on him.

The coast guards head out on the town to celebrate their last night on dry land. They run into the police and a barroom brawl ensues, Ma and a plain-clothed policeman beating each other with bottles, chairs and tables. A lot of spaghetti is thrown around. Eventually more police arrive to break it up, let off the policemen, including the plain-clothed copper who turns out to be Captain Chi's nephew, and arrest the coast guards. They are only freed the next day when the Admiral pulls rank.

All set to sail, the coast guards form up, troop the colour, present arms and watch their ships being blown up. They are promptly disbanded, and placed under the command of a young upstart, Inspector Tsu – who turns out to be the Captain's nephew and Dragon's opponent from the previous night. Cue lots of painful training exercises and practical jokes. Hearing that a dangerous criminal is in town, Ma and Tsu are sent undercover into the exclusive Hoover Club where he is thought to be hiding. A fight predictably breaks out, and the two gain respect for each other during the course of it. When Ma is prevented from apprehending the bad guy by Captain Chi, he throws in his badge in order to continue pursuing the man.

Jobless, Ma runs into his old friend Wei, now a petty criminal, and agrees to steal a shipment of rifles with him to make some money. Little does he know that Wei is fulfilling a contract to supply police rifles to the pirates. After throwing the Police Captain into the sea, the pair abscond with the rifles and hide them in a logging yard, marking the log they are concealed in with a red flag. But Ma returns later and marks all the logs, preventing Wei's employer from getting the rifles. Ma turns them over to the police, but the thugs who employed Wei are not happy and come after the friends. Some brilliantly choreographed fighting follows, including head-crushing stunts, as Ma manages to escape by getting himself arrested, climbing a flag pole and falling from a clock tower.

Meanwhile, the British Rear Admiral, on his way to sort out this frightful mess with the pirates, gets himself kidnapped. The ransom is the rifles, and the Secretary of Security is all ready to do a shady deal with the pirates when Dragon launches into a lengthy diatribe about national pride and persuades him to put his faith in the coast guard one last time. Reunited, the coast guards hook up with the police, resurrect their Admiral and embark upon Project A.

Posing as the gunrunner, Dragon makes his way to the pirates' island and befriends San-Po, while Inspector Tsu and the coast guards follow closely behind. On the voyage, Dragon runs into Wei, who is still trying to make a quick buck, and they agree to stay out of each other's way – as if that's going to happen. Dragon cases the joint and waits for back-up. Narrowly protecting his assumed identity, he distracts the pirates while the prisoners are released. When Tsu turns up, things start to go wrong. Against his better judgement, Wei comes back to help his friend and the three defeat all the pirates before turning their attention to the evil leader. The following three-on-one fight is spectacular. Eventually they catch the pirate captain in a carpet, and make sure he won't be appearing in any sequels. The day is saved.

CASTING: *Project A* is the film that made the 'Three Brothers' from the Chinese opera school – Sammo Hung, Jackie Chan and Yuen Biao – a bankable product. They had already collaborated on the highly popular, although occasionally misfiring, *Winners and Sinners*, directed by Sammo Hung, but this was the first feature in which they all had leading roles. The chemistry between the three, and the way their action and comedy styles complement each other, made *Project A* an instant success. Starring, written and directed by Jackie Chan, it would be easy to see this as a vehicle for the rubber-faced actor to star in, but that is not the case. Without the input of his opera brothers, the film would not have become the enduring classic that it unquestionably is.

Supported by the others' genius, Chan was finally able to make the film that suited his unique talents. Gone are the classic gung-fu pian training scenes, replaced by the action comedy that revived the genre in the 1980s. Showcasing his acrobatic skills, comic timing and willingness to throw himself off tall buildings in the name of entertainment, *Project A* is one of the finest examples of a style that has come to be known throughout the world as a Jackie Chan film. Light on plot, the film doesn't require much acting ability, but Chan is perfectly suited to playing the irreverent, inventive, upstanding Sergeant Ma: unsurprising when you consider that he wrote the part for himself. It is a classic Jackie role – well-meaning, put-upon, desperately unlucky and with no romantic interest to speak of.

Project A saw Sammo Hung perfect the role of the petty thief of which he became so fond and which he reprised several times. His character's grumpy reluctance to do the right thing, desperate pursuit of profit and frightening martial arts ability make for an entertaining mix which Sammo pulls off with ease. As always with the big man, his bulk belies his athletic ability and speed, and woe betide anyone who comes between him and his money. Experimenting throughout his career with a mix of comedy and action, changing the formula each time, as an actor Hung has rarely got it more right. He plays the perfect foil to Jackie Chan's righteous character, each tolerating what they consider to be the other's weaknesses. The fact that the two knew each other so well and had worked together for so long shines through and is a joy to behold, especially during their synchronised fight scene in the teahouse.

And so to the littlest brother. Cast as the straight guy, Yuen Biao develops the part of the earnest young police inspector from a stickler for routine into one of the most appealing characters in the film. The most acrobatic of the trio to come out of Yu Jim Yuen's opera school, Yuen has not had the outstanding success of the other two – in other words, he has never made it in the West. But it cannot be denied that he has been involved with some of the greatest martial arts films ever made. From *Prodigal Son* to *Zu: Warriors from the Magic Mountain*, Yuen Biao just keeps cropping up, astounding audiences with his athletic ability and winning hearts with his cheeky grin. Working with Sammo on many of his films, Yuen Biao was given the leading roles in *Knockabout* (1979) and *Prodigal Son* (1981). His big break came in 1980 with a part in Jackie Chan's *Young Master*, showing just how well the two stars were looking after their little brother. In *Project A* he is allowed to show off his skills as an actor as well as an acrobat and acquits himself well, although really the audience is just waiting to see him flying through the air in his black, Bruce Lee-style cat suit.

The success of bringing the Three Brothers together on screen continued with their next outing, *Wheels on Meals*, a bizarre story of Italian aristocrats, pickpocketing prostitutes and Chinese fast food sellers in Barcelona. The only reason the film wasn't called *Meals on Wheels* was that Golden Harvest had recently had bad returns on two movies that began with the letter 'M'.

The dominance of Yu Jim Yuen's students in the Hong Kong film industry created a whole sub-genre of its own. Given stage names that incorporated their instructor's family name, the involvement of a Yuen in a film from this era can be used as a benchmark of quality. They even made a film about their time in the opera school, *Painted Faces*. Although Jackie Chan and Sammo Hung took new names for themselves when they entered the film industry (helpfully adding to the vast number that they have each been known by), at school they were Yuen Lung and Yuen Lo respectively. Their classmate Mars went in a whole new direction when it came to his moniker, but Yuen Biao, Yuen Choi, Yuen Tak, Yuen Mo, Yuen Wah and Yuen Kuei still bear the name out of respect for their teacher. Mars apart, the other eight were known as the 'Seven Little Fortunes', a child acting troupe who proved very profitable for their teacher, despite the fact that he apparently couldn't count.

As always in martial arts films, the bad guy is central to the success of the production, and in Dick Wei *Project A* has the archetypal villain, in what was probably his finest hour and a half. Discovered by Chang Cheh, Wei was a martial artist before he was an actor and happily admits that he found his first roles a challenge when he was required to do more than just kick and hit. Working for director Sammo Hung, Wei enjoyed the fact that Hung's style of on-screen martial arts required every punch to impact. He believes that, following Hung's masterpiece *Prodigal Son*, all fight scenes for the next decade looked essentially the same. After being cast in the role of the bad guy in *Lucky Stars*, Wei was utterly typecast in the Hong Kong film industry, playing maybe two positive roles in his entire time in the business.

Project A is no exception. As the swashbuckling pirate San-Po, Wei hams it up in style, leering at the women and arm-wrestling the men. His tattoos add to his image, although they would be more convincing if they didn't rub off all over Dragon's shirt in the final fight scene. Wei's martial talents are undeniably awesome, and led to him being employed as the fight director in *Once Upon a Time in China 3*. Approaching the star of the film, Jet Li, five times Wushu Champion of China, he declared that he wasn't qualified to direct the star. Li apparently replied that he had no idea how free style fighting should work on film, and Wei should tell him what to do. His final fight in *Project A*, where he fends off all Three Brothers, is a testament to his martial skills. You wouldn't want to get in the way of one of those kicks.

MARTIAL ARTS: *Project A* is the perfect fusion of opera acrobatics with hardcore action, as one would expect from the Three Brothers, schooled at the China Drama Academy and hardened in the brutal world of Hong Kong movies. The action is fast and furious, and the long, drawn-out fight scenes that had previously characterised Jackie Chan movies are replaced by short bursts of action. *Project A* served as a prototype for the style of fighting that would later prove so effective in *Police Story*. Jackie Chan made the format his own – gimmicks abound, and each fighter is able to use his particular skills to emerge triumphant. So Sammo outmanoeuvres his opponents while clinging on to his winning mah-jong hand, Biao somersaults his way out of trouble and Jackie gets to mess around on a bike.

It was at this point in the development of the genre that martial arts moved beyond classic styles into theatrics. Real martial artists and acrobats were employed, but the style of fighting was heavily modified to look good on film, at the expense of authenticity. And why not? It was unlikely that many in the audience would be able to tell the difference. No matter how good the martial artists performing in the film were, it was down to the action director to bring out their best on camera and co-ordinate differing techniques to the best effect. As Lee Hoi-San, a master of wing chun who plays the evil sifu in Jackie Chan's early comedy *Drunken Master*, has said, 'I rarely used my own kung fu moves in the films. There is always an action director on set. All the actors have to follow his directions.'

Mixtures of styles were created, combining the flashiest elements of both northern and southern techniques with large, sweeping movements that looked good on camera. These were emphasised by exaggerated sound effects at the point of contact, so that every blow could be heard and almost felt by the viewer. Opera acrobatics were an essential part of the mix, and actors had to make sure they could perform any move required of them. Lee Hoi-San learned tumbling and jumping skills from Sammo Hung and Jackie Chan, while Yuen Biao studied traditional kung fu forms to make his fighting look more authentic.

In *Project A*, comedy and kung fu are seamlessly blended. This is epitomised by the Sammo/Jackie fight in the teashop. Teaming up to defeat their adversaries, the two synchronise their movements with comic effect and devastating accuracy. Although in awe at seeing them dealing with their opponents so effectively, the audience is also laughing at Sammo's mock outrage and the Brothers' ability to stay perfectly in time as they cosh the villains around the head. Training together for years in their youth paid dividends.

In the final fight scene, where the Three Brothers combine to bring down the pirate captain, the brilliance of their skill and its compatibility with screen presentation are obvious. At first, it doesn't look as though they will be able to overcome the mule-kicking San-Po, but then they start to warm up. With a mixture of broadsword swinging, carpet pulling and high-flying kicks, they succeed in wrapping the bad guy in a rug and stuffing a police issue grenade in with him.

STUNTS AND SPECIAL EFFECTS: In the new genre of wu da pian, the stunts make the movie, and *Project A* is no exception. Looking for new ways to thrill audiences, Chan and Co. go to extreme lengths to provide thrills and, quite often, spills. With casts almost entirely composed of Hong Kong stuntmen who had cut their teeth (and just about everything else) acting as body doubles for the actors of the 1970s, the opportunities to show real action were endless. Where once characters threw their hands in front of their faces at the crucial moment to disguise the fact that they had cunningly morphed into an entirely different person for the dangerous scene, action directors could set up long, continuous sequences with close-ups of the actors' faces, leaving the audience in no doubt about who was falling from the rooftops.

The need for actors who were also skilled stuntmen led to the repeated appearance of the same faces in all of the classic films from this era. Actors who had played characters killed off in a previous film would appear in totally different roles in the sequel. When a winning formula was found, it was repeated over and over again, sometimes with different actors in the lead roles, who might have played another part in earlier films. It has been suggested, somewhat tenuously, that this mix-and-match approach was made more viable in the south-east Asian film market by the pervading Buddhist culture and its belief in reincarnation.

Project A includes some of Jackie Chan's most famous individual stunts, which reflect the influence exerted upon him as a director by the silent movie stars of 1920s Hollywood. It was in this film that Chan first developed his 'money-shot' stunt: the reason that audiences would flock to see him time and again, and the reason no insurance company would ever give him cover. It appears in all of his later films: the stunt so insane that it is hard to believe that anyone is actually attempting it, let alone the star of the film. Needless to say, Chan has nearly got himself killed on a number of occasions.

The clock tower stunt in *Project A* brings together all of these elements. Handcuffed to a flagpole, Jackie shinnies up it to escape the bandits, smashes through a window into the clock tower, has a quick fight with one of the bad guys, falls out of the clock face and ends up clinging to its hands. It is pure Harold Lloyd in *Safety Last*, but the next bit is all Jackie Chan. Losing his grip, he falls through two flimsy awnings then crashes to the ground. Still handcuffed. All in one take. Apparently it took Chan a week to build up the nerve to complete the stunt. When he did it, it had only previously been tested with a bag of dirt. Having managed it once, he did it at least twice more – the replay shown in the film is clearly another take, and as the credits roll a third version is shown, with Chan falling on to his head and not getting up again.

Unlike the heroes of the wuxia pian, who either remain unscathed or die in tragic circumstances, the good guys in kung fu comedies always end up bruised, battered and playing it for laughs. The Three Brothers realised early on that there was more comic value in being beaten up than doing the beating (although they give as good as they get). In *Project A* the perfect example is when Jackie Chan and Yuen Biao smash each other over the back with chairs in the bar brawl, shrug it off manfully and then simultaneously retreat behind a pillar to writhe in agony. Slapstick is also part of the formula, and the brawl just wouldn't be the same without the plates of pasta that are flung in all the wrong faces. Although not as dangerous as the other stunts in the film, these episodes still required comic timing and careful planning.

There are also many extended action sequences such as the bicycle flight fight, in which Chan uses his bike as both a means of escape and a convenient weapon – along with everything else he can lay his hands on, including passers-by and doors. Leaping over obstacles as his bicycle goes beneath, then landing on it again, he manages to evade his pursuers. But, according to the rules, the good guy can't come off unharmed. His bicycle seat flies off just before he sits down with toe-curling force. This gives Chan a chance to perform his famous agonised gurning, while providing some comic relief in the tightly choreographed, frenetically paced action.

But even Jackie Chan's brilliance and fearlessness would be less thrilling were it not for the support of his opera brothers. The spectacle that the three provide, in their common willingness to go to any end to please the crowd and their physical ability to match their madness, makes the film a classic wu da pian. Hung and Yuen are absent from the sequel, *Project A Part 2*, and the film is the poorer for it. In contrast, the *Lucky Stars* series, directed by Sammo Hung, in which all of the Three Brothers appeared, albeit often in cameo roles, was one of the most successful in martial arts film history. The final stunt in *Project A* perfectly encapsulates the chemistry and sheer insanity of the former opera performers: blowing up the pirate captain sends them flying through the air with the force of the explosion, before they crash back down to earth. All three were hurt.

DIRECTOR: When it comes to the development of the comedy kung fu sub-genre that flourished in Hong Kong in the 1980s, Jackie Chan is the man. He didn't do it alone, of course, following in the footsteps of Michael Hui, writer and director of *The Private*

Eyes, released in 1976 and arguably the first of its kind. Chan worked with Yuen Woo-Ping on his early forays into this new arena, and ran side by side with Sammo Hung as the cult of Asian action-comedy grew. But Jackie Chan has eclipsed them all in his willingness to push the limits to stay ahead of the game. His style is always mimicked, so he is always reinventing it.

In numerical terms, Chan has not directed as many films as, for example, Hung, but those he has been in charge of have all been unique. The *Project A*, *Police Story* and *Drunken Master* films are all groundbreaking in their own way, and each revived the genre when it was sorely in need of it. A huge commercial success, *Project A* also rejuvenated Chan's career, which was floundering following his US flops at the beginning of the 80s, undermining the success he had achieved with *Young Master* and *Snake in the Eagle's Shadow*. Even when Chan has not been sitting in the director's chair, he has had a powerful influence on his movies. Which is why it is so odd to hear him say, 'I hate violence. Yes I do. It's a kind of a dilemma, huh?' He might not like it, but he's very good at it.

PRODUCTION: By setting the film in Hong Kong in the early 1900s, the filmmakers created a unique challenge for themselves. There were no existing sets and costumes that could be used, and the film needed a different feel from the period dramas and contemporary stories that were the norm. This end was achieved in a number of ways. Golden Harvest built a vast set in Hong Kong, which still stands to this day. The colour has a soft, pastel look, which gives a sense of stepping back into the past. The police uniforms with their conical hats are not only historically accurate but add a great comedy element, as does the sight of Jackie Chan in a sailor suit.

One of the most outstanding aspects of the film is the music, scored by Michael Lai. From the opening chords you know you are in for a comic treat. The bumbling marches, sea shanties and hectic chase themes, scored with a full orchestra, all add great atmosphere. As in the later *Police Story*, the same theme tune is used throughout (the music for *Police Story* became so recognisable that the Hong Kong Police used it in a recruiting video, starring Jackie Chan). The most effective use of music in *Project A* occurs when the coast guards and the police square off against each other in the bar, freezing as the music begins and then launching into furious fighting in time to the beat.

TRIVIA: *Project A* was the first Jackie Chan film to show failed stunt scenes during the closing credits. Ouch. Jackie Chan broke his nose during filming and, unsurprisingly, hurt his neck doing the clock tower fall. The film won the Best Action Design (awarded to the Jackie Chan Stuntmen Association) at the 4th Annual Hong Kong Film Awards.

THEMES: This is one of the first films in which Jackie Chan showcased his role of the underdog coming good. It was one that would be reprised in *Police Story* and went on to become a staple of the comedy-action film. The international success of these films was due largely to the slapstick humour embodied by these hapless heroes, a style that draws heavily on the silent comedians of 1920s Hollywood. Even some of the jokes are the same, like the reconstruction of a wall collapsing and the hero's head passing through a window, first seen in Buster Keaton's *Steamboat Bill Junior* and reprised in *Project A Part 2*. It is a ploy Chan uses throughout his films. In the mid-1980s every Hong Kong action flick included an element of comedy, and *Project A* can be held up as both a prime example and a leading influence in the genre.

The nostalgia that this referencing invokes is ideal for the colonial Hong Kong setting, a political situation like no other, which is directly commented on, and criticised, by Dragon in his passionate rant to the Secretary of Security. The golden age of Hong Kong cinema, supported by the unique style of film produced there, is paid homage by the use of a uniquely local setting. The swashbuckling action in *Project A* also harks back to a nobler time and to that very early gung-fu pian, *The Story of Wong Fei Hung, Part 1*.

PLACE WITHIN THE GENRE: *Project A* marked a turning point for many of the actors who appeared in it and sparked a series of copycat films that breathed new life into the industry. It established the ability of the Three Brothers to make consistently good films that drew massive audiences. Recognised as a classic now, the film was also appreciated when it was released in 1983 – it was hugely successful at the box-office, and won Jackie Chan his first nomination for a Golden Horse for Best Actor at the Hong Kong Film Awards.

Effectively linking comedy action with the insane stunts for which Chan was to become known, *Project A* was the first of a new breed of wu da pian, in which visual storytelling was key and dialogue secondary. Along with the universal appeal of its stars' sense of humour, this made the formula far more digestible to an international audience than previous examples of the genre. Suddenly there was more to martial movies than extreme violence and antiquated codes of honour, and consequently there was now more that just a cult audience.

Dispensing with both the far distant, or even legendary, past and contemporary society as a setting, the film creates a unique place for itself in the genre. It has managed not to become dated, and in relying on physical stunts rather than technology-based special effects its production hasn't aged either. Following the success of *Young Master* and *Winners and Sinners*, Golden Harvest was prepared to invest heavily in the film, and the company's faith in the project paid off.

Heroic Ones: Sammo Hung

- **AKA: Sammo Hung Kam-Bo, Hung Gam Bo, Sammo Hung Kam Po, Samo Hung, Sanno Hung, Hung Kam Po, Hung Kim Po, Hung Ching-Pao, Chin-Pao Hong, Jinbao Hong, Hong Jin Bao, James Hung, Kam-Po Hung, Yuanlong Zhu, Yuen Chu, Chu Yuen Lung.**
- **Birth name: Hong Jin Bao.**
- **Nickname: Big Brother.**
- **Not to be confused with: Jackie Chan – same sense of humour, different physique.**
- **Martial style: Trained at the Chinese opera school, Hung has incredible acrobatic skills and combines them with his own heavy-handed, ham-fisted take on traditional kung fu.**
- **Born: 7 January 1952 in Hong Kong.**
- **Biography: Raised by grandparents while his parents slaved in the Hong Kong film industry, Hung was born to perform. He begged his family to allow him to join the China Drama Academy, which he did at the age of eight. Rotund even then, Hung convinced his dubious sifu to allow him to train by displaying incredible acrobatic abilities and a stern manner that belied his youth. Surviving the rigorous training, he became the oldest member and leader (and**

bully, according to Jackie Chan) of the Seven Happy Fortunes, the opera's performing troop made up of children which also included Chan and Yuen Biao. In the 1970s Hung abandoned the opera for the more lucrative world of cinema, borrowing the name Sammo from a popular chubby cartoon character of the time. His skill and dedication made him the top action co-ordinator in Hong Kong before he began acting for the newly formed Golden Harvest studio. His heavy form and scarred face led to a number of bad guy roles until he teamed up with former classmates Chan and Biao for a series of the most successful martial arts films ever to come out of Hong Kong, including *Project A* and *My Lucky Stars*. These films revitalised the industry and secured the careers of the 'Three Brothers', even after relations between them soured. Working as both an actor and a director, as well as writer and producer, Hung has been nothing short of prolific. After trying his hand at TV in the US series *Martial Law* in 1998, which was cancelled after two seasons, he returned to Hong Kong to work on, among other things, a number of projects with his old friend Jackie Chan.

- Best kick flicks: *Enter the Fat Dragon* (1978), *Magnificent Butcher* (1979), *Prodigal Son* (1982), *Pedicab Driver* (1989).
- Trivia: Sammo Hung had a band named after him, a punk-pop group from Cardiff whose hits included *Stand Up and Swear*, but sadly they disbanded in November 2004. The prominent scar on his face was received in a bar brawl over a woman.
- Where are they now: Still a prolific actor and director, Hung's most recent project is 2005's *Dragon Squad*.

Heroic Ones: Yuen Biao

- AKA: Yuen Biu, Yuan Biao, Biao Yuan, Biao Yuen, Hsia Ling-Jun, Ha Ling Tsan, Bill Yuen, Jimmy Yuen, Jimmy Tuen, Biu Yuen.
- Birth name: Hsia Ling-Jun.
- Nickname: Little Brother.
- Not to be confused with: Jackie Chan, Sammo Hung.
- Martial style: Opera acrobatics, fast and furious.
- Born: 26 July 1957 in Hong Kong.
- Biography: At the age of five, Yuen was enrolled in the China Drama Academy. He was the youngest of his classmates, distinguished by an acrobatic ability that he has never lost, even in recent years. He was taken under the wing of fellow students Jackie Chan and Sammo Hung, the 'Dia Go' or Big Brother of the gang. Although he never achieved the fame of his colleagues, more often playing the acrobatic doubles for the stars of his movies, the three have remained lifelong friends. While the others headed for the Hong Kong film industry, their Little Brother stayed with the opera, travelling to Hollywood to

promote the art. After two years he realised that more success was to be had using his gymnastic skills on Hong Kong film lots than by waiting on American producers who were not interested in Chinese stars. Having played bit-parts in films such as the brilliantly titled *Stoner*, his career was boosted when his old friend Sammo Hung cast him as the lead in *Knockabout*. His real break came in 1982 with *Prodigal Son*, starring alongside Hung. Jackie Chan was now the biggest martial arts star in Hong Kong and in 1984 the three friends combined to create *Project A*, arguably the peak of Yuen's career. Never fully receiving the acclaim he deserved, he has forged a career in Japan and playing stunt doubles. Although he features in Tsui Hark's *Once Upon a Time in China*, many of his scenes were cut to reduce the film's monumental running time. Yuen dabbled in directing with *A Kid From Tibet* and did stunts in Jackie Chan's Hollywood project *Shanghai Noon*, but these days takes things a bit easier. He performs few roles, complaining that most of the scripts he is sent are poor.

- Best kick flicks: *Project A* (1983), *Zu: Warriors from the Magic Mountain* (1983), *Once Upon a Time in China* (1991), *A Man Called Hero* (1999).
- Trivia: Yuen Biao means 'Young Tiger'. Although he needs spectacles, he hardly ever wears them in his films and still manages to perform precise acrobatic feats.
- Where are they now: Playing golf in Canada, waiting for a good script.

Once Upon a Time in China
(aka *Wong Fei-Hung, Huang Fei-Hong*)

Hong Kong, 1991, 134 minutes

Production companies: Film Workshop Co., Golden Harvest
Director: Tsui Hark
Martial arts directors: Lau Kar-Wing, Yuen Cheung-Yen,
Yuen San Yee, Yuen Woo-ping
Producer: Tsui Hark
Executive producer: Raymond Chow
Screenplay: Tsui Hark, Yuen Kai-Chi, Leung Yiu-Ming, Tang
Pik-Yin
Directors of photography: David Chung Chi-Man, Bill Wong
Chung-Piu, Arthur Wong Ngok-Tai, Ardy Lam Gok-Wah, Chan
Tung Chuen, Wilson Chan Pui-Kai
Music: James Wong Jim

CAST: Jet Li (*Wong Fei Hung*), Rosamund Kwan (*Aunt Yee*),
Yuen Biao (*Leung Foon*), Kent Cheng (*Wing*), Jacky Cheung
(*Buck Tooth Soh*), Yuen Kam-Fai (*Kai*), Yam Sai-Kwoon (*Iron
Robe Yim*), Karel Wong (*Commander Man*), Jonathan James
Isgar (*Jackson*), Lau Shun (*Naval Commander*), Wu Ma (*Old
Man*), Sunny Yuen (*Manchu Soldier*), Mark King (*Wickens*), Steve
Tartalia (*Tiger*), Sek Kin (*Wise Old Man*): Jimmy Wang Yu, Yuen
Cheung-Yan, Yuen Kam Fai

PLOT: Wong Fei Hung is back! Again! The most frequently
portrayed hero in martial arts film history gets a makeover in this
tale of his early days as a teacher. All the moral, political and
pacifist principles that defined the character played by Kwan
Tak-Hing are present, but when he is forced to fight, Wong Fei
Hung now has the martial skills of Jet Li in his prime. His talents
are immediately apparent as he saves a lion dance from disaster
when the lead dancer is shot, performing a high-wire act that
leaves his 'tail' dangling far behind. And why was the lead dancer
shot? The lion dance is taking place on board a Chinese navy
junk, and the sound of firecrackers going off draws return fire
from a nearby British ship. The stage is set for a story fuelled by
racial tensions, British buffoonery and some of the most acrobatic
martial arts ever seen on screen, all taking place against the
backdrop of nineteenth-century China, which foreign powers are
carving up between them.

Having saved the dance, Wong Fei Hung is entrusted by the
Naval Commander with a fan, on which are painted the unjust
treaties forced upon the Chinese, and with the task of
transforming the Black Flag troop into a local militia. The
Commander himself is off to Vietnam to fight the French, and
fears for his country in his absence. Clashes of culture are seen
early in the film, with a Chinese teashop band trying to drown out
the singing of some Jesuit priests, and then in the arrival of Wong
Fei Hung's Thirteenth Aunt. By marriage. Having studied in the
West for the last two years, Aunt Yee has returned clad in
Western garb, her head filled with the wonders of steam engines
and photography. Her understanding of such technology is
revealed to be imperfect, however, when she manages to fry a
songbird with her camera flash. The other revelation is that there
is a certain frisson between Fei Hung and his 'Aunt': she is no

wizened relative, but rather the lovely Rosamund Kwan. Fei Hung is both pleased and alarmed when his Great Uncle entrusts him with her safety.

Back at Hong's Lam Chi Bo clinic, wannabe Wong-disciple Leung Foon mistakes American-Chinese herbalist Buck Tooth Soh for the master and ends up with his arm and leg in plaster before realising he will not be learning any kung fu from the medic. Played by Yuen Biao, he still manages to perform a series of somersaults while trying to impress 'Wong'. Soh's Chinese is less than perfect, since he was raised in America, and Wong's other students tease him mercilessly for his inability to speak his 'native' language.

Returning to the theatre where he is trying to become an actor, Foon manages to throw a bucket of pitch over Aunt Yee, resulting in him getting a good ogle at her when she is changing, and a secondary (unreciprocated) love interest plot. Pursuing Yee to return her umbrella, Foon falls foul of the Shaho triad gang who have been trying to extort money from his theatre boss. Porky Wing (another of Wong's disciples and the title character of *Magnificent Butcher*, the earlier Wong Fei Hung film starring Sammo Hung and Kwan Tak-Hing) comes to his rescue, calling on the Black Flag Militia to protect their new brother. An enormous fight breaks out, involving a range of unusual weapons including shop signs and pigs' legs.

Meanwhile Wong Fei Hung has gone to meet the British General Wickens, Jackson, head of the Sino-American Corporation, and the local Mandarin to try to resolve the shooting of the lion dancer in a peaceful manner, using Soh to translate. Told to keep out of it, he demands to know why the British and Americans can set up no-go areas in the country. His diatribe is interrupted by the arrival, crashing through the restaurant windows, of his students and the triads, still embroiled in their fight. Demanding that his militia stop fighting – they are now using plates, cutlery and musical instruments as well as their fists – he tries to prevent them, but ends up getting drawn into the fight. The local police finally turn up to end the riot and the militia are threatened with arrest. More worryingly, they have earned the displeasure of their sifu.

Always interfering where he sees injustice, Fei Hung arrests the leader of the Shaho gang when he finds him trying to take protection money from a teashop owner. Unable to persuade anyone to act as a witness to the crime, Wong, who has put his trust in the law, realises that it favours the strong when the triad leader is let go. Deciding that their lives would be a lot easier without Wong around, the triads burn down the Lam Chi Bo clinic. No one is hurt, but Aunt Yee allows the Commander's fan to be burnt while she takes photographs of the clinic. Wong reacts badly to this, telling her she is just like the Westerners and has all her priorities screwed up.

The triad leader enlists the help of Jackson, whose human slavery business is also under threat from the do-gooder, to kill Fei Hung at a theatre performance. Foon and Wing stand in for the actors whom Wing has mistakenly sent away, Aunt Yee is the very model of formal Chinese propriety and Tiger, Jackson's henchman, shoots the Jesuit priest who was willing to stand as witness against the triads who burnt Wong's clinic. All hell breaks loose, with Fei Hung, Wing and Foon taking on the gangsters, the British shooting the audience and the soldiers arresting Fei Hung.

Foon leaves the theatre and becomes the disciple of Iron Robe Yim, who is determined to seal his reputation as a martial artist by defeating Wong Fei Hung. Allowed to heal the wounded before going to gaol, Wong discovers that one of them is a Chinese worker who has escaped near-slavery in the West. Yim and Foon arrive to challenge him and, although Wong points out that it really isn't a good time, Yim forces him to fight. Fei Hung is distracted, and Yim claims victory before the soldiers arrive. Aunt Yee, Soh and the Chinese worker escape while Fei Hung is taken away.

Fleeing for the docks, they fall foul of the triad gang who kill the old man and take Yee prisoner to sell to Jackson as a prostitute. Soh escapes and heads for the gaol, where Fei Hung is refusing to escape, despite being freed by an honourable soldier. When he hears that Aunt Yee is in danger, however, he changes his mind and, with the militia, charges off to rescue her. Meanwhile, Yim has joined forces with the triads, agreeing to teach them in return for cash, causing great discomfort to Foon, who knows a gang of bad guys when he sees them. He tries to save Aunt Yee and gets strung up for his trouble. Tricking the American soldiers into letting them into the compound, the Black Flag Militia, headed by Wong, arrive to save the day. Cue showdown between Yim and Fei Hung, a battle with the Westerners, and righteousness winning out.

CASTING: Tsui Hark's casting of Jet Li as the legendary martial artist was a stroke of brilliance that revived Li's career and made both the actor and the film an international success. Famous throughout south-east Asia for his role in *The Shaolin Temple*, Li had subsequently experienced a series of failures, particularly when attempting modern roles. Hark, who had worked with him on the shelved project *The Master*, saw the potential to remake the actor in the mould of Wong Fei Hung, casting him in the period drama genre that suited him so well. Just as Kwan Tak-Hing was chosen to play the legendary Wong Fei Hung because of his martial abilities, so Jet Li is utterly convincing in the role because of his phenomenal wushu skills. Sadly, due to injury, Li is doubled in a number of the fight scenes in *Once Upon a Time in China* by Hung Yan Yan, so the audience does not experience the full range of his brilliance.

Having a new actor playing the traditional role so heavily associated with Kwan Tak-Hing emphasises the film's themes of continuity and change. Li is a far more flexible actor, capable of reaching across cultural and national boundaries, which the tradition-bound Kwan could not. Li himself had had to deal with a changing political situation in China, and he brings a deep level of understanding to the cultural challenges faced by Wong. Although he plays the part with gravitas and sincerity, Li's youth also allows him to inject some uncertainty into the character. Not yet the implacable master played by the mature Kwan, Li's Wong, while certain of his moral position, still suffers doubts about how best to pursue his ends. He eschews violence and tells his men not to fight, but is himself driven to attack those who act unjustly. Refusing to break China's laws for his own sake, he does so to save a family member. Not wanting to be typecast as Wong Fei Hung, Li declined to appear in part 4 of the *Once Upon a Time in China* series. The role was filled by Zhao Wen-Zhou, and the film is weaker for the lack of Li.

The casting of Yuen Biao as wayward disciple Leung Foon is equally impressive. The fresh-faced actor swings from self-pity to self-sacrifice while flinging his body through a series of incredible aerial stunts. Due to the film's epic running time, many of his scenes were cut, which is a tragedy. The audience is denied some classic Biao action – he arrives on stage in full opera costume, and then quickly exits without performing a single move. Because the actor was disappointed that so much of his character ended up on the cutting-room floor, he declined to appear in the sequels to *Once Upon a Time in China*.

The wide-eyed Rosamund Kwan does well as the Westernised Aunt Yee, trying to balance her modern way of thinking with the traditions of her culture. She is both yielding and tough, recognising when to bow to Fei Hung's sense of propriety and when to speak her mind. Kwan also provides continuity, reprising her role in all but one of the five films in the series.

Veteran Hong Kong stuntman and action star Yam Sai-Kwoon is surly and desperate as Iron Robe Yim, the martial master who has fallen from grace and sold his integrity for silver. Believing himself impervious to bullets, he is driven by pride to challenge Wong Fei Hung, but accepts the other's superiority and wisdom in the end. Yam, whose career flagged in the late 80s when the genre's popularity slumped, recognised *Once Upon a Time in China* as his way back and gave the role his all. He brings to it a level of emotion missing from his earlier parts, such as his appearance in Jackie Chan's *Fearless Hyena* (although, to be fair, no one is very good in that film), battling his conscience for the sake of survival. Unable to bend and adapt to the changing times in China, his character clings to heroic values that are inappropriate to the new society – he wants to battle his countrymen for supremacy instead of uniting with them against the common Western enemy. His solitary character, who refuses to take advice from his student, harks back to the roles played by Jimmy Wang Yu in the films of the 60s and 70s. By casting an actor from this period, Hark is clearly marking the link between the anachronistic values of the early kung fu films and those of the character Yim. This is emphasised by the casting of Jimmy Wang Yu in *Once Upon a Time in China*, and of David Chiang Dai-Wai, another star from the former era, in the second film in the series.

Yam cites *Once Upon a Time in China* as his favourite film because of the strength of the character he plays, although sometimes he prefers a more evil role: 'When you are playing the bad guy the beginning of the film is dead easy – you bully and kill people.' Apparently, his favourite way to be injured is falling off horses. Tsui Hark cast Yam in several of his later martial arts films, including *New Dragon Gate Inn*, *Swordsman 2* and most notably *Iron Monkey* in 1993. He also incongruously appears on the right side of the moral line as Chung in *Once Upon a Time in China 2*.

MARTIAL ARTS: The true martial artist practises for physical health, self defence and spiritual enlightenment, and the character of Wong Fei Hung resists violence unless it is unavoidable. Fortunately for the kick flick fan, in *Once Upon a Time in China* it proves to be unavoidable on a regular basis, to spectacular effect. The film revived a genre in which violence is central, and did so by taking the filmic representation of Chinese martial arts to a new level, setting a standard for fight choreography that has rarely been surpassed. By combining the skills of some of the best fighters in the industry with imaginative choreography and advanced special effects, the filmmakers have created action that is both convincing and thrilling. The credit sequence that shows Jet Li training his militia men on the beach is a classic moment, and reflects the superiority of the martial arts in this film over those of its predecessors (although it becomes a bit reminiscent of *Chariots of Fire* when they start jogging up the sand). The scene is both beautiful and brilliant, something that can't be said about the mass training sequence on Han's island in **Enter the Dragon**.

In trying to produce a fresh approach to fight scenes, Tsui Hark moved away from the opera-influenced syncopated style of earlier films. The Beijing opera music used in King Hu's movies has been abandoned, and with it the flips and somersaults of staged martial arts (although Yuen Biao still gets to perform a few). Introducing a high degree of athleticism, the martial arts in the film are at times exaggerated but never fantastical. The action takes place on a number of different physical levels: swinging through the rigging of a ship, leaping between ladders, climbing on cotton bales. Says Tsui, 'I'm a great fan of people doing things on top of tables, on top of posts.' So Yim leaps, somewhat unnecessarily, on to a table to challenge Wong.

Using a combination of action co-ordinators, the director manages to create a build-up that climaxes in the final confrontation. The early fight scenes in the film are directed by Lau Kar-Wing, and exhibit his trademark realism. Based on the ground, they take full advantage of the skills of the actors and employ some imaginative weapons, including a cello and a pair of violins. An element of slapstick is introduced when Jet Li kicks the triad leader in the back of the head while facing him, with such speed that the gangster is utterly confused about who has just hit him. Wanting a greater level of flamboyance in the later action sequences, Tsui called upon the services of Yuen Woo-Ping, who takes the fights and throws them up in the air. The ladder sequence is one of the finest martial arts battles ever filmed. Taking place between Wong and Yim, it is effectively the film's ultimate confrontation, if not its last. The scene took over a month to film, and involves Wong Fei Hung and Iron Robe Yim twisting ladders through the air, running up them as they fall, balancing with infinite skill on vertical ones and smashing through them with hands and feet. It is the perfect showcase for Jet Li's flexibility of both physique and style.

Once Upon a Time in China does not totally abandon the traditional take on martial arts common to many films in the genre. Individual techniques are cited as central to a character's strength. Hence the focus on Yim's Iron Robe style, as well as his desire to fight Wong Fei Hung in order to defeat the latter's famed Shadowless Kick – which Li demonstrates at the theatre – and the Ten Forms Fist. The mastery of special techniques is central to many kick flicks, from *The Stormriders* to the unabashed tribute films *Kill Bill Volumes 1 & 2*. Li was initially uncomfortable with the fantastical elements of some of these moves, but Tsui Hark convinced him that once the audience believed in the character, they would believe in his ability to do anything.

There is a strange contradiction in the film's attitude to martial arts. Wong Fei Hung tells his students not to fight, and prevents them from doing so by using martial techniques to disable their knees and relieve them of their weapons. Unlike previous outings in the genre, martial arts are not seen as all-conquering. While Fei Hung is the undisputed master, this is partly because he recognises that guns are superior to hands and feet (unless you can kick them out of your enemy's grasp before he can fire them, as Wong proves at the theatre). Master Yim's Iron Robe technique, which can deflect swords, cannot protect him from bullets, as he learns to his cost, finally admitting to Wong as he dies that kung fu cannot stop bullets. He is killed because he was determined to be the best martial artist in town. The day is saved by non-martial artist Buck Tooth Soh, who uses his ability to speak English to get inside the American compound and redirect the British firepower.

Nonetheless, this is a martial arts film, and despite admitting that 'Fists cannot fight guns', when Wong Fei Hung witnesses the British troops gunning down the theatre audience, he defeats them with kung fu. He kills Jackson at the film's climax by firing a bullet from his fingers, demonstrating that perhaps a mixture of Chinese and Western weaponry is the ultimate answer.

STUNTS AND SPECIAL EFFECTS: If *Once Upon a Time in China* took cinematic martial arts to a new level, it is partly because of the advanced enhancement techniques that its editors were able to take advantage of. The use of wire-work is more subtle than in the early, high-flying wuxia pian, but is nonetheless apparent throughout, from the lion dance to the finale. When Wing and Yim fight in the rain, they kick an enormous log between them. Although it is suspended on wires, the care with which these have been removed from the film makes the scene almost believable.

The props are imaginative and diverse, particularly the hanging street signs that play such a large role in Wing and Foon's fight with the triads. Crashing into each other like dominoes, they are kicked into adversaries, broken over heads and used to swing on. Flying plates and cutlery come into play in the restaurant, along with joints of pork. This use of unusual props is carried on into the sequel for Jet Li's spectacular fight against Donnie Yen, using a twisted sheet as a weapon.

DIRECTOR: Tsui Hark is responsible for the reinvention of the martial arts genre in the 1990s. Languishing in the depths of repetitive rip-offs of winning formulas from the early 80s, it needed a new direction, which Tsui discovered by taking it back to its roots and improving each of its component elements – production values, settings, martial performances and cast. The first of the new wave modern wuxia directors, he was not scared to return to the traditional recipe, providing continuity and development rather than a stale product. Tsui had already shown his fondness for the wuxia genre with the 1983 offering *Zu: Warriors from the Magic Mountain*, starring Yuen Biao, a modern take on the fantasy style. With *Once Upon a Time in China* the director also draws more on the history of the gung-fu pian, and the film includes many of the ingredients of the work of Chang Cheh and his fellows.

Tsui's belief that, with the approaching handover of Hong Kong to China, the colony needed to take a realistic, open-minded approach to the coming changes and prepare itself to compromise over issues of national identity is an omnipresent theme in the film. He uses a historic setting, when Chinese culture was coming under threat from foreign powers encroaching on its land, to comment on modern problems. 'It connects to who we are now and the situation we are in now ... If I had the chance, I would link Wong Fei Hung with every incident in the modern history of China.' He emphasises adaptability and flexibility as the means of dealing with change. Educated in Hong Kong but trained in America like the character Buck Tooth Soh, Tsui has a strong sense of what it is to be separated from one's roots as well as the need for an international perspective.

Writer as well as director, Tsui Hark had firm control over the way in which Wong Fei Hung is portrayed in the film. Despite having grown up with the original *Wong Fei Hung* films, instead of the morally unassailable Wong created by Kwan Tak-Hing, Tsui develops a character who is not comfortable with his role of folk hero and resists the expectations of others. A complicated, flawed character who does not always make the right decisions, and has to learn to become less unbending in his ways, Tsui's Wong Fei Hung is hindered by his traditional training which cannot deal with modern problems. The director was also concerned to make his lead character accessible to an international audience that wasn't grounded in those traditions. 'You have this character coming from the past,' says Tsui. 'If you want the films to succeed, you better present the character in a way that people from a different culture will find him easy to accept.'

PRODUCTION: Using dusty, almost sepia shades of brown and yellow, the film's army of directors of photography manage to create a real sense of the past, complemented by authentic costumes and sets. Nothing looks temporary or shoddily created, as it often did in the plethora of cheaply produced Hong Kong films in the late 80s. The complexity of each shot gives the film a depth and epic quality in keeping with its subject matter.

Much of the dramatic action occurs in extremes of weather, bringing a dark aspect to the proceedings. Yim's fight with the Broadsword Master is made more dramatic by the storm, with the fire's flames and the swordsman's severed queue flying in the wind. Yim's degradation and fall into disgrace are emphasised by the pouring rain that often dogs him. Performing for coins in the street and forcing Wong Fei Hung to face him, he is drenched by the rain of misery. When Wong's vision is clouded by the torrent, the camera lens is also blurred, giving the viewer a sense of how difficult it is to fight in these conditions.

The camera work mirrors the action at certain points in the film. As Aunt Yee takes a final photograph of the Lam Chi Bo clinic, the frame is frozen for a second, just as the clinic is frozen in time. Slow motion filming is used to great effect, both dramatically as Master Yim snaps spears with his neck and comically, when the bucket of pitch lands on Aunt Yee. It often accompanies the demonstration of a traditional act, as with the lion dance, representing the contrast between tradition and the speed of modern life.

TRIVIA: Daaaa daaaa da da da da daaaaa . . . The epic theme music of the *Once Upon a Time in China* series was so rousing and recognisable that the stuntmen would turn up on the set of the second episode singing it. When Jet Li jumped from the teashop balcony and was borne to the ground by his umbrella, he injured his knee badly and it had to be put in plaster. To disguise this, many of the shots of him after this point are from the waist up. When Fei Hung is kicked into his clinic during his fight with Yim, his clothes are dry, despite having been fighting in the pouring rain.

THEMES: There are a number of powerful themes running through the entire *Once Upon a Time in China* series, many of which were clearly preying on the mind of director Tsui Hark when he made the film in 1991. The impending handover of Hong Kong from Britain to China was fuelling a bubbling anxiety beneath the surface of the colony. In the film, kung fu is used as a metaphor for old traditions which must be updated in the face of change, represented by foreigners and their guns. It raises questions about the contemporary situation in Hong Kong – would old values continue to be important, would people lose their sense of identity?

Because of censorship, filmmakers could not directly comment on political situations, especially one as sensitive as reunification, so Tsui had to approach it in an oblique way. The use of real historical events and characters is an announcement that the film takes both Chinese history and the themes it portrays very seriously. That Western culture cannot simply be laid over the surface of China is shown when Aunt Yee tries to make Fei Hung shake hands with Joanna – instead of saying 'How do you do?' he parrots 'Kill you!', causing the good lady some consternation.

The film is anti-colonial in its position, but its themes go a great deal beyond that, focusing on what it means to be Chinese as well as their varying reactions to the invasion of the foreigners. Leung Foon calls Soh a banana – yellow on the outside, white on the inside – for his inability to speak Chinese. His command of English, however, is shown to be a strength when he tricks the American guards and he comes to save Foon, whose kung fu has failed to beat the gangsters. Wong Fei Hung criticises the Manchu official for favouring the foreign devils over his countrymen, before one of the foreign devils turns the insult back on him, revealing that he can speak Chinese and claiming that he has as much right to be in China as Wong.

Unlike many martial arts films, the lines between good guys and bad guys are blurred, and, despite the racial tensions portrayed, these lines are not drawn between nationalities. The Jesuit priest, symbol of the encroachment of Western ways, proves himself to be noble and selfless, testifying against the leader of the triad gang before throwing himself between Wong Fei Hung and the bullet meant to kill him. Unscrupulous Chinese rob their countrymen and sell them into near-slavery in America. Despite being Westerners, the Americans and British clearly do not consider themselves to be on the same side, as both are trying to wring the maximum profit out of China. Wong's main adversary, Yim, is not a villain, but rather a man who cannot see beyond the ways of the past and tries to fight Wong for supremacy over a martial world that no longer exists.

Although technology is presented as inevitable and necessary, Wong refuses to accept that it is by definition good. He threatens to break Aunt Yee's camera, and says he will only wear a Western suit when all Chinese men do. That he relents on both issues at the end of the film is indicative of both the inconsistent nature of Jet Li's Wong Fei Hung and his development throughout the course of the film as he becomes more flexible. From a position of security in his world and abilities, he has to face uncertainty and the possibility that he must learn new skills.

The student-sifu relationship is central to the narrative: Foon's choice of sifu dictates his course through the film, and only at the end is he redeemed when he abandons Yim to train with Wong. Porky Wing is punished for his disobedience by being sent to kneel outside the school, and is offered the ultimate threat when Wong says he will stop teaching him. Wong's power over his disciples is shown when he overcomes their lack of appetite by instructing them to eat in the manner of a training session.

The romantic relationship in the film between Fei Hung and Aunt Yee is also strictly controlled by the rules of Chinese society. Emotions are repressed, and only spoken of in general terms, as when Aunt Yee admits she missed Fei Hong while she was overseas. Despite her Western outlook, it is obvious that she still accepts him as the dominant one, fearing his displeasure and never pushing him too far.

PLACE WITHIN THE GENRE: This new wave kung fu films, with *Once Upon a Time in China* at the forefront, took themselves more seriously than their predecessors. Gone was the high comedy, replaced by more subtle humour and broader political issues. The new wave was created by filmmakers who had been born in Hong Kong (although Tsui Hark was actually born in Vietnam), had no direct connections to China and had trained in the West. Their films are a product of their background, and take a different view of Hong Kong's history. In commenting on the reunification, *Once Upon a Time in China* was not so groundbreaking – this was a theme that had obsessed Hong Kong filmmakers for the previous decade. It is the way in which it approaches the issue that is so different from its predecessors.

The film pays its respects to those that went before with nods to the original *Wong Fei Hung* series, in the character of Foon and the opening lion dance. *Once Upon a Time in China* was itself the start of a long-running series, with the character of Wong Fei Hung developing throughout, learning from those around him as well as handing on wisdom to his students. Its English title reflects the view that director Tsui Hark had of its subject matter – events such as these could happen at any time in China's history, and the people had to learn to change and adapt with them.

Heroic Ones: Donnie Yen

- **AKA:** Yen Chi-Tan, Yan Che Dan, Yen Ji-Dan, Zidan Zhen.
- **Birth name:** Donnie Yen Ji-Dan.
- **Not to be confused with:** Bruce Lee, however much he might want to be.
- **Martial style:** Originally trained in t'ai chi and modern wushu, Yen later experimented with a wide variety of styles, including Western kickboxing and tae kwon do. Specialises in mimicking other styles, and claims, like Bruce Lee, to have developed his own system of universal martial arts.
- **Born:** 27 July 1963 in Canton, China.
- **Biography:** The son of famous wushu and t'ai chi instructor Bow Sim-Mak, Yen was taught martial arts by his mother as soon as he could walk. When he was two, the family moved to Hong Kong, then relocated to Boston, Massachusetts when he was eleven. Here he became obsessed with kung fu films, discovering that through his classical training and thirst for knowledge of other styles he could copy the martial arts moves of the stars he idolised. When he fell in with the wrong crowd in Boston, his mother sent him to train with the Beijing Wushu Team, under the same instructor as Jet Li. The first non-PRC Chinese to be admitted to the organisation, he opened the way for others to follow. After two years, Yen travelled to Hong Kong where he met Yuen Woo-Ping, who had directed *Snake in the Eagle's Shadow* and catapulted Jackie Chan to fame. Having convinced the director of his martial skill, Yen, at the age of nineteen, gained his first starring role in Yuen's *Drunken Tai Chi*. Several classics followed, including the *Tiger Cage* series. Jet Li personally requested that Yen fight opposite him in *Once Upon a Time in China 2*, and their duels in that film are among the finest ever shot. The early 90s saw fallings out with directors and a rumoured cocaine habit. Yen changed his focus to television, starring in and directing *Kung Fu Master*. In *Fist of Fury*, a mini-series development of the Bruce Lee film, Yen plays Lee's character Chen Jun and constantly references the dead star's style. Profits from the TV shows allowed Yen to make his own films, directing *Legend of the Wolf* and *Ballistic Kiss* (once described by a reviewer as 'Ballistic Shit').

These were followed by work in Hollywood, including *Highlander: Endgame*, *Blade 2* and *Shanghai Knights*.

- Best kick flicks: *Once Upon a Time in China 2* (1992), *Iron Monkey* (1993), *Wing Chun* (1994), *Hero* (2002).
- Trivia: Yen is a classically trained pianist. He is fluent in Mandarin, Cantonese and English.
- Where are they now: Yen has recently finished work on Tsui Hark's latest film, the period martial arts flick *Seven Swords*.

Summary

When discussing classic kung fu films, it is the era of *Enter the Dragon* and *36th Chamber of Shaolin* that comes to mind. Forget the dramatics of wuxia or sweeping historic epics, these films are about the demonstration of martial arts and very little else. The themes are basic kick flick fodder – the tournament, brutal training, kung fu philosophy, revenge and family loyalty – and the male protagonist dominates. Between them they perfectly represent the gung-fu pian, and are among the most famous films in the genre. But despite these similarities the films are very different. For the purist, *36th Chamber of Shaolin* is a contender for the best kick flick ever made, true to the traditions of Shaw Brothers production and gilding the legend of Shaolin with its authentic training sequences. *Enter the Dragon*, on the other hand, can be described as a mangled attempt at combining too many ideas and influences, which never really makes the most of its star. But it is also the most popular martial arts film ever made, which is why it rates inclusion in this book, above other Bruce Lee vehicles such as *Fist of Fury*, which is, by the benchmarks of this genre, a better film.

All the world loves Jackie Chan, and *Project A* is the best of his 80s comedies. It is also the film in which the Three Brothers fulfil their true potential as a filmmaking trio, perfectly combining their individual skills to create a movie that is the epitome of all that is great about the decade's martial arts films. And it's fun too. From the kitsch costumes to the death defying stunts, *Project A* looks, sounds and feels good.

At the other end of the scale *Once Upon a Time in China* takes life much more seriously, reawakening the appreciation of historic chivalry and reinventing the legend of Wong Fei Hung for a new generation. Beyond the high ideals and socially conscious messages, this film is all about Jet Li doing what he does best. From the moment he leaps to catch the lion head midair until he fires a bullet from his fingers with deadly speed, this is classic martial arts cinematography.

Heroic Ones: Cynthia Rothrock

- **AKA:** Cindy Rothrock, Law Foo Lok, Luo Fu Luo.
- **Nickname:** Queen of the B-Grade Kung Fu Movie.
- **Not to be confused with:** Anyone, probably – she has a style all her own.
- **Martial style:** Kung fu, karate and kickboxing, although she has studied a range of other styles. Famed for her scorpion kick and weapons skills, including the double broad swords, nine-section steel whip chain and iron fan.
- **Born:** 8 March 1957 in Delaware, USA.
- **Biography:** Rothrock began training in martial arts at the age of thirteen and was soon competing in her native America and on the international circuit. Her on-screen career began with a Kentucky Fried Chicken advert, but it was her attendance, as a joke, at an open audition for a male martial arts actor that launched her as a film star. D&B films recognised her skill and cast her opposite Michelle Yeoh in *Yes, Madam*, having rewritten the part for her. As a result, Rothrock became the first non-Asian star in Hong Kong, opening the way for Western men such as Jean-Claude Van Damme to come after. She was the heart and black soul of the 'evil foreign chick' genre of films. Despite her success, Hong Kong producers were wary of showing her too much favour, and she became something of a gimmick, only appearing in cameo roles in the late 1980s. Golden Harvest attempted to launch her in America with the *China O'Brien* films, but discovered that her martial arts did not have the draw in the States that they did in the East. In the end, her fame has endured as a martial artist, rather than a film star.
- **Best kick flicks:** *Yes, Madam* (1985), *Righting Wrongs* (1986), *China O'Brien* (1990).
- **Trivia:** Rothrock has five black belts in Chinese and Korean martial arts and was five times undefeated World Karate Champion in forms and weapons, competing against men. She was the first woman to appear on the cover of a martial arts magazine and has a video game character based on her – Sonya Blade in *Mortal Kombat*.
- **Where are they now:** Teaching martial arts in her studio in California and writing martial arts books.

Return of the Deadly Blade: Modern Asian Classics

Martial arts films, with their tales of suppressed minorities, lawless heroes and nostalgic images of a culture that no longer exists, have always been escapist. Upstanding individuals who fight for family, friends and national pride and are endowed with superhuman fighting skills function within a society structured by the traditions of the martial arts school, where sword and fist are used to gain power or dispense justice. The portrayal of the fantasy-land of the jianghu or a contemporary society where wrongs are always righted is particularly appealing to emigrant communities looking for a link back to the traditions of their homeland. While this is particularly true of Chinese and Hong Kong films, it can also be seen in other Asian productions, particularly those from Thailand, where muay thai is intrinsically linked to the history of the country.

Films of 'mythic remembrance', epitomised by the work of King Hu in the 1960s and Tsui Hark in the 80s and early 90s, have increased in relevance with the growth of Chinese communities outside Mainland China. With increasing numbers of Chinese people living overseas, the need for an easily accessible link to the homeland – or a nostalgic version thereof – has become more pressing. At the same time, as Chinese culture has been disseminated around the world, Western interest in the country's way of life has expanded to embrace everything from Zen Buddhism to Chinese New Year. Also, having received the international cold shoulder for decades for its political position and attitude to human rights, China has been in sore need of a positive PR campaign.

Enter the modern Asian classic. Or, more accurately, enter *Crouching Tiger, Hidden Dragon* – the film that brought martial arts into the mainstream, proved language was no barrier to empathy with human tribulation and sparked a new wave of big-budget kick flicks. Extolling the virtues of the wuxia, rooted in decades of filmmaking history, these films have allowed martial arts movies to reinvent themselves one more time, thrilling a new generation of moviegoers around the world.

The twenty-first century has seen a resurgence of the wuxia genre, with the creation of these modern classics, in which successful Asian directors have returned to what they think of as their roots and made ultra-traditional martial arts films with modern production techniques and special effects. Plots may be more intricate, characters more complex, the casts composed of trained martial actors and there may even be sex scenes, but the path of the modern classic along the road already trodden can nonetheless be easily mapped. These films are stylised, located within Chinese society and history but with strong fantasy elements, and focus on the skills of some exceptional martial artists. The period dramas that regained popularity in the 1990s on the back of *Once Upon a Time in China* have been infused with contemporary plot-lines. The characters are seen breaking free of the strictures of society, overturning rules of class, respect for elders and patriarchy. Forbidden love is pursued not repressed, and the master-student relationship has been reinterpreted to suit modern expectations.

This immortal genre has continued to supply the links to traditions and culture desired by expatriates throughout the world, while engaging a contemporary audience that does not comprehend the moral codes of previous generations. The one constant is action, translatable into any language, something made clear by the Hong Kong slapstick kick flicks of the 1980s. For these reasons, modern Asian classics have proved incredibly successful in crossing over to the Western cinema screen, making them some of the most popular, highest-grossing foreign language films ever. They have entered the mainstream – and it all began with Taiwanese director Ang Lee's desire to make an epic wuxia pian.

Heroic Ones: Jet Li

- AKA: Jet Lee, Li Lian-Jie, Lian Jie Li.
- Birth name: Li Lian Jie.
- Nickname: The New Bruce Lee.
- Not to be confused with: Bruce Lee.
- Martial style: Modern wushu, mixed for filmic purposes with traditional t'ai chi and kung fu. Kicks so fast the film has to be slowed down to show his legs moving.

MARTIAL ARTS Return of the Deadly Blade

- Born: 26 April 1963 in Heibei, Beijing, China.
- Biography: For a small guy, Jet Li has made it really big, starring in some of the seminal Chinese kung fu movies, the crossover modern Asian Classic *Hero* and Hollywood mainstream and martial arts outings. His high-speed kicks and precision moves have become a trademark, whether hamming it up, on his dignity as Chinese paragon Wong Fei Hung or killing the bad guys with acupuncture needles in *Kiss of the Dragon*. Born in April 1963, the youngest of five children raised by a widowed mother, this future movie star was a cosseted, protected child until he began wushu training in 1971, when his incredible talent was revealed. He won the only prize awarded at a national wushu competition only a year after taking it up. Success led to punishment as he embarked upon a brutal training regime. At eight he joined the Beijing Wushu Academy, at eleven he won gold at the national championships, competing against adults. Taken under the wing of teacher Wu Ben, Li was pushed to the limit to develop his monumental potential. In his teens he became a national coach and travelled to the US on a goodwill mission to perform before President Richard Nixon, who probably didn't know what hit him. His fame led to him being cast in *Shaolin Temple* in 1979. This shy, quiet man, who only wanted to promote the art of wushu, became a Chinese superstar. He achieved his aim as interest in the sport exploded, but found himself thrust into a new world. Sequels followed, as did an unsuccessful venture into directing with *Born to Defend*. In search of an international audience, Li moved to the US in 1988, where he began to work with director Tsui Hark. After failing to make an impression in the States, Tsui persuaded Li to return to Hong Kong, where their collaboration resulted in one of the greatest martial arts films ever made, *Once Upon a Time in China*. After three massively successful films in the series, Li, amid rumours of disputes with Tsui, went on to work with Corey Yuen Kwai, famed director and martial arts co-ordinator, on *The Legend of Fong Sai Yuk*. He reprised his role as Wong Fei Hung, this time playing it for laughs, in *Last Hero in China* – which includes the unlikely spectacle of Li dressing up in a chicken suit – then moved on to romance with *The Bodyguard From Beijing*. In 1994, he finally had the chance to address his nickname of 'The Next Bruce Lee', which had dogged his entire career. Yuen Woo-Ping and Gordon Chan were remaking Lee's classic *Fist of Fury*. Anxious not to tarnish the memory of Lee, while making the film his own, Li hit the perfect balance with the fantastically successful *Fist of Legend*. In 1997 Li made the devastating (for martial arts fans everywhere) decision to give up acting and retire into a life of contemplation and Buddhism. Fortunately, he soon came to the conclusion that he could spread the word to a worldwide audience far more effectively through the medium of celluloid than by sitting in a cave staring at the wall for ten years. And so he returned. Seemingly obsessed with the legendary hero, Li again played Wong

Fei Hung in *Once Upon a Time in China and America*, before having another bash – literally – at the US market. As the villain in *Lethal Weapon 4*, he was so popular that promoters added his image to the movie poster after the film had opened. Starring roles in Hollywood followed, including the enormously enjoyable *Kiss of the Dragon* and the equally entertaining but extremely silly *The One*, in which he fights himself and demonstrate the advantages of harmony over force in kung fu. With the exception of Jackie Chan, Jet Li is the biggest Asian star in the world. Give him time: he's got a few years of catching up to do.

- Best kick flicks: *Once Upon a Time in China* (1991), *The Legend of Fong Sai Yuk* (1993), *Fist of Legend* (1994), *Hero* (2002).
- Trivia: The name 'Jet' came from a distribution company in the Philippines, who shortened Li's given name, Lian Jie, when they released *Shaolin Temple*. Apparently he liked it. If you touch his hair, he'll kill you. Li narrowly escaped the December 2004 tsunami while on holiday in the Maldives: he injured his foot running for higher ground, carrying his daughter. He turned down the role of Li Mu Bai in *Crouching Tiger, Hidden Dragon* because he promised his wife he would not work while she was pregnant.
- Where are they now: Having released the Luc Besson movie *Unleashed* (co-starring the equally vertically challenged Bob Hoskins) in 2005, Li is working on the story of legendary martial arts master Fok Yuen-Gap. Quotes from Li, reported in the Chinese newspaper *Shenzhen Daily*, have suggested he is about to end his martial arts acting career. Fans can only hope that he doesn't mean it this time either.

Crouching Tiger, Hidden Dragon
(aka *Wo Hu Zang Long, Ngo Foo Chong Lung*)

USA/China/Hong Kong/Taiwan, 2000, 120 minutes

Production Companies: Golden Harvest, Edko Films, Zoom
Hunt International Production
In collaboration with: China Film Co-Production Corporation,
Asia Union Film & Entertainment
Presented by: Columbia Pictures, Sony Classics, Good
Machine International
Director: Ang Lee
Action choreographed by: Yuen Woo-Ping
Assistant martial arts co-ordinators: Ku Huen-Chiu, Wong
Kim-Wai

Executive producers: James Schamus, David Linde
Producers: Bill Kong, Hsu Li-Kong, Ang Lee
Screenplay: James Schamus, Wang Hui-Ling, Tsai Kuo-Jung
Based on the novel by: Wang Du-Lu
Cinematographer: Peter Pau
Music: Jorge Calandrelli, Tan Dun, King Yong

CAST: Chow Yun-Fat (*Li Mu Bai*), Michelle Yeoh (*Yu Shu Lien*), Zhang Ziyi (*Yu Jen*), Chang Chen (*Lo*), Lung Sihung (*Sir Te*), Cheng Pei-Pei (*Jade Fox*), Li Fa-Zeng (*Governor Yu*), Gao Xian (*Bo*), Hai Yan (*Madam Yu*), Wang De-Ming (*Tsai*), Li Li (*May*), Huang Su-Ying (*Auntie Wu*), Zhang Jin-Ting (*De Lu*), Li Kai (*Gou Jun Pei*), Feng Jian-Hua (*Gou Jun Sihung*): Yang Rui, Du Zhen-Xi, Xu Cheng-Lin, Lin Feng, Wang Wen-Sheng

PLOT: Unusually for a martial arts film, even an esoteric wuxia pian, *Crouching Tiger, Hidden Dragon* makes you wait for the action. Rather than immediately thrill its audience with flying warriors and flashing swords, it spends quite a long time setting the scene – which is just as well, because there's a lot of scene to set. Based on the fourth in a popular series of wuxia pulp fiction by Wang Du-Lu, the story takes place in nineteenth-century China, amid the strictly controlled and structured society of the Qing Dynasty at the height of its power. A legendary warrior from Wudan Mountain, Li Mu Bai, has decided to exchange his righteous adventuring for a life of peaceful meditation and hang up his sword – or, rather, give it to Sir Te, his mentor and father figure since the death of his kung fu master. The task of transporting his famous Green Destiny sword to Beijing he entrusts to Yu Shu Lien, who runs a security firm, is a pretty fine fighter herself – and happens to be the unacknowledged love of his life.

Shu Lien duly heads for the capital, while Mu Bai returns to Wudan to pay his respects to the spirit of his master, who was murdered by the outlaw Jade Fox. It is Li Mu Bai's final quest to apprehend the criminal and make her pay for the crimes for which she has so far gone unpunished. Why he gives up his sword before heading after a woman capable of slaying a Wudan master is anyone's guess.

In Beijing, Shu Lien delivers the Green Destiny, an exquisite jian (straight sword), to Sir Te, and meets one of his guests, Yu Jen.

The daughter of Governor Yu, Jen is preparing to marry a worthy but dull business acquaintance of her father's. The Green Destiny and Shu Lien's life as a swordswoman fascinate Jen, who reads the stories of the wuxia warriors and longs for their life of adventure. Shu Lien tries to point out that it is not all glory and honour, but also hardship and pain. When asked why she never married, she reveals that her fiancé – Li Mu Bai's martial brother – was killed fighting, and out of respect for his memory she could not wed another. Women are not allowed to train at Wudan, so she has not even had the solace of becoming a fully-fledged Wudan warrior. Shu Lien points out that she too has had to do her duty as a woman, for all that Jen believes her life to be one of freedom and choice.

That night, the Green Destiny is stolen and, when a guard raises the alarm, Shu Lien sets off in pursuit of the masked bandit. Flitting up walls and across rooftops, the two battle it out in spectacular style but the thief finally escapes. Hearing of the stolen sword, a police inspector on the trail of Jade Fox is convinced that she is the perpetrator of the crime. He and his daughter are seeking revenge for the murder of his wife, killed by Jade Fox. Li Mu Bai arrives unexpectedly, claiming that he has come to present his sword to Sir Te, but in reality hoping to see Yu Shu Lien. She admits that the sword is lost, but reveals that she has her own suspicions about its whereabouts. Following her, Mu Bai sees wanted posters for Jade Fox and realises his nemesis must be near at hand.

The police inspector and his daughter track down Jade Fox and challenge her in a graveyard. She kills the policeman before Li Mu Bai arrives, ready to take revenge for the death of his master. But before he can dispatch the evil crone, the masked bandit arrives and saves her, challenging Mu Bai with his own sword.

Yu Shu Lien, now itching with suspicion, has a cunning plan. She invites Jen to tea, where she makes it known that she has discovered who has Mu Bai's sword, but will not tell as long as the sword is returned. She also does a neat trick with a teacup to test Jen's reactions, discovering them to be as fast as a trained warrior's. That night the thief brings the sword back, but Li Mu Bai is standing guard, and the two fight. Appreciating the raw talent of his adversary, Mu Bai offers himself as teacher, but he is rebuffed and the thief escapes. Returning to the Governor's house, the bandit is his feisty young daughter, who has been getting cheap, non-aristocratic kicks running around the rooftops of the city at night. Her governess is revealed to be the wicked Jade Fox, who has taught her charge martial arts from a manual stolen from Li Mu Bai's master when she killed him. A man creeps into Jen's bedroom and, before she attacks him, Jen recognises her long-lost lover, Lo.

Cue flashback to a caravan making its way across the desert, Jen and her mother travelling in its midst. The caravan is attacked by Dark Cloud and his villainous band of ruffians, and Jen is unable to resist peering out of the window, drawing the attention of the bandit leader, Lo (for it is he). He steals her comb and, rather than let him take it, she throws caution and her mother's good advice to the wind, grabs a horse and charges after him in the headstrong fashion that is to become her trademark. Relying on natural talent alone, Jen fights off the bandits, and gives Lo a good kicking before he overcomes her. Taking her as his prize, he retreats to his cave in the mountains and ties her up in case she starts kicking him again. Deciding that she really is too pretty to go to waste, Lo has his wicked way with her and she decides she really rather likes it. After a period of living happy and wild in the desert, they are tracked down by Yu's soldiers and Lo sends Jen away, promising he will make himself respectable and come to claim her.

But he never turned up, and here she is, preparing for her marriage to the tedious Gou. Lo begs her not to go through with it but she has little choice – a Chinese girl must follow the wishes of her parents. When the wedding procession is taking place the next day, Lo tries desperately to reach his lover but is apprehended by Shu Lien and Mu Bai. He tells them of his troubles and they – star-crossed lovers themselves, who have revealed to the audience, if not to each other, that they are in love but can never admit to it – agree to help him.

After the wedding, Jen disappears along with the Green Destiny, Li Mu Bai takes Lo to Wudan Mountain and Shu Lien heads home. Jen has gone off in search of the adventure she has always craved, seemingly having forgotten about Lo since he hasn't come to get her. Dressed as a boy, she turns up at an inn and is challenged by the local martial artists to show what she can do with her flashy sword. She proceeds to hammer the lot of them, taking down most of the inn in the process. Unsure what to do next, Jen turns up at Shu Lien's house, asking for advice. Not liking what she hears – that she should head home and do as she is told – she attacks Shu Lien and the two fight, Shu Lien making her way through a staggering array of weapons trying to find one that will overcome the Green Destiny.

Just as she is about to gain the upper hand, Li Mu Bai arrives and Jen escapes. Mu Bai pursues her across a bamboo forest, deflecting her attacks and offering to teach her, despite the fact that women are not welcomed at Wudan. She refuses and, when he throws the Green Destiny into a lake, she dives in after it. Rescued by Jade Fox, Jen is taken to a cave, where her former governess drugs her. Jade Fox feels betrayed by Jen, who could read the Wudan manual better than she, and has far outstripped her teacher in the level of her kung fu. Jade Fox is determined that Jen will never leave her again. Once more, Li Mu Bai and Yu Shu Lien arrive to save the day, and Mu Bai gets his revenge on Jade Fox, finally killing her to avenge his master. She had just cause, however: while he was happy to sleep with her, the master refused to teach her, so she was only getting her own back. She has done so again: even as she dies, she knows Mu Bai will too. He has been struck in the neck by one of her poison darts.

While Jen rides desperately to Shu Lien's home to prepare an antidote, the two would-be lovers spend their last minutes together. Shu Lien urges Mu Bai to save his energy, but he insists on telling her of his love at last. Only during this final tragedy can they speak of their feelings. Jen returns, too late, and Shu Lien tells her that the only way she can make up for her selfish behaviour is to be true to herself, as she and Mu Bai could not. Journeying to Wudan Mountain, Jen is reunited with Lo, but realises that she cannot live the life he wants for them and commits the ultimate sacrifice, flying from a bridge to fall to the bottom of the mountain.

CASTING: Jet Li was the first actor to come to director Ang Lee's mind when he began planning his martial epic, but when the wushu star couldn't commit to the project, it changed the tenor of the film entirely. Needing a recognisable name – the film stars two of Hong Kong's most bankable actors, helping to make it more digestible in the West – Lee chose Chow Yun-Fat, casting him in the flowing-robed, long-haired, sword-swinging period role the actor had sworn never to play. Despite his oath, he took the part, which was substantially rewritten as more of a romantic lead than a martial arts hero. The size of the role increased, and Chow plays it with a sensitivity and grace that make up for his lack of kick flick bravura. Despite having little martial arts experience, Chow threw himself into the role. 'He'd maybe only done one or two action films before, and it was his first time with wire-work, but I was amazed. His movement was great. Maybe he saw a lot of Hong Kong movies,' muses action director Yuen Woo-Ping.

The only trained martial artist of the three leading players, Michelle Yeoh was also the only one who was the first choice for the part. She didn't get the chance to show off all of her skills, however, injuring her knee early in the shoot schedule and spending a lot of the scenes shot after that point standing behind pot plants or sitting down with her leg hidden under a table. Lee refused to replace her, having cast her despite the fact that she didn't speak Mandarin, the language *Crouching Tiger, Hidden Dragon* is recorded in. Initially Lee considered dubbing Yeoh, but decided that no one else could do the part justice. Says Yeoh, 'It was intimidating because I was working with actors who knew Mandarin as their first language, and I didn't have the rhythm, and I didn't know what I was saying . . . I talked like a robot.' While the accents of the Cantonese-speaking stars – the dialect is also Chow's first language – may undermine the film for a Mandarin-speaking audience, they make little difference to the rest of the world, which understands the language less than Yeoh. An icon from the golden age of Hong Kong movies, Yeoh is the making of the film with her portrayal of Shu Lien's rigid moral code, aching heart and devastating martial moves.

Lee initially cast popular martial arts actress Shu Qi in the role of Jen, but when her agent pulled her from the film to do a Pepsi commercial he went for the more fresh-faced yet determinedly driven Zhang Ziyi, tailoring the part to fit his budding star. (Shu Qi has since sacked her agent.) A troubled teenager in her own right, Zhang manages to keep her schizophrenic character believable. In only her second film, the dancer and actor had the advantage of playing a self-taught martial artist, and her enthusiasm for the action far outweighs her lack of martial training. Fresh out of college, she handles the journey from innocent to lover, cross-dressing warrior to melancholy heroine with maturity and style.

An inspired piece of casting resulted in the appearance of Cheng Pei-Pei, who, in the guise of Golden Swallow, was the heroine of a dozen kung fu films in the 60s. Her presence in the film creates a direct link between *Crouching Tiger, Hidden Dragon* and the wuxia pian of earlier decades. Concerned that she might not want to tarnish her reputation by playing the evil Jade Fox, Ang Lee actually found her more than willing. She oozes vitriol against the men who would bed Jade Fox but not teach her kung fu, inspired perhaps by her real feelings for the men who created the male-focused gung-fu pian, writing her out of a genre she had made her own. No longer the lithe girl of her youth, Cheng's heavy movements, twisted expressions and palpable desperation as she sees Jen slipping from her grasp add power and poignancy to the core themes of the film.

Among the smaller parts in the film, Lung Sihung in the role of Sir Te is a staple of Ang Lee's previous Chinese films, reprising his role of father figure and adding a quiet dignity to the piece.

MARTIAL ARTS: Although *Crouching Tiger, Hidden Dragon* has been cast in the mould of the wuxia genre, the martial arts it contains differ in a number of ways. The film employs the talents of Yuen Woo-Ping, a veteran of Hong Kong kick flicks dating back to the 1970s – although, on the release of *Crouching Tiger, Hidden Dragon*, the Western press insisted on giving him the suffix 'of *Matrix* fame' – to plan the choreography, but the fight scenes are shorter and more individual than in his earlier movies. There are no huge set pieces with massed martial artists battling it out, and dialogue frequently punctuates the action. The lack of practical experience among the actors – with the exception of Yeoh and Cheng – is compensated for by spectacular wire-work.

There are four central fight scenes between the protagonists, each quite different in character, reflecting the dramatic development of the film. First there is the night flight over the rooftops, as Jen tries to escape with the Green Destiny with Shu Lien hotly in pursuit. Then Jen takes apart an inn and all its occupants, in true Golden Harvest style – on what looks like a set from an earlier GH film. Arriving at Shu Lien's home, the two fight in her training room with an educational display of the ancient weapons of kung fu, before Jen takes on Mu Bai atop a bamboo forest. Each of these scenes has a different feel and colour: black, brown, grey and green. The settings reflect classic scenes from the genre. Rooftop combat marks the climax of *The Duel*, **Dragon Gate Inn** is the genesis of kung fu pub brawls, the training room is the setting for display fights from **36th Chamber of Shaolin** to *The Matrix*, and conflict in the bamboo forest is ubiquitous throughout the genre. As an added twist, this time the combatants duel above the trees rather than beneath them.

The advantage of focusing on individual duels is that the audience does not get lost in the action and can follow every move. This is particularly beneficial to an international audience not schooled in the appreciation of Asian action flicks – it takes practice to pick out the artistry amid the general carnage. Every leap and thrust is marked, with frequent switching to high-angled shots to provide context. The fighters complement and contrast: Michelle Yeoh's stylish, economical moves are the antithesis of Cheng Pei-Pei's brute force and battering weapons, while Zhang Ziyi's wild athleticism rebounds against the controlled, tight movement of Chow Yun-Fat.

When James Schamus produced the first draft of his script, the extent of the description of the action scenes was 'They fight'. The rest came from the imagination of one man. Action choreographer Yuen Woo-Ping has found his return to the heroic chivalry genre a liberating experience. 'We went back to swashbuckling heroics, where you have a freer hand with the choreography . . . I am more into the softer styles, rather than the hard, fast cut-cut-cut of a lot of movies.' His use of wire brings out a more flowing, harmonised style. The film marks a change from Yuen's early Hong Kong movies, which focused on authenticity. When he first started on films like *Iron Monkey*, the martial arts he choreographed were very down to earth, using a more practical and realistic approach. This direction was abandoned in *Crouching Tiger, Hidden Dragon*: 'I was trying to express the more magical characteristics of old-fashioned wuxia. You might notice that they fly through the air, but for every leap they make they come back down to earth.' The film never explains how and why people can walk up walls – when you're trained with the arts of Wudan, you can just do that sort of thing.

As with many Hong Kong films, the martial arts provide the draw – the bridge to an international audience that may not understand the subtleties of Chinese culture in the nineteenth century or the motivations of the characters but definitely understands the action. Just as Jackie Chan broke into the Western market with his kung fu comedy, so Ang Lee has found a way to introduce the wuxia pian to the world without the world realising he was doing it.

STUNTS AND SPECIAL EFFECTS: In *Crouching Tiger, Hidden Dragon*, Yuen Woo-Ping elevates wire-fu, that staple of Hong Kong martial movies, into an art form. The most complex sequence he composed was the duel that takes place in the branches of the bamboo forest – a familiar setting which is almost a prerequisite for any wuxia film. Using a challenging yet surprisingly basic technique, the actors, wearing heavy canvas harnesses, were suspended 75 feet in the air, dangling from industrial cranes. The cables supporting them weighed more than the actors, causing their cargo to swing in unexpected directions, so that the 'pullers' controlling them had to be constantly alert. These puppeteers also had to work in tandem with the other teams to avoid collisions.

After that, what you see is what you get. Says Yuen, 'There is no computer trickery involved – the only "special effect" is when we remove the wire in post production.' The action director claims he never uses CGI, and the only difference between the work he does now and the films he made in the 70s is that he can set up much longer shots. Entire martial exchanges can be completed in a single take, much to the relief of the actors. Michelle Yeoh insists that it all looks easier than it is. 'It's a difficult and very subtle process. When you're doing it, you can't eat, breathe or speak!' At least these days the cables don't snap, which is just as well given that more than 300 were used in the bamboo sequence alone, operated by forty people – usually it requires only fifteen.

DIRECTOR: Ang Lee is far from a kick flick specialist, a fact that he recognised when creating *Crouching Tiger, Hidden Dragon* by employing Yuen Woo-Ping to choreograph the action. His previous films have dealt with everything from a gay Chinese immigrant in New York in *The Wedding Banquet* to Jane Austen's *Sense and Sensibility*, and are generally marked by their slow, stately pace, the antithesis of the Hong Kong aesthetic. Lee did, however, grow up on a diet of wuxia in his native Taiwan, and was determined to create his own take on the genre at some point in his career. 'To me it is important after three English-language films to go back to my cultural roots, to fulfil my boyhood dreams.' Lee sees those roots as being entwined with the work of King Hu and Chang Cheh rather than the directors of the late 70s and 80s. 'It's the storytelling that really grabbed me, the fantasy storytelling, about power, about personal transcendence, about romance. Morality tales.' He does, however, admit to owing a debt to some of the classic fight sequences of the 80s and 90s.

Lee also believes that *Crouching Tiger, Hidden Dragon* benefited from the experience he gained working on his previous films, even though at first glance his Hollywood productions bear little resemblance to a genre considered by many to consist of Chinese B-movies. He cites similarities between his other films and his wuxia pian that make them all part of a uniquely Ang Lee-styled back catalogue: 'I had to bring in drama, I had to bring in women, I had to bring in beauty and whatever I feel added quality to it. It became an Ang Lee movie.' But beauty, women and drama have all been part of the genre since its inception in the 1920s. These elements are not unique to the director and, while their presence attests to Lee's roots in the wuxia genre, it is surprising that he fails to acknowledge their history.

Two things that Lee did bring to the film were US backing and a Western audience. Thanks to his early days on the New York independent film circuit and his home in Westchester, New York, he was able to present himself as a US director with an Asian background, and so was far more palatable to American studios. His independent film *The Wedding Banquet* had already proved that Lee was capable of crossing international boundaries in both content and context. With *Sense and Sensibility* and *The Ice Storm* Lee broke out of the art-house cinemas to which Asian directors are so often consigned, and his name became linked to mainstream movies in the minds of Western filmgoers. These factors contributed to the enormous success of *Crouching Tiger, Hidden Dragon* in the West, where its popularity eclipsed all previous foreign language films.

But despite these advantages, Lee set himself a challenge by trying to make a traditional Chinese film with mainstream international appeal. 'I have two sons in America, and all they care about in Chinese culture is Jackie Chan and Jet Li. Those movies present probably the worst, most raucous part of Chinese culture.' With *Crouching Tiger, Hidden Dragon*, Lee wanted to bring another side of Chinese society to Western viewers. The film is anything but raucous. As a result, it failed to attract the audience it should have been able to take for granted. Although it did very well in Asia, the film was less of a hit in Hong Kong than expected, proving to be too slow for viewers raised on a diet of frenetic action.

PRODUCTION: The budget for *Crouching Tiger, Hidden Dragon*, while small for a Hollywood movie, was enormous for a Chinese martial arts film. This unheard-of wealth fuelled Ang Lee's ambitions and caused him to drive the project almost to the point of disaster. The initial shoot in the Gobi Desert was beset by disaster – they got lost, trapped in a sandstorm and then hit by flood. In a desert. Worse was to come. When Lee announced that the fight in the bamboo forest was to take place above the trees, his crew initially refused. It had never been done before, and was considered impossible. Lee says, 'We live in a place with gravity. I sort of underestimate that.' He forgot that his actors couldn't really fly. As well as gravity, he had to contend with nature. The leaves of the bamboo would begin to dwindle as soon as it was cut, reducing shooting time to half an hour before the vegetation had to be replaced.

Colour plays an important part in the composition of the film. The action swings from the passion and heat of the red desert – the tiger – to the cool, green, internalised world of the forest. 'The colour green is really the Hidden Dragon for me in the movie, against the colour of red in the desert flashback. The crouching one, the forbidden one is green. The Green Destiny. Jade Fox,' says Lee. This focus on colour and texture is apparent in the early work of King Hu, and Zhang Yimou further develops the style in *Hero*, where each sequence has its own defining pigment.

Moods are also switched in *Crouching Tiger, Hidden Dragon* by changes of pace, swinging from quiet contemplation in a teahouse to the frenetic fighting of the bar brawl. The machine-gun editing common to the genre has been abandoned in favour of Lee's trademark poetic compositions, made possible in an action film by developments in stunt techniques which allow for long, continuous shots. These are underscored by the soundtrack, which ranges from the single drum beat of the rooftop fight to soaring strings over sweeping shots of Wudan Mountain. There is even the ubiquitous sentimental love song over the closing credits.

TRIVIA: The closing love song, *A Love Before Time*, is sung by CoCo Lee, Hong Kong's answer to Celine Dion. The lyrics were penned by scriptwriter and producer James Schamus: on reflection, perhaps he should stick to screenplays. In April 2001, in response to the huge success of *Crouching Tiger, Hidden Dragon*, the Sultan of Perak state in Malaysia awarded Michelle Yeoh the royal title of Dutak. The Chinese names of the characters Lo and Jen mean, respectively, 'Little Tiger' and 'Little Dragon', while the Green Destiny is actually 'Green Dark World Sword', named for the place where the Chinese believe the dead reside.

THEMES: 'Crouching tiger, hidden dragon' is a quote from Chinese mythology, referring to the practice of hiding your true nature and strength from those around you. The dragon represents secret desire and social taboos. This is obviously a dominant theme in the film: many of the characters disguise their motivations and identities. Jade Fox, thief and murderer, poses as a harmless hand-matron while Yu Jen pretends to be a dutiful aristocratic daughter awaiting her marriage, when her heart is running wild in the desert with her lover and her spirit wants to break into the jianghu. Jen literally disguises herself with a mask to steal the Green Destiny, and again as a boy when she goes adventuring, thereby reviving the tradition of women in drag in the wuxia pian. Yu Shu Lien and Li Mu Bai act out the fantasy that they are just good friends, refusing to admit their love to themselves or each other. Li claims that he wants to leave the life of a warrior, but as soon as he discovers Jen he offers to teach her; he is clearly not yet ready to quit the world of Wudan. Shu Lien is adamant about her duty and her place as a woman, but cannot hide her disappointment when Li Mu Bai offers Jen the chance to train at Wudan, an opportunity she was denied because of her gender. Even the policeman who is hunting Jade Fox hides his identity while trying to trap his quarry.

The setting of *Crouching Tiger, Hidden Dragon* is typical of the wuxia genre, a mystical version of late Qing Dynasty China, considered a golden age in the country when it stood separated from other nations and secure in its sense of superiority. Thus the conflicts of the characters are confined within their own society. The Qing are sure of their hold on the country, which has yet to be undermined by internal corruption or the invasion of foreign devils. The Manchurian Dynasty is still portrayed as an usurping power, however: when Lo accuses Jen of being a Manchu, she furiously retorts that she is pure Han.

One of the social conflicts is between the generations, represented by Jen and Lo, desperate to live their own lives and fighting against the conventions of their culture. As an outlaw he could never hope to marry a noble woman, so he seeks to rise above his class through wealth and power – not an accepted route in Qing China, where precedence through birth was everything. Lo tries to convince Jen to abandon the wedding her parents have arranged for her, and defy them. She in turn seeks to break free from the influence of Jade Fox, whom she has surpassed in martial arts, and rebuffs the advances of Li Mu Bai and Yu Shu Lien, who want to bind her within the moral codes of Wudan. The comparison with the older warriors emphasises the theme: while they are strictly controlled, she does as she pleases. Shu Lien refrains from cutting Jen when she bests her in their fight. Jen shows no such compunction, slashing her across the arm. It is only after Li Mu Bai's death that Jen realises the errors of her headstrong, self-centred ways, although in taking her own life she in turn denies Lo the chance of happiness with her.

By emphasising the generation gap, a feature of all his films, Ang Lee reworks the sifu-student relationship. Rather than trying to convince a master to teach her, as Foon courts Wong Fei Hung, Jen has two teachers vying for her attention: the powers of light and darkness. She ignores the advice of both and, while Lee acknowledges that the next generation will surpass the last, as Jen surpasses Jade Fox, when Jen ignores the advice of her elders she and everyone around her ultimately suffer. The blazing love affair between Jen and Lo also contrasts with the gentle sorrow of the other pair of lovers, who are unable to break the bonds that restrict them.

By focusing on romance, the film acknowledges *Once Upon a Time in China* and the earlier *Golden Swallow*. It ignores the gung-fu and wu da pian, and focuses on the aspects of martial arts beyond the brutal training regimes, such as calligraphy and meditation, which are shown to be as important as swordplay. Like many wuxia pian, *Crouching Tiger, Hidden Dragon* revolves around a set of righteous knights battling evil. But this is not a uniquely Chinese theme: it bears more than a passing resemblance to the legend of King Arthur, appealing to those who grew up with a different set of swashbuckling heroes. The wicked witch, the noble warrior, the doomed lovers, the magic sword being cast into a lake: it's all there. Each character has their own quest, for love, power, revenge or peace. 'Arthur' even dies at the end of the tale, in the arms of his would-be lover, passing the task of preserving Wudan's honour on to another.

Feminism – and femininity – is also a strong theme in *Crouching Tiger, Hidden Dragon*. The women, denied access to Wudan's teachings, steal the knowledge, empowering themselves by developing skills restricted to men. The balance between masculine and feminine is another area of conflict, with Jen being pulled between the two sides of her personality. Jade Fox encourages the masculine, teaching her to fight, which results in her dressing up in male drag and running off to battle bandits. Shu Lien represents the feminine, bringing Jen female clothes to wear when she turns up at her house. Although Shu Lien is the most balanced character, retaining her femininity while acknowledging the need for strength – she prefers to fight with the machete, but switches to a heavy sword to overcome Jen – she has failed to find contentment. She has achieved a level of equanimity by repressing her desires, but in doing so only intensifies them. Ultimately, Jen recognises that she cannot live the life she wants in her current form and sacrifices herself on Wudan Mountain, hoping, perhaps, to be reborn as a man.

Sexual relationships receive a more public airing in *Crouching Tiger, Hidden Dragon* than in most wuxia pian, although the characters' real desires are often hidden. This is true of all the modern Asian martial arts films, thanks to relaxation of censorship, a more liberal society and the demands of a twenty-first century audience. The initial sex scene between Lo and Jen is blatant and relatively brutal, although Ang Lee's sensibilities mean the viewer doesn't actually see much. While their relationship is transparent, the same cannot be said of the feelings of others. Jade Fox's attentions to Jen and her accusations that Jen has betrayed her hint at a more intimate relationship than that of student and teacher. Li Mu Bai's intentions are also questionable. Shu Lien is clearly jealous of the attention he shows Jen, who in turn is not too keen on the idea. When he offers to take her to Wudan she screams, 'Wudan is a whorehouse!' and it would appear that she is not wrong: Jade Fox reveals that Li's master used her for her body. Jen challenges Li in the cave, baring her breasts and demanding if it is the sword he wants or her.

PLACE WITHIN THE GENRE: *Crouching Tiger, Hidden Dragon* is a film of many facets, not just in its themes but in the different reactions it arouses among critics and audiences, and the several genres it brings together. A direct descendant of the wuxia pian, in many ways it is a very traditional film made with modern techniques and money. But it also lacks some of the characteristics of that genre. It was created to bridge the gap between Asia and the West, and in attempting to appeal to both audiences it succeeds in creating a new place for itself as action-art house.

Ang Lee wanted a Chinese blockbuster that would do well on the international festival circuit. He got something that was almost the complete opposite: the biggest foreign language film ever, making more money and winning more Oscar nominations that any that had gone before, *Crouching Tiger, Hidden Dragon* was trailed in the West without dialogue, implying that the action and the drama were more important than the language. It brought martial arts films from the cult into the mainstream, while broadening the acceptance of subtitles in the UK and the US – in many other countries, subtitles or dubbing have long been the norm. In China, however, the film was more of a curiosity: related to popular kick flicks, but subtly different, with Cantonese actors speaking Mandarin (badly, some pointed out). It did well, but maybe not as well as might have been expected.

A crossover was achieved, however. Compact, Westernised narrative structures were introduced into a Chinese film, while Chinese culture and filmic eccentricities were laid before

Above Out with the old:
The climax of *Enter the
Dragon* shows that ageing
drug lord Han (Shek Kin)
is no match for Lee (Bruce
Lee, here seen modelling
his favoured shirtless,
blood-spattered style)
(Warner Bros/Ronald Grant
Archive)

Right Time to die:
Oharra (Bob Wall) comes
to a bloody end at the
hands of Lee (Bruce Lee)
in *Enter the Dragon*
(Warner Bros/Ronald Grant
Archive)

Left This one's on him: Tsu (Yuen Biao) helps Dragon (Jackie Chan) to a drink in *Project A* (Paragon Films/Ronald Grant Archive)

Below left All together now: In *Project A* Jackie Chan and Sammo Hung use their opera training to bash their opponents in perfect harmony (Paragon Films/Ronald Grant Archive)

Below right Chariots of Fire: Wong Fei Hung (Jet Li) leads a training session on the beach in *Once Upon a Time in China* (Film Workshop/The Kobal Collection)

Right Lethal weapons: Yu Shu Lien (Michelle Yeoh) demonstrates her preference for twin machetes in *Crouching Tiger, Hidden Dragon* (Sony Pictures/Ronald Grant Archive)

Below Caught in the act: Li Mu Bai (Chow Yun-Fat) and Yu Jen (Zhang Ziyi) pause mid-battle in *Crouching Tiger, Hidden Dragon* (Columbia/Sony/The Kobal Collection/Chuen, Chan Kam)

Left Faster than a speeding arrow: *Hero*'s Nameless (Jet Li) after clearing the sky of flying missiles
(Elite Group Enterprises/ Ronald Grant Archive)

Below Foregone conclusion: Nameless (Jet Li) strikes the fatal blow in his mental battle with Sky (Donnie Yen) in *Hero*
(Beijing New Picture/Elite Group/The Kobal Collection)

Above Blood brothers: Leo (Andy Lau) and Jin (Takeshi Kaneshiro) duel to the death at the climax of *House of Flying Daggers*
(China Film Group Corporation/The Kobal Collection/Bai Xiao Yan)

Below Deadly blade: Blind dancer and *House of Flying Daggers* assassin Mei (Zhang Ziyi) reveals that she's more than just a pretty face
(China Film Group Corporation/The Kobal Collection/Bai Xiao Yan)

Above Winning streak:
The Karate Kid – otherwise
known as Daniel-san
(Ralph Macchio) – proves
the virtue of quality over
quantity in the final
tournament
(Columbia Pictures/Ronald
Grant Archive)

Above inset Wax on, wax
off: Mr Miyagi (Noriyuki
'Pat' Morita) shows Daniel
(Ralph Macchio) what all
those chores were for in
The Karate Kid
(Columbia Pictures/Ronald
Grant Archive)

Left Blood bath:
Kurt (Jean-Claude Van
Damme) proves that
he's a real *Kickboxer* by
destroying the evil Tong
Po (Michel Qissi)
(Kings Road Entertainment/
The Kobal Collection)

Right Girl fight: In *Kill Bill Volume 1* O-Ren Ishii (Lucy Liu), garbed in the world's most inappropriate martial outfit, prepares to take on The Bride (Uma Thurman), who sports a tracksuit inspired by Bruce Lee's wardrobe in *Game of Death*
(Miramax Films/Ronald Grant Archive)

Right Fist of fury: Pai Mei (Gordon Liu) shows Beatrix (Uma Thurman) how to punch her way out of a coffin in *Kill Bill Volume 2*
(Miramax Films/Ronald Grant Archive)

Below Mirror image: The training scene in *Kill Bill Volume 2* references the opening sequence of *36th Chamber of Shaolin* – both feature Gordon Liu
(A Band Apart/Miramax/ The Kobal Collection)

Above Muay thai warrior: Ting (Tony Jaa) prepares himself to fight in the old style and win back the *Ong-Bak* Buddha (Baa-Ram-Ewe/The Kobal Collection)

Above Monkey magic: The Monkey King (Masaaki Sakai) struts his stuff in the TV series *Monkey* (20th Century Fox TV/ Greenway Prod/The Kobal Collection)

Below Kung fu chop: *The Green Hornet*'s trusty sidekick Kato (Bruce Lee) demonstrates a move that Austin Powers would be proud of (NTV/Ronald Grant Archive)

international audiences in a format they could digest. Says Ang Lee: 'I took great care in making it an A-movie – to portray the martial arts in a realistic and genuine manner and to verbalise the romance.' It has also strengthened the options for co-financing, with the international film industry recognising the potential profit to be made from the genre – and starting to realise that the genre is 'martial arts' rather than the all-encompassing 'foreign language'. *Crouching Tiger, Hidden Dragon* has created a new place for the martial arts film, resurrecting it once more and opening the door for Zhang Yimou's epic *Hero* and complex *House of Flying Daggers*. Tsui Hark has been inspired to return to Hong Kong, where he is filming a sequel to *Zu: Warriors from the Magic Mountain* and trying to push the genre to even greater heights.

Heroic Ones: Michelle Yeoh

- **AKA:** Michelle Khan, Yang Ziqiong, Yeung Chi-King, Yeoh Chu-Keng.
- **Birth name:** Yeoh Choo-Kheng.
- **Nickname:** The Queen of Martial Arts.
- **Not to be confused with:** Anyone – ever.
- **Martial style:** Originally trained as a ballet dancer, Yeoh came to martial arts relatively late in life. Since becoming an action heroine, however, she has played everything from a judo instructor to a wing chun aficionado to a machete-wielding kung fu mercenary.
- **Born:** 6 August 1962 in Ipoh, Malaysia.
- **Biography:** The woman who was to become the most famous female martial artist and movie star in the world never planned to be either. Her first love was ballet. She represented Malaysia in youth competitions for swimming, diving and squash, and was the country's Junior Squash Champion. At 15 she moved to England with her parents, later attending the London Royal Academy of Dance. A spinal injury cut short her dancing career and she turned to choreography. Returning to Malaysia for a holiday, she discovered that her mother had entered her in the national beauty contest. She won and was catapulted into the public eye. Hong Kong businessman Dickson Poon chose her to star in a watch advert with Jackie Chan, and another with Chow Yun-Fat. He also offered her a film contract and, some years later, a wedding ring. Poon's D&B Films, run in partnership with Sammo Hung, launched Yeoh's career. Eager to work on action films, she became the icon of the 'girls with guns' genre when she starred with Cynthia Rothrock in *Yes,*

Madam. As a female action star, Yeoh stands apart, not least because she does her own stunts. This is not without its risks. During the course of her career she has ruptured an artery in her leg, dislocated her elbow and shoulder, been burned, re-injured her spine and had to have screws inserted in both her knees. Her marriage to Poon in 1988 instigated a brief period of retirement, but when the marriage ended her career was kick-started by *Police Story 3: Super Cop*, in which she traded blow for blow with Jackie Chan. The film broke box-office records in Asia, and Yeoh has never looked back. A series of classic martial arts films followed, before she was launched on to the international scene in 1997, playing the Bond Girl who fights back in *Tomorrow Never Dies*. While this film didn't garner Yeoh the attention she deserved, the same cannot be said of Ang Lee's modern Asian classic *Crouching Tiger, Hidden Dragon*. The true female star of this film – with respect to Zhang Ziyi – Yeoh steals the show in her weapons and open hand fight scenes. Her acting is also sublime, made even more remarkable by the fact that the script was written in Mandarin, a language she does not speak. Each line had to be learned by rote before shooting. In 2000 she set up her own production company, Mythical Films, in partnership with Media Asia, and has produced as well as starred in the films *The Touch* and *Silver Hawk*.

- Best kick flicks: *Butterfly and Sword* (1993), *Tai Chi Master* (1993), *Wing Chun* (1994), *Crouching Tiger, Hidden Dragon* (2000).
- Trivia: Yeoh is one of the few female stars whom Jackie Chan allows to perform her own stunts, and after filming *Tomorrow Never Dies*, Pierce 'James Bond' Brosnan said she could definitely take him. In 1993 she released a single, *Love Quite Like a Comet*.
- Where are they now: Still the most prominent Asian actress in the world, Yeoh has recently finished work on *Memoirs of a Geisha*. She is tipped to star in a film about the Chinese historic heroine Hua Mulan.

Heroic Ones: Chow Yun-Fat

- AKA: Chow Yuen Fat, Chow Yun Fat, Yun Fat Chow, Zhou Run Fa, Amon Chow, Donald Chow.
- Birth name: Chow Yun Fat.
- Nicknames: Fat Tsai, Fat 'Kor' (Big Brother).
- Not to be confused with: Sammo Hung – Chow is only Fat in name.
- Martial style: Spiritual kung fu, gun-fu, toothpick wielding. More a character actor than a martial artist.
- Born: 18 May 1955 on Lamma Island, Hong Kong.
- Biography: While not a martial artist, Chow Yun-Fat does have the distinction of being a god to his fans and appearing in some classic kick flicks. Born on an island in Hong Kong Harbour, Chow moved to the mainland when he was

ten, and in 1973 attended a casting call for TVB, the television division of Shaw Brothers. Originally cast as a heartthrob in TV roles, he changed all that when he played the white-suited crime boss Hui Man-Keung in the massive Hong Kong hit *Shanghai Beach 2* in 1983. He then came to the notice of director John Woo, who cast him in the gangster flick *A Better Tomorrow* in 1985. Following this film, half of Hong Kong ran out to buy the long wool 'mark coats' sported by Chow, despite the humid weather. In the West he is known for his performances in Hong Kong action thrillers, but in his native land Chow is the ultimate character actor. He proved his talent to international audiences as the long-suffering mercenary from Wudan, Li Mu Bai, in *Crouching Tiger, Hidden Dragon*. On the few occasions when he lays down his brace of pistols to take up the t'ai chi sword or crossbow, Chow shows himself more than capable of working in the martial arts idiom.

- Best kick flicks: *The Postman Fights Back* (1982), *Crouching Tiger, Hidden Dragon* (2000).
- Trivia: Chow turned down the part of Morpheus in *The Matrix*. At 6'1", he is unusually tall for a Hong Kong actor, and usually towers a head above his co-stars.
- Where are they now: In pre-production on *The Wretched*, in which he plays a zombie-catching bounty hunter.

Hero

(aka *Ying Xiong, Jet Li's Hero*)

China, 2002, 96 minutes

Production companies: Edko Films, Zhang Yimou Studio
In collaboration with: China Film Co-Production Corporation, Sil-Metropole Organisation Ltd, Beijing New Picture
Distribution Co.
Director: Zhang Yimou
Action director: Tony Ching Siu-Tung
Martial arts choreographer: Ting Wei
Executive producers: Dou Shou Fang, Zhang Wei Pin,
Producers: Bill Kong, Zhang Yimou
Screenplay: Li Feng, Zhang Yimou, Wang Bin
Director of photography: Christopher Doyle
Music: Tan Dun

CAST: Jet Li (*Nameless*), Tony Leung Chiu-Wai (*Broken Sword*), Maggie Cheung Man-Yuk (*Flying Snow*), Zhang Ziyi (*Moon*),

Chen Dao Ming (*King of Qin*), Donnie Yen (*Sky*), Liu
Zhiong-Yuan (*Scholar*), Zheng Tian-Yong (*Flying Snow's
servant*): Qin Yan, Chang Xiao-Yang, Zhang Ya-Kun, Ma
Wen-Hua, Jin Ming, Xu Kuang-Hua, Wang Shou-Xin

PLOT: Very little actually happens in *Hero*, but the events that do
occur are examined in exquisite detail. Three times. Some 2,000
years ago, during the Warring States period, what is now China
was composed of seven kingdoms. The King of Qin was busy
trying to reduce this number to one, namely Qin, and everyone
else was busy trying to assassinate the King of Qin. *Hero* tells the
story of one of those assassination attempts.

A minor local official is summoned to the King after claiming
that he has killed three warriors from Zhao, all of whom had
previously tried to assassinate the monarch. The official, Nameless
– so called because his family was killed before they could give
him one – has brought the weapons of the three assassins with him
to prove his story: Sky's silver spear and the blades of Flying Snow
and Broken Sword.

Nameless describes how he defeated Sky at a chess house after a
battle of wills, using the incredible speed of his sword, which he
has been honing for ten years. After killing Sky, he goes after
Broken Sword and Flying Snow, lovers who are hiding in a
calligraphy school. He tells the King that the two have not spoken
since Flying Snow had an affair with Sky. This is news to the King.
Nameless sets the cat among the pigeons by telling the warriors
that he killed Sky, and that Sky told him on his death that he only
cared for one person, and she would avenge his death: Flying
Snow. Nameless tells her to meet him at the Qin camp if she wishes
to do so. Wild with jealousy, Broken Sword has meaningless sex
with his assistant, Moon, so Flying Snow stabs him. She also kills
Moon when she comes seeking vengeance, and, distraught, is
killed by Nameless when she goes to meet his challenge.

All very well, says the King, but he thinks he knows them
better: Flying Snow and Broken Sword came to kill him three
years before, and he found them to be noble warriors, not given to
petty arguments and random stabbings. He goes on to give his
own version of events. He believes that Sky and Nameless were
old friends, and Sky allowed Nameless to kill him as part of a final
desperate attempt to assassinate the King. Since the last attack, the

ruler has let no one near him, but decreed that whoever rid him of the threat of Sky could come within twenty paces. The perceptive monarch outlines how Nameless must have convinced Flying Snow and Broken Sword to let him kill one of them so he could win the right to halve his distance from the King, having shown them that he is unstoppable from ten paces. Stabbing her lover to prevent him from sacrificing himself, Flying Snow allows Nameless to kill her, and he takes her sword as proof. Broken Sword and Nameless then fight to honour Flying Snow. The anguished Broken Sword gives the would-be assassin his weapon as well, so that his sword and Flying Snow's will never be parted, then kills himself.

Unfortunately for the conspirators, the King has some magic lamps that flare up and reveal Nameless' murderous intent. Unfortunately for the King, he has already allowed Nameless within ten paces of him, and his guards are 100 paces away. Nameless admits that he is actually from Zhao. Qin soldiers killed his family, and he was adopted in Qin. Ten years ago he discovered his true identity, and vowed to train until he had the skill to kill the King. He has perfected the descriptively named move, Death Within Ten Paces.

But Nameless hesitates. There is more to this story than the King has guessed. Back he goes again to the calligraphy school where Nameless reveals that his sword is so accurate, he can plunge it right through someone, missing all their vital organs, without killing them. Sky has recovered fully, and Nameless offers to do the same to one of the lovers so they can trick the King. But everyone has underestimated Broken Sword, who doesn't actually want to kill the monarch. Three years ago, he failed to strike the final blow, greatly annoying Flying Snow, whose homeland was ravaged by the Qin and who isn't of a mind to be forgiving. Broken Sword says the King must not die, and he will stop their plan. Flying Snow attacks her lover and, with the help of Nameless, stabs him. Moon gets very upset and attacks Nameless, but is no match for him. Flying Snow gives Broken Sword magic healing medicine so he can recover while she fights Nameless.

Flying Snow falls on Nameless' sword, and he sets off to fulfil his plan, but is stopped by Broken Sword who explains why he didn't kill the King before and doesn't want him to die now. Writing 'All under Heaven' in the sand, he tries to convince

Nameless that only the King of Qin can bring the peoples of the Seven Kingdoms together and stop the bloodshed, which gives Nameless something to think about. The King asks how he was planning to perform Death From Ten Paces without a sword, and Nameless tells him he was planning to use his. The King gives it to him, turns his back and waits for death. But Nameless is a convert to Broken Sword's convictions, and chooses his own death for the greater good, allowing the King's guards to shoot him down, proving himself to be the hero of the new Empire.

Now Flying Snow is really annoyed. She cannot believe that Broken Sword has betrayed her again, and demands that he prove his affection as she attacks him. He does so by unexpectedly refusing to defend himself, and she mortally wounds him. Realising that she now has nothing to live for, she stabs herself with the sword that has passed through his body. The King is safe, the assassins are dead and the reign of the First Emperor begins with the foundation of the Qin Dynasty (not to be confused with the Qing Dynasty, house of the last Emperor of China, which features in so many Chinese martial arts films).

CASTING: Who other than Jet Li could be cast in the role of Nameless? Mainland China's hero, its most famous acting export, a wushu warrior and a man who likes to put a bit of philosophy into his films along with the high kicks and flying swords, Li is the ideal choice for a modern wuxia pian that was released around the world. He gets to speak Mandarin instead of being dubbed into Cantonese, so the audience can fully appreciate his acting as well as his martial abilities.

A devout Buddhist, Li is uncomfortably aware that many of his films promote violence as a solution to problems. In America, his popularity is based on his uniquely violent skills, because he has rarely displayed anything other than the physical manifestation of martial arts. 'I haven't had the opportunity to show them that the important thing is not kicking people's asses. If you understand the yin and yang balance, maybe you will grow up.' In Hero, Broken Sword uses persuasion and reasoning to sway Nameless, and Li's character chooses the greater good rather than personal vengeance. 'In my 22-year career of making movies, this is the first script that has made me weep. It is an incredible story . . . about what kind of person we can call a hero.'

Maggie Cheung, Tony Leung Chui-Wai and Zhang Ziyi get an acting and martial workout in *Hero*, as they reinvent their characters for each version of the story, living, reacting and ultimately dying differently, and subtly altering the ways in which they interact with each other. By casting some of the biggest stars in martial arts films, Zhang Yimou makes a statement about the kind of film he is producing and just how good the fight scenes are going to be. Donnie Yen appears only briefly as Sky, but his two fights are technically brilliant. Similarly, Leung is convincing as the greatest swordsman in Zhao, pulling off the kind of flamboyant yet efficient moves that audiences have come to expect since *Butterfly and Sword*. He handles his development from stroppy lover to selfless imperialist with care, and even manages to make calligraphy look dramatic, exciting and violent.

But it is the female characters that drive the action onwards. Maggie Cheung underwent months of training to take on the character of swordsmaster Flying Snow, but it is her ability to mix immovable determination with undying tenderness that completes the character. Particularly memorable is her condescension towards Moon, when she refuses to fight her, then wearily agrees that she is clearly very keen to be killed and obliges her. Zhang Ziyi also had to train for the part, learning to wield Moon's crescent knives. She smiles only once in the entire film, spending most of the time crying, defending her master's honour and generally being devoted to a man who is clearly in love with someone else. The part does not really do her justice, with its single emotional motivation. The actress is better served by the feistier roles she plays in *Crouching Tiger, Hidden Dragon* and *House of Flying Daggers*.

MARTIAL ARTS: *Hero* takes the core concepts of kung fu to a higher level, with Jet Li's character expounding on the similarities between fighting and music, how both are in reality quests to attain a state of ultimate perfection. Like *Crouching Tiger, Hidden Dragon*, the film reveals that there are other elements within kung fu, beyond how good you are at fighting. Broken Sword's skills are rooted in his calligraphy, and Nameless studies the character he writes for 'sword' in an attempt to understand his power. The King finally gets it, stating that the aim is to reach a point where one does not have to fight. That said, there's still plenty of hardcore action to enjoy for those who prefer to watch Jet Li concentrating on the physical rather than the spiritual.

Many of the conventions of fight scenes in the genre are observed, although there is no bamboo forest (Zhang Yimou rectifies this omission with some style in *House of Flying Daggers*). Thus Sky takes on seven lesser opponents and easily dispatches them before discovering that he is unable to defeat Nameless. In martial arts films there is rarely any suspense in the action, as it is usually obvious who will win a fight. *Hero* takes this one stage further, since the characters either agree who will triumph beforehand or even, in the case of Sky and Nameless, fight the entire battle in their minds before ever crossing spear and sword. When a martial artist reaches the peak of proficiency there is no need to fight, as the outcome is already decided. Zhang depicts this concept in the mental battle that is going on behind the warriors' eyes – which, by being shut, show just how confident the assailants are in their abilities.

The weapons used are highly significant, reflecting each opponent's style and temperament. The armies of Qin bludgeon their enemies with walls of arrows fired by ranks of archers, and execute the undefeated Nameless in the same way. The hero fights with a plain sword, sharp as cut glass, its simplicity befitting the position of a lowly county official. Flying Snow carries her father's sword, which happens to be very feminine, straight and slender, with a white handle. Broken Sword is named for his weapon, which he handles with such skill that its missing point is no handicap. The crescent blades used by Moon reflect her name and match her short, passionate temper, while Sky shows off with his silver spear, an unusual, flashy weapon which he flourishes extravagantly.

The fighting is stylised, in keeping with the preordained nature of the fights, using special effects and wire-work to create dazzling displays. Action director Tony Ching Siu-Tung's roots in Hong Kong action are apparent in his puppets' gravity-defying behaviour and larger-than-life abilities. They can even bounce on water. Ching has been working on wuxia films since the 80s, and is one of the pioneers of the technique of wire-work mixed with tight editing to create fast-moving action sequences, such as those seen in *A Chinese Ghost Story* and Tsui Hark's *New Dragon Gate Inn*. Ching's influence on *Hero* is immense, as Zhang Yimou readily admits his lack of experience in filming martial arts action and left control largely in the hands of Ching and choreographer Ting Wei. Zhang clearly had some influence, however: many of the action sequences occur in slow motion, of which the director is obsessively fond.

STUNTS AND SPECIAL EFFECTS: Whereas Yuen Woo-Ping disdains CGI in *Crouching Tiger, Hidden Dragon*, Zhang Yimou goes the whole hog with *Hero*. Using a device first seen in the appalling Kevin Costner vehicle *Robin Hood: Prince of Thieves*, the camera follows the flight of an individual arrow as it shoots towards the calligraphy school. The wire-work enhances the action but the CGI serves to undermine it, at times looking tacky and obvious. Extra arrows are added to the hail fired by the Qin archers, appearing as unconvincing black streaks on the film.

Zhang Yimou concentrates on gravity-defying, mind-bending effects rather than incredible, bone-breaking stunts. It's all about the look of the thing, style above content, which is pretty much what you would expect from this director. It almost seems a waste of the talents of Jet Li and Tony Leung: the poignant pinging of a drop of water from one sword to another and on to the face of Flying Snow is the climax of their fight, rather than a fantastic finale. Even the encounter between Li and Donnie Yen, the best martial artists in the film, is about the effects of slowly dripping water and Nameless running faster than the rain can fall rather than the incredible interplay of sword and spear. Maggie Cheung doesn't even try to block Zhang Ziyi: she simply flies out of the way, mirroring the swirling red leaves, which seem to be the main point of the scene's creation.

DIRECTOR: Zhang Yimou was a photographer and cinematographer (and actor) before he was a director, and it shows. So dedicated is he to his art that as a young man he sold his blood to pay for his first camera. *Hero* is a contender for the title of most beautiful film ever made, every shot perfect in its composition. Zhang's lack of experience in the wuxia genre is apparent, but at least he recognises it, and has not made the fatal flaw of limiting the action in favour of extended dialogue. The fighting tells the story and, along with the blatant symbolism and unsubtle colour coding of the different scenes, this makes the film easily translatable into any language.

But sometimes the art is allowed to eclipse the emotion. Says Maggie Cheung, 'What Zhang wants he gets. He visualises things so clearly that if [cinematographer] Chris Doyle moved the camera one inch, it would spoil things for him.' The desire to focus on sweeping scenes and stylised characters at times denies the human side of the story. 'Zhang lacked something for the drama. When I saw the film, I wasn't touched by it at all. Every time I read the script, by a certain point I would be crying. That had disappeared,' laments Cheung.

Following in the footsteps of the highly successful *Crouching Tiger, Hidden Dragon*, Zhang's decision to make a wuxia pian has brought him an international audience, hungry for new martial arts films, and lifted him out of the art house and into the unexpected position of China's most celebrated director. *Hero* was as popular in American cinemas as the *Kill Bill* films, proving that it doesn't have to be in English to be big. As Ang Lee says, making a wuxia is just one of those things a Chinese director has to do, even if they have no real grounding in the genre. Zhang certainly does not claim to be an expert, having seen no more than twenty wuxia films. 'My favourites are Hu Jing-Chuen's [King Hu's] *Touch of Zen* and Tsui Hark's *[New] Dragon [Gate] Inn*,' says the director. 'You've got to remember growing up during the Cultural Revolution, I had no access to watching kung fu and wuxia films.' But, he says, 'It seems to me that every Chinese filmmaker has a sort of cultural obligation to make at least one wuxia movie during their career.'

Zhang is one of the so-called Fifth Generation directors, who have been a staple of the Chinese independent film scene for the last two decades. Once censored and even banned, his earlier films were largely psychological melodramas infused with subtle political comment. Now he is making promos for the government and apparently producing films that advocate the stability of the state over the suffering of individuals. This appears to be a massive departure for the director. The work of the Fifth Generation often includes criticism of feudal patriarchy of the type represented by the King of Qin in *Hero*. Father figures in Zhang's films are usually ravaged and twisted, and get their comeuppance at some point in the story. The questioning of the father figure has long been seen as a criticism of Chinese society – hence the censorship.

Hero, however, seems to be a complete about-face, representing the King of Qin as an almost benevolent father figure and making a statement about the importance of unity that would have had Chairman Mao dancing with glee. Zhang himself claims that he is not interested in politics, refusing to discuss the themes in *Hero* in that context. He will admit, however, that his greatest desire is to make a series of films about the Cultural Revolution – which would perhaps have Mao turning rather than jigging in his grave.

PRODUCTION: Unless you're cripplingly colour-blind, the most striking thing about *Hero* is the use of colour to define each scene. This is more than just a device to differentiate the versions of events narrated by Nameless and the King: the colours have meanings in their own right. The initial version, rife with betrayal, intrigue, lust and needless violence, is red, the colour of blood. The second telling, offered by the King and strangely the most flattering to his enemies, is blue. It creates a soft, idealised representation of Broken Sword and Flying Snow's love, with each planning to stab the other to save their life (Snow gets in there first) and then die magnificently for their love. When Sword recounts how the lovers went to kill the King three years previously, they are clothed in green, the colour of hidden purpose and meaning, representing his betrayal of Snow's trust. The final version of events is draped in white. In China, white is the colour of death and mourning, and the sequence ends with the death of all three assassins. The designated colours are picked out in every detail, from Flying Snow's earrings to the furniture, to the swirling leaves and sand. Coloured filters add to the effect, and different shades are used for each character – pale and subtle for the women, strong and vibrant for the men. Nameless and the King, in their roles as narrators, wear black.

Zhang Yimou adds various artifices of his own to the film which break the mould of the martial genre. When Sky and Nameless fight in their minds, we see it in black and white – usually a chopsocky ploy, alien to wuxia – while the music of the blind zither player slows the action. In the lake fight, water becomes solid matter. This scene took three weeks to film, as Zhang insisted the surface be totally flat, meaning that the crew could only work for two hours a day, when the tide was not running, and had to start at five in the morning.

TRIVIA: Jet Li is said to have insisted that the part of Sky be given to Donnie Yen, just as he asked for Yen to appear in *Once Upon a Time in China 2*. The role of the King of Qin was offered to Jackie Chan but he declined, which is just as well, as it might have been hard to take him seriously. Traditionally, Nameless would have presented the King with the heads of his enemies, rather than their weapons, but Zhang Yimou decided that severed heads are not very picturesque. Besides, Nameless had left them all alive.

THEMES: Revenge. There's a lot of it about. Nameless is revenging himself on the killer of his family, Flying Snow on the oppressor of her country and Moon on anyone who hurts her master. Patriotism and filial loyalty are also thrown into the mix, along with the ideal of sacrificing the individual for the good of the community. Zhang appears to be taking a nationalistic line and suggesting that people should put their trust in powerful men and suffer personal deprivation for the goal of ultimate peace. But it is possible to read an underlying subversion of this theme, which would be more in keeping with the director's earlier work. Broken Sword writes his message 'All under Heaven' in the sand, and it is blown away almost as fast as he writes it. In the most moving scene of the film, when Snow takes her life and carries her lover home, it is clear that she does not accept the greater good in Sword's sacrifice, and neither can the audience.

In the splendid tradition of *Crouching Tiger, Hidden Dragon*, no one in *Hero* is really who they appear to be at first glance. Nameless is the hero of Qin, then is revealed as an assassin, before becoming the saviour of the new Empire when he declines to murder the first Emperor. Broken Sword's motivations only become clear at the end, and the King is far from the merciless tyrant that his reputation suggests. This representation caused a great deal of controversy in China, since many consider the founder of the Qin Dynasty to have been a tyrannical despot. He buried 400,000 Zhao soldiers alive and even in the film he orders the death of the man who has just spared his life. *Hero* does offer an apology for this behaviour, with the King's ministers insisting on the death of Nameless, but, given that the King held absolute power, this is an anachronism.

The film's political stance is not unequivocal however: Nameless is shown looking deeply pained at the idea of a single writing system being imposed across the country. In any case, the film is not just the product of China. It has a multinational crew, and, at the end of the day, perhaps Zhang, as he claimed, has simply produced a historical epic that looks really good.

On a lighter (and sometimes darker) note, romance and violence towards loved ones are recurrent themes of the film. Snow's attack on Broken Sword is reminiscent of Qi Pei's mutilation of Fang Gang in *One-Armed Swordsman*. She certainly regrets it afterwards. The achievement of oneness with the sword, of every movement coming from the heart, and of finally discarding the need for violence is driven home. Unlike traditional wuxia, no one actually gains their revenge: Moon is defeated, Snow kills herself and Nameless stoically accepts his execution even after having left the King alive.

PLACE WITHIN THE GENRE: *Hero* is the next stage of development of the wuxia tradition. Even without the precedent of *Crouching Tiger, Hidden Dragon*, the international fame of Jet Li would have been enough to make it a hit, but with that precedent the film managed to leapfrog the art-house hurdle and land straight in the multiplex. *Crouching Tiger, Hidden Dragon* opened in 151 sites across the UK. *Hero* commanded 250, and only 50 of those were art-house. It went straight into London's West End. In the US it opened as number one in the box-office. Miramax paid a reported $20 million for the English-language release rights, so the film is in effect another internationally co-funded production.

At home, *Hero* was a strike for domestic productions against the encroachment of the Hollywood fare that has stolen so much of the market. It has proved that the Chinese film industry can produce a big-budget version of a traditional format and sell it all around the world. The film builds on the foundations laid by *Crouching Tiger, Hidden Dragon*, and surpasses its achievements, not least because it is better. *Hero* has been more successful in the Chinese market, not grating in the way that the earlier film did. It is a tighter, slicker production, with plot, action and actors working in harmony.

Heroic Ones: Maggie Cheung

- **AKA:** Maggie Cheung Man-Yuk, Cheung Man-Yuk, Zhang Man Yu, Cheung Man-Yu.
- **Birth name:** Cheung Man-Yuk.
- **Not to be confused with:** Maggie Cheung Ho Yee, star of *When a Man Loves a Woman*.
- **Martial style:** Sci-fi kung fu (Keanu Reeves isn't a patch on this woman) and exquisite swordplay.
- **Born:** 20 September 1964 in Hong Kong.
- **Biography:** Jackie Chan once said of Maggie Cheung that 'She wouldn't mind me kicking her down a flight of stairs', after which he promptly hired her. The former model, who had been appearing in various TVB television shows, got her big break on the strength of Chan's good opinion (and the strength of her bones) when she won the role of his hapless girlfriend May in the *Police Story* films. Raised in England, Cheung returned to Hong Kong when she was 17, came second in the Miss Hong Kong pageant and was spotted by the Shaw Brothers' TV station. Stereotyped as the clumsy May, Cheung sought more serious projects under the guidance of director Wong Kar Wai, but never abandoned the martial arts. In *Police Story 3: Super Cop*, she is upstaged by the inestimable Michelle Yeoh, but then proceeded to hold her own, matching blow for blow with the kung fu star, in *Heroic Trio* and *Executioners*. When she took a break from acting in 1994 the Hong Kong paparazzi had a field day, assuming she had broken down and would never work again. She proved them wrong, however, returning in glorious style with several acclaimed art-house films and, more excitingly, *Augustin, King of Kung Fu* (in French, no less). Her martial pedigree was completed in 2002 when she starred as the tragic lover and deadly sword mistress Flying Snow in Zhang Yimou's *Hero*.
- **Best kick flicks:** *Police Story* (1985), *New Dragon Gate Inn* (1992), *The Eagle Shooting Heroes* (1993), *Hero* (2002).
- **Trivia:** Cheung has been given every role she has played since she was eighteen without an audition. From the age of eight, she grew up in Bromley, Kent.
- **Where are they now:** No current projects are publicised, but we can only hope to see her soon.

House of Flying Daggers

(aka *Shi Mian Mai Fu, Ambush From Ten Sides*)

China, 2004, 119 minutes

Production companies: Edko Films, Zhang Yimou Studio
In collaboration with: Beijing New Picture Film Co., China
Film Co-Production Corporation
Director: Zhang Yimou
Martial arts co-ordinator: Chen Xiao-Dung
Executive producer: Zhang Weiping
Producers: Bill Kong, Zhang Yimou
Screenplay: Li Feng, Zhang Yimou, Wang Bin
Cinematographer: Zhao Xiao Ding
Music: Shigeru Umebayashi

CAST: Takeshi Kaneshiro (*Jin*), Andy Lau (*Leo*), Zhang Ziyi (*Mei*), Song Dandan (*Yee*): Wang Yabin, Zheng Lu, Wu Weifeng, Yan Yan, Zheng Jie, Zhao Hongfei

PLOT: The characters in *Crouching Tiger, Hidden Dragon* are all concealing something, and no one in *Hero* really is who they say they are, but you ain't seen nothing yet. *House of Flying Daggers* caps the lot with its mélange of double agents, double crossing and double takes. The main players spend a lot of time doubling back, as well. Absolutely nothing is as it appears.

The year is 859, and the revered Tang Dynasty is going the way of every historic Chinese government, disintegrating under the weight of corruption and brutality. Secret societies have formed to challenge those in power, among them the House of Flying Daggers, whose members can be identified by their pouches of curved knives, which they fling with deadly, reality-bending accuracy.

Jin and Leo are two police captains, responsible for hunting down the Flying Dagger clan. Or are they? They have killed the old leader, but a new one has arisen and they need to find out where she is hiding out. They've heard that one of the dancers at the Peony Pavilion is really a Flying Daggers assassin and over a few cups of rice wine they hatch a plot to smoke her out. Cut to Jin entertaining himself in the brothel, having consumed considerably more rice wine, engaging in a tug of war with the resident ladies and then demanding to see the new dancer. He discovers she is blind, but this is no bar to her breathtaking dancing, or her stunning beauty. Apparently overcome with lust, he grabs her, but is stopped mid-grope by the arrival of the police led by Leo, who 'arrests' him, and then threatens to arrest the blind dancer Mei for appearing in a state of undress. The brothel's madam is distraught at the thought of losing her prize attraction, and begs for leniency, whereupon Leo agrees to let her go if she will play the echo game with him.

The echo game is very simple. Leo flicks beans at a circle of drums, and Mei has to hit the drums he strikes – with her ten-foot-long sleeves, while performing a series of acrobatic moves. When Leo throws the whole bowl of beans at the drums, Mei strikes them all, then grabs his sword and tries to kill him. Despite her blindness, she comes within a hair's breadth of slitting his throat. They fight their way through the brothel, and he only overcomes her when he lures her into a room filled with running water and clattering beads, deafening her.

Back at the police station, Mei refuses to reveal what she knows, although Leo suspects that she is the blind daughter of the old leader of the House of Flying Daggers. He threatens her with torture, then leaves her to stew. Meanwhile, he concocts another deception: rather than hand Mei over to the General, he proposes that they trick her into leading them to the Flying Daggers, thus winning a greater prize to present to their superior. Jin agrees to pose as an itinerant warrior and 'rescue' her from the police before offering to reunite her with her clan, keeping in touch with the police all the while. The fact that she is very beautiful and he likes to flirt doesn't hurt either. Leo warns him not to forget that it is all a ruse.

Jin spirits Mei away, introducing himself as Wind, her suitor from the brothel, a good-time guy who comes and goes as he pleases. She is suspicious of his motives, but believes him after he fights off the police that pursue them, killing four with his bow. These 'corpses' are later resurrected: he shot them through their clothes, with astonishing accuracy. Mei believes she has discovered his true motivation when she realises he is watching her bathe. She reasons that this is a just reward for saving her life. He gives her men's clothes to wear, then finds he can't resist the sight of her in drag and jumps her. After initially responding, she draws away, leaving him somewhat frustrated.

Heading onwards, they stop to mess about in a meadow but are attacked by more policemen. Jin is surprised, having told Leo to keep his men at bay, especially when they wound him in the back and he realises they are for real. Mei and Jin are fighting for their lives and about to be overwhelmed when a wave of sharpened stakes comes flying out of the woods and takes out the policemen. Jin accosts Leo in the forest and demands to know what is going on. Leo tells him the General has taken over the operation and all the fighting will now be for real. He offers Jin more arrows but Jin quits, not keen to play a game where his life is at stake. He has to decide what to do about Mei, however.

The blind girl insists he leave, saying she has left the Flying Daggers and does not wish to return to them. He obeys but turns round, realising that he cannot abandon her. Which is just as well, as she has got herself into a bit of a fix in (where else?) a bamboo forest. Jin arrives in the nick of time and, attacked on all sides, they fight back to back before being caged in bamboo. They grasp hands and wait to die, but the policemen are felled by the Flying Daggers. Back in their camp, Nia, the leader, offers Mei to Jin as a wife. In fear of his life, he accepts and, as he bows, is captured in a net. Leo is brought in bound – the Flying Daggers have apparently discovered their plan. It becomes apparent that Mei has also been playing a part: she is neither blind nor the daughter of the old leader.

Nia marches Leo into the forest to kill him, but she cuts his bonds instead of his throat; it is revealed that he is in fact a Flying Daggers secret agent who has spent the last three years infiltrating the Tang police force. Nia is sending him back undercover but, as a reward for his loyalty, he gets to spend some time alone with Mei, the love of his life, of whom he has been dreaming all the while. They play a variant of the echo game with bamboo and knives, showing the significance of their interaction in the brothel. All is not hunky-dory, however: although he burns with passion for her, she appears to have fallen for someone else – Jin. This is understandably frustrating for Leo – he has been waiting three years, while she has known Jin for three days. He tries to force himself on her but gets a dagger in the back for his trouble, and is sent away by Nia to rejoin the police.

Mei is told to kill Jin. She reminds him that she told him to go, and it's not her fault. In the end she cannot do it and releases him. They share a passionate moment in the meadow, and he tries to convince her to come with him. She refuses and he leaves, but this time it is her turn to double back, and she chases after him. Before she can reach Jin, she is brought down by Leo, who, driven mad by his love, cannot live without her and won't allow her to live without him. Jin comes back for her, and he and Leo fight, neither caring if he dies, only desperate to kill each other. Mei has the final say, however, bloodily sacrificing herself to save Jin.

CASTING: As in *Hero*, Zhang Yimou has kept the number of speaking parts in the film small, and filled them with some of Asia's biggest stars. With *House of Flying Daggers*, Andy Lau has added another string to his already very well-strung bow. After his career as one of the kings of Canto-pop, the Hong Kong megastar is most famous for his gangster gun-fu movies: for many years he was a side-kick to Chow Yun-Fat and has recently been seen in the violent cop flick *Infernal Affairs*. Unlike Chow, Lau had appeared in several kung fu films before being cast in a modern wuxia, notably Jackie Chan's *Drunken Master 2* and *The Duel*. In *House of Flying Daggers* he proves his ability as a convincing martial actor, as fanatically driven playing a double agent in ancient China as when he is portraying hard-bitten cops in contemporary Hong Kong. His intense, hawk-like visage becomes increasingly strained throughout the course of the film as he watches another man woo his love, until the final scenes where grief has overtaken reason and he pulls off a great line in psychotic desperation.

With Takeshi Kaneshiro the film has ensured its appeal across all the Asian markets. The multilingual star, who began public life as a teen idol, has a huge following in Japan, Taiwan, Hong Kong and China. In the Japanese sci-fi film *Returner* he showed off his kicking and wire-work skills, but this is his first pure martial arts movie. He carries it off in style, looking as comfortable swinging a broadsword as brandishing a gun (or a can of pineapple – see *Chungking Express*). Like Lau, he has played policemen before, but never in Tang Dynasty China.

Zhang Ziyi has become a permanent fixture of the modern Asian classic, almost defining the sub-genre on her own. In *House of Flying Daggers* she benefits from a far more complex and demanding part than she was given in *Hero* – in that she gets to do more than just cry – and rises to the challenge. Graduating from her previous martial arts films, in which she played characters with inferior or poorly trained skills, in this latest offering she gets to demonstrate what she has learned. Zhang looks far more competent and skilled than in her previous outings, even when pretending to be blind, and is finally given the chance to fully develop a role.

MARTIAL ARTS: Because of Zhang Yimou's relative inexperience in the genre, the choice of fight director was always going to define the film's martial style. The director wanted to produce something different from his previous martial arts film, with a more practical, emotional take on the action rather than the philosophical and theoretical treatment that kung fu gets in *Hero*. The choice was between Yuen Woo-Ping, Yuen Kwei and Chen Xiao-Dung, all recommended to Zhang by Jet Li. The director made his choice based on his desire to fit the action to the plot. 'What I really liked about Chen is that he keeps with the story-line best and all his fights tell a story beautifully and romantically.' Beautiful and romantic the fight scenes may be, and a far cry from the bloody chopsocky of the 70s, but the body count is still enormous. The final fight scene is at once epic, bloody and poetic, as the seasons turn around the exhausted fighters, whose dying desire is the death of the other.

Unsurprisingly, daggers play a big part in this film and they are used imaginatively, swinging round corners, thrown in pairs and boomeranging to pierce people in the back. They are filmed from all directions and, although the 'dagger's eye view' along the blade becomes somewhat repetitive towards the end of the film, the suspense of guessing where it will land is never lost. Other innovations include the incredible echo-drum sequence and Zhang Yimou's interpretation of the traditional bamboo fight scene. 'Bamboo forest fights have been seen in many wuxia films like in *A Touch of Zen*, so this had better be unique,' says Zhang. He knew that he had to make it special and spent three days discussing possibilities with Chen. 'Those good chase scenes in American films where you have helicopters chasing cars through busy streets and firing at each other: I just took that concept and put it into a bamboo forest.' The end result has Jin and Mei fleeing along the forest floor while the government forces swarm through the bamboo above them, raining down sharpened stakes. The effect is more chilling than any helicopter chase.

STUNTS AND SPECIAL EFFECTS: Chen Xiao-Dung is known as one of the fathers of wire-fu, and with this film he has literally taken the art to new heights. His wire-work has a great sense of gravity: the characters do not just launch themselves into the air and fly around, but rather complete huge leaps and bounds, propelling themselves from the ground and pushing off against objects rather than floating through the atmosphere.

The sheer scale of the massed battles stretched budgets and technology to the limit. 'In the bamboo forest sequences, actors were flying at the top of the bamboo. No other film has wired up so many actors,' says director Zhang. When Yuen Woo-Ping did it in *Crouching Tiger, Hidden Dragon*, only two people were fighting, and they floated above the forest, rather than flying into the thick of it. It took four hours to wire up all the actors for a single hour of shooting. Added to this inconvenience was the risk inherent in what they were trying to do. 'Wires can easily become entangled. It was very dangerous. I feel very lucky that we managed to finish the bamboo sequences safely,' recalls Zhang.

DIRECTOR: Between *Hero* and *House of Flying Daggers* Zhang Yimou developed as a director, becoming far more accomplished in handling the genre. The fight sequences are blended into the story, rather than appearing as a series of stylised set pieces. 'My goal is to make the fights in my wuxia films beautiful and poetic . . . the final fights in American films, they're usually in dark places where the actors are sweaty, bloody, messy and realism is emphasised.' By contrast Zhang recognised that in wuxia films, like the kung fu novels on which they are based, the last fight is between two heroes, in a beautiful and often famous place in China.

PRODUCTION: Beauty is everything to Zhang Yimou and, as with *Hero*, colour is of vital importance to the narrative of *House of Flying Daggers*. The darkness of the prison; the golden meadow where Jin and Mei fall in love; the deep green of the bamboo forest where everyone's true identities are revealed; the white snow, splashed with blood, in the place where the heroes fall. It is more like a painting than a film. Shooting in the Ukraine and Sichuan Province, China, with a budget of $20 million, Zhang had the scope to create the sweeping, epic beauty he wanted.

But all did not run smoothly; the filmmakers discovered that they had more to deal with than the usual issues of running over deadlines and budget. In the flower meadow things began to go wrong. People were injured: Lau was cut in the eye by a sword, Zhang Ziyi twisted her ankle and got a swollen eye, Kaneshiro was injured and accidentally stabbed Chen, who was also hit by an arrow. The horses acted strangely and the crew was unsettled. Zhang Yimou discovered that the field was the site of a Ukrainian battle and a large, unmarked grave. Chinese beliefs held that there could be a lot of ghosts remaining on the battlefield, so the crew attempted to appease them in the traditional way. 'We burned incense and asked for protection, but it didn't help. We thought since these were foreign ghosts, the incense didn't work. Different ghost rules, so to speak,' recalls Zhang.

The sets are spectacular, the Peony Palace one of the most intricate ever created for a Chinese film. Imagination is evident everywhere, as production designer Huo Tingxiao and art director Zhong Han stretched their minds to the limit. Bamboo canes become cages, stakes and spears, the outdoor locations swing through the seasons, and, from the forest hideout to the brothel, the sets feel permanent. The only let-down in the artful cinematography is the fireside scene with Jin and Mei, so unconvincingly lit and obviously in a studio that it appears to have been added as an afterthought.

TRIVIA: In preparation for her role as Mei, Zhang Ziyi spent two months living with a girl who had been blind from the age of 12. The final fight scene was filmed in the Ukraine, and it unexpectedly started snowing while they were filming. To take advantage of the situation, the script was changed so that the epic fight appears to begin in autumn and end in winter. *House of Flying Daggers* was to be Anita Mui's last film, but the Hong Kong superstar died of cancer before her scenes were shot. Out of respect, Zhang Yimou rewrote the script to remove her part rather than recasting it. Her name still appears in the credits.

THEMES: 'Are you for real?' Mei demands of Jin at several points in the film, and well she might. He isn't, but then neither is she, or anyone else, which perhaps accounts for her paranoia. Even the leader of the Flying Daggers has a stand-in. The ulterior motives, hidden feelings and secret identities are all brilliantly interwoven. Watching the film for a second time, when everyone's true story has been disclosed is a revelation, almost like watching a different movie. Jin is the only character who reveals his true nature to the audience, but he is forced to lie to the one person he wants to be truthful to. Leo has been lying for so long it drives him mad, and Mei is eventually able to lie to everyone but herself. The literal English translation of the film's Chinese title is 'Ambush from Ten Directions': none of the characters knows whence friends or foes will come.

Telling the story of virtuous rebels fighting a corrupt government that is happy to kill its own soldiers, *House of Flying Daggers* is far less pro-state than *Hero* appears to be, and more in line with what one expects from the work of Zhang Yimou. The depiction of the imperial army hunting a shadowy terrorist organisation has a less than flattering contemporary resonance. Politics are less important here than the romance: Jin suggests to Mei that they run off and leave the opposing sides to fight it out – they are merely small cogs in the wheel after all, and no one will miss them. This is a very different perspective from that of *Hero*, in which everyone is prepared to sacrifice themselves for their principles. One thing the films do have in common, and with *Crouching Tiger, Hidden Dragon*, is that none has a routine Hollywood-style happy ending. Heroes die, no one gets to ride off into the sunset, and love is never allowed to conquer all.

PLACE WITHIN THE GENRE: *House of Flying Daggers* was intended to be a sequel to *Hero*. Zhang Yimou conceived the idea for the film while working on his first wuxia, binding his three main characters into the original story-line. Andy Lau would play the Emperor's bodyguard, Takeshi Kaneshiro the ruler's son, and Zhang Ziyi an assassin sent to kill him. The characters are still essentially there, but the story they move through has altered, arguably for the better.

House of Flying Daggers fulfils Zhang Yimou's intention of taking the genre another step further. If *Crouching Tiger, Hidden*

Dragon recreated traditional wuxia in a modern mould, and *Hero* refocused it on the roots of martial arts, *House of Flying Daggers* brings both aspects together and twists them into an enthralling story. Riding on the back of the earlier films, it had a readymade international audience which was educated about the genre, knew the stars and had heard of the director. Unlike *Hero*, there was no delay in its overseas release. There was no doubt that it would be an international hit.

What it was not, however, was a massive hit in China. Just as they didn't appreciate Ang Lee's offering, Chinese critics have labelled *House of Flying Daggers* soporific, illogical and not a real kung fu movie. Zhang Yimou freely admits that he was aiming for a foreign market, in order to recoup the massive investment made in the film. Perhaps he went too far and lost his native audience through trying to appeal to Westerners. While action and a good love story should appeal to anyone, the Asian audience generally requires these ingredients in larger measures. Apparently there is still some distance to go before everyone is happy.

Heroic Ones: Zhang Ziyi

- AKA: Ziyi Zhang.
- Nickname: Little Gong Li, not for her resemblance to the Asian superstar, but rather because she is rumoured to have had an affair with director Zhang Yimou, Gong Li's former lover.
- Not to be confused with: Gong Li.
- Martial style: Trained as a dancer, not as a martial artist. Nonetheless, plays impossibly beautiful yet bloody-minded girls with incredible martial arts skills.
- Born: 9 February 1980, Beijing, China.
- Biography: Zhang has quickly become one of the most recognised, and lusted after, Asian actresses in the business. Raised in urban Beijing, the daughter of a kindergarten teacher and an economist, her first interests were dancing and gymnastics. But despite studying at a school linked to the Beijing Dancing College and winning an award at the National Young Dancer competition, at fifteen she decided that she would rather act. She attended the Central Drama Academy in Beijing before being discovered by Zhang Yimou when she auditioned for a shampoo commercial he was shooting. The director of *Raise the Red Lantern* decided Zhang was perfect for the role of a schoolgirl in love with her teacher in his 1999 offering *The Road Home*, a film

which has been re-released on the back of her new-found success. Despite her lack of martial arts training, director Ang Lee chose her to play the precocious aristocrat Jen Yu in his kung fu epic *Crouching Tiger, Hidden Dragon*. She more than justified his faith in her. Starring alongside action superstars Michelle Yeoh, Cheng Pei-Pei and Chow Yun-Fat propelled her on to the world stage, and her graceful dance moves and flying acrobatics led to roles in the modern martial classics *Hero* and *House of Flying Daggers*. She also stopped off in Hollywood, playing the villain opposite Jackie Chan and Chris Tucker's bumbling cops in *Rush Hour 2*, a part she managed to perform without speaking a word of English. Having worked with some of Asia's greatest directors in the most high profile martial arts movies of recent years, Zhang's future in the genre seems assured – as long as Hollywood doesn't snap her up.

- Best kick flicks: *Crouching Tiger, Hidden Dragon* (2000), *Hero* (2002), *House of Flying Daggers* (2004).
- Trivia: When she worked on *Rush Hour 2*, Jackie Chan had to translate everything the director said to her. The Chinese edition of *Forbes* magazine ranked her the country's second most popular celebrity in 2004, after NBA basketball player Yao Ming.
- Where are they now: Zhang has just completed work in Los Angeles on the film *Memoirs of a Geisha* with Michelle Yeoh, for which she had to learn to speak English – with a Japanese accent.

Summary

Although the films covered in this chapter have only been produced in recent years, it is not a misnomer to describe them as classics. This is not due to their popularity or the fact that they will be remembered by posterity as great films – although it is likely that they will – but rather because they include all the fundamental, traditional elements of the martial arts masterpiece. But although they can all be categorised as wuxia for the twenty-first century, and have many features in common, from their use of wire-work to their historic Chinese settings, there is still much to differentiate the movies. In lumping them all together one risks failing to appreciate their finer points.

Crouching Tiger, Hidden Dragon has many fine qualities, and has served an important purpose in opening the vault of long-forgotten wuxia to a new audience. Many people in the West had never seen anything like it, and, after watching it, decided that they wanted to see more. The action is carefully assembled and the story poignantly told, while the cast rise to the myriad challenges with grace and style. Viewed in the context of modern Asian classics as a whole, this is not the greatest martial arts film among them, and certainly not, as some claim, the greatest ever made. It suffers the effects of being made for an international audience by a director struggling to harness influences from both Asia and the West, and cannot compete with *House of Flying Daggers* for intrigue or heart-thumping action, largely because it lacks mass fight sequences. But it's still great fun to watch, and without *Crouching Tiger, Hidden Dragon*, it would be fair to ask, where would the genre be now?

In the hands of *Hero*, quite possibly. Even without the introduction provided by Ang Lee's film, this beautiful, stylised movie, which showcases the talents of some of the industry's best martial actors, would have made its mark on world cinema. Domestic reviewers can argue over the political motivations of its director, but the enduring image is not of the First Emperor in his stone hall but of Jet Li and Maggie Cheung deflecting a hail of arrows from the roof of the calligraphy school in a swirl of movement.

House of Flying Daggers has many of the attributes of Zhang Yimou's earlier film, and the intricacies of the plot leave nothing to be desired, except, perhaps, a less tragic ending. But it would not be the same film without it. The true mastery of the movie lies not in the stunning martial action – although that is original enough, and the drum sequence ranks as one of the most visually stunning ever shot – but in its depth. Every repeat viewing, even when the twists of the plot are known, reveals added subtleties and shades of what is already a complex concept.

Exit the Dragon, Enter the Tiger: Hollywood

Although *Enter the Dragon* has long been hailed as the crossover film that brought the martial arts genre to the West, and *Crouching Tiger, Hidden Dragon* as the one that made it mainstream, the first international kung fu movie success was the little known *King Boxer*. Before it agreed to finance Bruce Lee's 1973 hit, Warner Brothers had done its research, keeping an eye on the impressive box-office takings of Hong Kong films that had started to penetrate the markets in other Western countries. In 1972 the company decided to get in on the action, importing a few films from Shaw Brothers as well as releasing the pilot for the television series *Kung Fu* starring David Carradine, to great acclaim. Testing the waters on the cinema circuit, they re-titled *King Boxer* as *5 Fingers of Death* to cash in on the fascination for killer kung fu, and watched it climb to the top of *Variety*'s box-office grosser chart. *Duel of the Iron Fist* followed, and within months Bruce Lee's first films were released in the US. Then came *Enter the Dragon*.

Not willing to let the genre fade with the death of Bruce Lee, Hollywood began to produce its own martial arts films, casting Western actors in lead roles to prove that karate and kickboxing were not the preserve of Asian superhumans, and to broaden the movies' appeal to Western audiences. Despite the Hollywood casting, writing and production, these films follow the model of the traditional martial arts movie very closely, choosing not to tamper with a winning formula. The tournament, the student-master relationship, the revenging of wrongs done to family and friends, and, most importantly, the arduous training sequences are all present and correct.

And then came the infiltration of Asian martial arts into Hollywood action films, along with Asian martial artists and action directors. These days, no one will credit a superhero, secret agent or über-villain who cannot literally kick butt. Frank Sinatra started the trend in *The Manchurian Candidate* in 1962 and now even James Bond does it. In the latest of the Batman series, *Batman Begins*, a young Bruce Wayne heads off to the Orient to learn his crime-fighting skills – Bat style kung fu perhaps? There are even reports of a martial arts version of *Snow White and the Seven Dwarfs* being produced by Disney and directed by Yuen Woo-Ping.

Hand-to-hand combat in the movies has stepped up a gear with the acceptance among audiences that martial arts are not the preserve of Chinese monks and small Japanese men. From the moment *The Karate Kid* hit the screens in 1984, the West realised that all it needed was a few months with a sensei, a computer programme jacked straight into the brain, or training with an assassination squad, and anyone could be a master. Western martial artists such as Jean-Claude Van Damme and Steven Seagal used their abilities as the sole basis for their acting careers, and today's actors undergo months of training to learn Eastern fighting moves that look good on the big screen.

The Matrix and the *Kill Bill* films have taken martial arts, specifically kung fu, and made them the stylish, indescribably cool side of Hollywood violence – with the help of Hong Kong legend Yuen Woo-Ping, who provides some HK authenticity. 'American actors aren't brought up in the Hong Kong tradition,' says Yuen. 'Jackie Chan and Jet Li will already know how to fight, whereas those in Hollywood have to be trained.' Keanu Reeves trained for just four months before taking on the role of the CGI-assisted Neo in *The Matrix*. But Yuen believes there is a place for both types of actor. 'I wouldn't call it devaluation; it's just a different way of working. You tailor-make the movement to the physicality and flexibility of the actor or actress.' *The Matrix* is not a martial arts film however: Keanu cannot be compared to Jet or Jackie in martial terms, and audiences do not go to watch his movies for his fighting skills.

As well as turning its own actors into martial arts 'experts', Hollywood has taken to its heart the heroes of Hong Kong and created a new kind of martial arts film combining Western themes and settings with traditional ingredients, often including a good dose of comedy. Jackie Chan's *Rush Hour* and *Shanghai Noon* and their sequels are cases in point. The *Shanghai* movies overtly exploit the appeal of martial arts films in Hollywood because of their similarity to its great founding genre, the Western. Both are set in a more lawless time, where everyone must fight to survive and the hero is the most successful killer, who battles for ultimately righteous reasons despite the bloody retribution he inflicts.

The Karate Kid

USA, 1984, 122 minutes

Production companies: Delphi II Productions, Columbia
Pictures Corporation
Director: John G Avildsen
Martial arts choreographer: Pat E Johnson
Executive producer: RJ Louis
Associate producer: Bud S Smith
Producer: Jerry Weintraub
Screenplay: Robert Mark Kamen
Cinematographer: James Crabe
Music: Bill Conti

CAST: Ralph Macchio (*Daniel LaRusso*), Noriyuki 'Pat' Morita
(*Mr Kesuke Miyagi*), Elisabeth Shue (*Ali Mills*), Martin Kove
(*John Kreese*), Randee Heller (*Lucille LaRusso*), William Zabka
(*Johnny Lawrence*), Ron Thomas (*Bobby*), Rob Garrison
(*Tommy*), Chad McQueen (*Dutch*), Pat E Johnson (*Referee)*

PLOT: This has all the elements of a classic martial arts film –
romance, the tournament, good versus evil, thumping action and
an enigmatic martial master – but given an added twist: it's set in
California. *The Karate Kid* follows the adventures of angst-ridden
teenager Daniel LaRusso, uprooted from his home in New Jersey
by his mother's new job and dumped in the middle of LA where
the kids just don't play nice. Cast in the mould of the righteous
hero who tries not to get beaten up too much, Daniel heads to a
beach party with his neighbour, exhibits his soccer skills and chats
up local rich girl Ali. Then her motorbike-riding, karate-kicking
ex-boyfriend Johnny arrives and starts causing trouble. Our
skinny hero tries to step in, but is left dumped on the ground with
sand kicked in his face for his trouble, looking like a wimp in
front of his swiftly exiting new friends.

Hiding his black eye from his mother, Daniel heads to high
school, only to discover that the punks from the previous night all
hang out there. On the plus side, so does blonde, bouncy Ali.
Unable to keep his mouth shut, or stay away from the girl with the
ex from hell (Johnny hasn't quite accepted that it's over), Daniel

comes in for a series of beatings, and starts avoiding everyone. He ends up hanging out with Mr Miyagi, the taciturn handyman at his apartment block, who also does a good line in grooming bonsai trees. Having failed to teach himself karate from a book, and discovering that his tormentors train at the local Cobra Kai dojo, run by psycho ex-Green Beret Kreese, Daniel has abandoned all hope of learning to fight back.

Fulfilling Daniel's wish to be the invisible man, Mr Miyagi sends him to the school Halloween party inside a shower curtain. He pours water all over Johnny (will he never learn?) and ends up running for his life, shower rail trailing. Almost home, the thugs catch him and administer a brutal beating, following their sensei's imperative to show no mercy. But before they can finish off their prey, Mr Miyagi, demonstrating surprising athleticism, vaults the fence and dispatches the villains with ease.

Mr Miyagi agrees to teach Daniel the karate he learned from his father in Okinawa, on the condition that it is for self-defence only, and he does not use it like his 'friends'. Realising that the root of the thugs' issues is their slavish devotion to their insane sensei, Miyagi takes Daniel to the Cobra Kai dojo to ask Kreese to hold them off. Instead he gets his new student involved in the local karate tournament, on the condition that the Cobras will leave him alone to train. Miyagi then has two months to turn the skinny runt into a karate champion.

The Miyagi training programme consists of a series of household tasks, including the famed 'wax on, wax off' car polishing. Despite having managed to catch a fly with a pair of chopsticks, proving that he can accomplish anything, Daniel is frustrated with the drudgery and threatens to quit. All becomes clear, however, when his mentor shows him that the repetitive movements have trained his muscles to block punches and kicks. He then spends a lot of time in the sea and messing about on boats to gain balance.

Meanwhile Daniel's relationship with Ali is on the rocks because of their social differences and Johnny's inability to take no for an answer. Coming to the rescue once again, Miyagi, who we learn is a decorated war veteran and broken-hearted widower, gives him a car and a karate suit for his birthday. He uses the first to woo Ali and the second to look the part at the next day's tournament.

Stolen black belt in place, Daniel leaps into the ring, with no idea of the rules and only a few blocks and punches up his baggy white sleeves. But quality outshines quantity and he progresses to the semi-final. Realising that the runt might prove too much for his little soldiers, Kreese instructs his student to damage Daniel's leg in the fight, getting himself disqualified but disabling the hero. A bit of Miyagi magic later, however, and Daniel is back in the ring to face Johnny in the final. Despite his opponent's underhand tactics, Daniel uses a ridiculous crane kick to fell him, winning the tournament, the girl and the respect of his peers. And an excessively large plastic trophy.

CASTING: The curse of the martial arts genre is that actors appearing in a successful series become typecast, and for no one is this more true than Ralph Macchio. Twenty years after he first starred as Daniel-san, *The Karate Kid* is still the film with which he is most strongly associated. Actually 23 when he played the 16-year-old Daniel (although Elisabeth Shue was only a year younger), Macchio's baby face did not desert him for the three films in the series, although it curtailed his chances of winning more serious roles later in his career. The film obviously left a deep impression on the actor: in 1996 he named his new-born son Daniel.

As the kid from the wrong side of the tracks Macchio is a class act: just the right amount of rebellious teenager mixed with respectful disciple, his quick mouth and bad luck offset by his ability to grasp the spiritual side of karate. Having already played troubled teenagers in *The Outsiders* and the TV show *Eight is Enough*, he had a natural, off-hand delivery that was tailored for the part. Tall and lanky, Macchio was no teen idol – although those 'baby browns' did win him a host of female fans – and he appears almost incapable of getting his limbs under control long enough to perform any karate. Fortunately for the untrained actor, the role only required him to practise a limited number of moves, and his awkwardness fits the part better than a sudden transition into an all-kicking, all-punching Daniel-san. He has the spirit, and the moves will come later.

The real star of the show is, of course, the Yoda-like Noriyuki 'Pat' Morita, who gets all the best moves and all the best lines – 'Either you karate do yes, or karate do no. You karate do "guess so": squish, just like grape.' Despite appearing in more than a hundred films and TV series, including *M*A*S*H* and *Happy Days*, for an entire generation of moviegoers he will always be Mr Miyagi. He almost wasn't, however. Morita was initially rejected for the role because of his reputation as a comedian – he started out in stand-up, under the stage name The Hip Nip – but in the end no one bettered his reading of the part. The humour he brings to the film, along with his ability to look enigmatically threatening when staring Kreese down in the Cobra Kai dojo, makes the part a classic. Jackie Chan recognised in the 70s that humour could make a martial arts film, and *The Karate Kid* is no exception to this rule.

Morita had never appeared in a kick flick before, and had no training in karate. Not that you'd know it from the way he chops the tops off beer bottles with his bare hand. The famous silhouette of Miyagi doing crane kicks on a wooden post was in fact performed by a stuntman in a 'bald wig'. In fact, after contracting spinal tuberculosis as a child, Morita was told be would never walk again. If his kicks seem a little stiff, it can be attributed to Miyagi's age, not lack of skill. His serenely unruffled sensei is the ideal contrast to Martin Kovc's testosterone-fuelled Kreese and Macchio's tempestuous Daniel. Morita was the first Asian-American actor to be nominated for an Oscar, and it was for his role in *The Karate Kid*. The film clearly left as indelible an imprint on him as it did on Macchio: he owns a Japanese-style restaurant on Sunset Boulevard called Miyagi's.

Of the other 'fighters' in the film, William Zabka had never done Asian martial arts before, although apparently he was a good wrestler. The referee in the All Valley Championship final is Pat E Johnson, who instructed movie stars including Steve McQueen in karate, was martial arts co-ordinator on the film and was a former student of Chuck Norris. Norris himself turned down the role of psycho sensei John 'No Mercy' Kreese because he thought the character was too violent and would give karate a bad name. Martin Kove, who took the part, has said that kids have been known to come up to him and abuse him for hurting Daniel, his character being as universally hated as that of Darth Vader. Before becoming an actor, Kove was a substitute maths teacher. Perhaps it helped him prepare for the role.

MARTIAL ARTS: Karate is the ideal martial art for this type of film. Instantly recognisable, it mixes just enough Eastern mysticism with rigid, kinetic action to fuel the plot. Moreover, the basic moves are simple enough to replicate that the lead actors, none of whom was trained in the style, could give convincing impressions of competence to fool an audience not immersed in a tradition of martial arts, on-screen or off. None of the techniques used in the film are flashy or complicated, but they appear effective. There is a great deal of bouncing about, not seen in martial arts films since the death of Bruce Lee (who did it in an altogether more threatening manner), but then what can you expect from a gang of energetic teenagers desperate to prove their mettle?

The best martial sequence is that performed by Daniel when he realises that all that waxing and washing has enabled him to block Mr Miyagi's punches, and the audience is invited to share his feelings of disbelief and exultation. Miyagi himself demonstrates the other side of karate, when he confronts Sensei Kreese and fences with words rather than fists to gain the advantage. Asking Daniel why he wants to learn to fight, he is satisfied with the reply: 'So I don't have to.'

Much has been made of the fact that the final crane kick used by Daniel to win the competition is not a karate move, but was made up for the film by martial arts advisor Darryl Vidal (who plays the semi-finalist beaten by Johnny at the tournament, competing under his own name). This may be the case, but the basis of the kick, flicking upwards to the throat, has long existed as part of Crane style kung fu. Why you would raise your arms above your head and not keep them down to guard your body, as demonstrated in the film, remains a mystery. Do not try these moves at home. Not because you might hurt someone, but because they probably won't work.

STUNTS AND SPECIAL EFFECTS: The only effect used in *The Karate Kid* is a lot of very fast editing to make the actors appear more skilled than they are. Some of the fight scenes are pretty brutal however, with lots of kicks to the face and bloodied noses. Rather than using Hong Kong-style sound effects to emphasise blows, the grunts and groans of the afflicted prove much more realistic. When the Skeletons attack Daniel on Halloween, the last spin kick he receives to the head actually connected, injuring Macchio.

DIRECTOR: John G Avildsen is most famous as the director of *Rocky*, and on the release of *The Karate Kid* many critics accused him of simply remaking his earlier film for teenagers. But does it really matter if he did? Avildsen manages to pump all the same excitement, entertainment value and pseudo-suspense of an essentially predictable plot into *The Karate Kid*, and it does not come off badly in comparison to the massively successful boxing movie.

Like Robert Clouse of **Enter the Dragon**, Avildsen is not a martial arts expert. Unlike Clouse, he did not have Bruce Lee to rely on for the choreography. The fight scenes are over in a few moves, leaving little for fans to get their teeth into. The action is concentrated in the build-up to the fights rather than in the karate itself, which is probably due to the director compensating for his untrained cast. To his credit, Avildsen does not try to gloss over the cerebral side of karate, allowing plenty of screen time to Mr Miyagi's philosophising and Daniel's gradual realisation of what is really meant by the way of the 'empty hand'.

PRODUCTION: *The Karate Kid* is awash with continuity errors, although this does little to undermine enjoyment of the film. Characters switch hands, clothes and bruises with alarming regularity but such good grace that the audience must forgive them for it. Most notable are Daniel's cuts and grazes, which disappear in time for him to meet Ali's parents, before re-emerging the next day. In addition to the lapses in continuity, the shooting style is quite lazy, using wide angles and dissolves typical of the early 80s. The shot in which Ali is framed in Daniel's thighs on the beach is outrageously corny, but generally the actors are just left to get on with it. This serves the purpose of enhancing the overall feel of gritty realism and lack of artifice.

The Karate Kid Part 2 was filmed only ten days after the release of the first movie, so at least none of the actors had a chance to age. An alternative ending was filmed for the original when it was made, with Mr Miyagi and Kreese engaging in a violent showdown outside the tournament arena, but it was never added to the film and instead became the prologue to *Part 2*.

TRIVIA: Mr Miyagi is named after Chogun Miyagi, founder of Okinawan goju-ryu karate. The Karate Kid himself is a character from DC Comics' League of Superheroes, and the filmmakers had to get special permission to use the name. The catching-flies-with-chopsticks scene is an obscure reference to the 1956 Japanese film *Miyamoto Musashi Kanketsuhen: Kettô Ganryûjima*, which includes a very similar sequence. If you look closely, you can see the wire from which the fly is suspended.

THEMES: The sensei-student relationship is clearly the central theme of the film, wariness growing into respect and then affection on both sides. The humour and obvious connection between the characters, despite their differences, are deeply satisfying and contrast well with the action sequences. The great master taking on the underdog disciple is a classic device, appearing in a host of Jackie Chan films, notably *Drunken Master*. Our hero is not only looked down on by his rich schoolmates, he is repeatedly beaten up by them: shades of Fang Gang in *One-Armed Swordsman*. Daniel manages to excel and beat the bullies at their own game by mastering the inner fundamentals of an art that they think is all about violence. The good and evil motifs are a little overdone, however, the only rehabilitation of the bad guys coming right at the end when Johnny proclaims that Daniel is all right because he has succeeded in kicking him in the face.

Confused teenagers are a major motif: Daniel throws strops at his mother, while the students of the Cobra Kai dojo mindlessly repeat their lack of mercy and the need to strike first and hard. When it comes down to it, however, and their sensei tells them to cheat and cripple Daniel, they are shocked. Despite being happy to beat him up on dark hillsides, breaking the rules of a tournament is almost a step too far. The tournament itself is, of course, a staple of the genre. And where would anguished teenagers be without a bit of romance, here seen in the form of Elisabeth Shue? Proving one's manliness and stealing the girl from a rival is standard fare for the genre, although *The Karate Kid* differs in that it seems to be entirely on the girl's terms, and there is a happy ending: this is 80s Hollywood after all. *Part 2* falls more into line when it opens with the announcement that Ali has fallen for a UCLA football player and dumped Daniel, and ends with his new love staying in Okinawa without him. Such fickle girls.

There is even a splash of social commentary in the film, with Miyagi talking about how his wife died in a relocation camp for American-Japanese during World War II. But this theme too has been seen in martial arts films before: Bruce Lee takes the segregation of Chinese (and dogs) very badly in *Fist of Fury* and Jet Li objects to the encroachment of foreigners in *Once Upon a Time in China*. The reference to the war allows another East/West contrast to be shown: on the wall of Kreese's dojo is a portrait of himself in full combat gear, while Miyagi wears his uniform only to commemorate his wedding anniversary, and hides away his valour medal. Karate, we are told, comes from the head and heart, not from belts and medals.

PLACE WITHIN THE GENRE: Although they might be reticent in admitting it, *The Karate Kid* is the first martial arts film that several generations of Westerners saw. As a film it should be bad: it's clichéd, predictable, badly edited, contains some appalling 80s fashions and music, and fails to hit the heights of martial excellence. But none of these things matter. They simply serve to increase the affection in which this film is held by its fans, along with its quotability and enduring appeal: 'Daniel-san' has forever eclipsed David Carradine's 'Grasshopper'. The critics who thought the film was just *Rocky* for kids ignored the wealth of martial tradition of which *The Karate Kid* is unarguably a part. It resulted in thousands of kids (and adults) heading for their nearest dojo, and even more heading to the video shop to find more of this karate stuff.

The high-school setting, appealing characters and happy ending, along with having American leads and English as its first language, allowed this film to bring martial arts to the masses. It was more accessible to Westerners than even Jackie Chan's international humour, and refined the genre to the point where its legacy can be identified in every Hollywood kick flick that followed.

Heroic Ones: Chuck Norris

- Birth name: Carlos Ray Norris.
- Not to be confused with: David Carradine, Jesus.
- Martial style: Karate. Ranger-craft.
- Born: 10 March 1940 in Ryan, Oklahoma, USA.
- Biography: Martial arts star and instructor Norris was allegedly encouraged by pupil Steve McQueen to go into acting. Although he had an established empire of 32 martial arts schools, Norris decided to try this new avenue. He is most famous in the kick flick genre for his fight scene opposite Bruce Lee in *Way of the Dragon*. The bearded star's best-known role, however, is as the eponymous Walker in the TV series *Walker, Texas Ranger*. He was offered the role of Sensei John Kreese in 1984's *The Karate Kid* but turned it down, not wanting to be associated with such a brutal character. Despite his martial training, he is famous for trying to find non-violent solutions to problems. In 1988 he wrote his autobiography *The Secret of Inner Strength*, which he followed up with *The Secret Power Within: Zen Solutions to Real Problems*. He runs the 'Kick Start' programme which helps troubled kids.
- Best kick flicks: *Way of the Dragon* (1972), *Enter the Dragon* (1973), *Slaughter in San Francisco* (1974).
- Trivia: Norris campaigned for George Bush in the 1988 US Elections. His brother, Wieland, was killed in Vietnam. He was six times World Karate Champion and is an eighth degree black belt in tae kwon do, as well as a committed Christian.
- Where are they now: Having played himself in 2004's *Dodgeball: A True Underdog Story*, Norris has just finished work on *The Cutter*.

Kickboxer

USA, 1989, 105 minutes

Production company: Kings Road Entertainment
Directors: Mark DiSalle, David Worth
Fight scene director: Jean-Claude Van Damme
Producer: Mark DiSalle
Associate producer: Charles Wang
Written by: Mark DiSalle, Jean-Claude Van Damme, Glenn
Bruce
Cinematographer: Jon Kranhouse
Music: Paul Hertzog

CAST: Jean-Claude Van Damme (*Kurt Sloane*), Dennis Alexio (*Eric Sloane*), Dennis Chan (*Xian Chow*), Tong Po [Michel Qissi] (*Tong Po*), Haskell V Anderson III (*Winston Taylor*), Rochelle Ashana (*Mylee*), Steve Lee (*Freddy Li*), Richard Foo (*Tao Liu*)

PLOT: There's very little here that can be described as original, but then, is that really what one looks for in a martial arts film? This one is hammered out on the trusty anvil of tried and tested plot-lines. Eric Sloane is the 'World' Kickboxing Champion, having, in the traditional Yank manner, beaten everyone in America and considered that enough to claim world dominance. His younger, more sensitive brother Kurt is his corner man, and excels in holding his towel and telling him to be careful. When Eric wins the US title belt, a reporter asks him if he is planning on proving he is the best in the world by going to Thailand and taking the Thais on at their own game. Eric, full of testosterone, thinks this is a great idea, although he appears to be somewhat confused about where he's headed, determined as he seems to be to get to Taiwan.

The brothers head to Bangkok and take an educational tour of the city, where the reason for their wildly differing accents becomes clear: Eric was raised by their father in the States, while Kurt was brought up by their mother in Europe to appreciate the more cultured side of life. Why the two brothers look so different, however, is something that never becomes clear. Still, they are now reunited, and Kurt is clearly devoted to his Neanderthal sibling. So much so that he tries to convince him to back out of the fight against Thai champion Tong Po after he sees the local giant battering concrete pillars with his shins. Eric is having none of it, secure in his skills – although he has been spending rather too much time in bars and not enough time training of late. He soon realises his mistake when it becomes apparent that the rules, and the standards, are somewhat different in Thailand. Tong Po takes him to the cleaners and, for good measure, breaks his spine with a late blow after Kurt has thrown in his trusty towel.

The brothers are left on the street, but Kurt manages to convince emotionally tortured Vietnam vet Winston Taylor to drive them to a hospital. Eric is in a bad way: paralysed, he won't be out of hospital for months. Which gives Kurt just enough time to learn the ancient art of muay thai and get his revenge on Tong Po for damaging his obnoxious brother. No one in Bangkok will teach the foreigner, however, especially when they learn that he wants to challenge their hero. There is only one option left: a reclusive old hermit living in the mountains whom Winston happens to know. Things don't get off to the best start when Kurt is caught in a booby trap and Master Xian taunts him for being a dumb American. He also points out that he doesn't teach any more. Kurt wins him round by explaining that he is seeking revenge for his family's loss of honour, and Xian, wise in the ways of kick flicks, changes his mind.

Kurt, of course, already knows karate. This explains the big muscles and his ability to beat up thugs in the local shop, much to the displeasure of Mylee, Xian's niece and the local shopkeeper. Still, she's not too upset to help her uncle with Kurt's instruction and take moonlit walks with his new student. The training montage follows, including some eye-watering tree kicking and pulley-aided stretching techniques. Deciding that his charge is ready, Xian takes him to a bar and sets him up, not only telling all the other patrons that Kurt thinks their mothers had sex with mules but also encouraging Kurt to dance, proving that this is a comedy after all, and that Van Damme needs to be physically restrained in the presence of 80s soft rock.

Dispatching his opponents with ease, Kurt takes on a Thai fighter to prove that he is ready to fight the champion. Winning with bloody skill, he is hailed as the 'White Warrior' by the crowd. Cue a match-up with Tong Po, fighting in the old style with glass-coated fists. But the plot thickens! Eric, newly released from hospital, is kidnapped by promoter Freddy Li to encourage Kurt to throw the fight. To make doubly sure that Kurt realises how evil they are, Tong Po rapes Mylee while the bad guys stab Xian's dog.

While Kurt is dutifully allowing himself to be beaten up – he has been told he must last the fight, as well as throw it – Winston overcomes his fear of doing anything in case he lets his friends down and rescues Eric, bursting through a wall in an armoured truck before mowing down everyone in sight. They rush to the ringside, releasing Kurt to beat the hell out of Tong Po. He then runs to celebrate with his brother, dog and girlfriend, in that order.

CASTING: 'Action has a new hero!' exclaims the *Kickboxer* tagline. This film was supposed to be the vehicle that squeezed Jean-Claude Van Damme into the muscle vests of Arnold Schwarzenegger and Sylvester Stallone. Unfortunately it didn't quite go the distance, largely because its star decided that it would also be his opportunity to act. He should have concentrated on flexing his muscles, or, like Arnie, stuck to roles where a mechanical delivery was all that was required. As it is, he overplays the sensitive younger brother – petting bunny rabbits? – and goofs his way through the love scenes. His one saving grace is an inability to get embarrassed, however ridiculous the demands upon his character. The proof of this is the bar brawl. Trained as a ballet dancer, you'd expect Jean-Claude to have some moves – and he does. Perhaps he truly was as drunk as he was pretending to be, but in any event this is one of the funniest scenes in any martial arts film ever, and it wasn't even meant to be. Jackie Chan may be able to fight to music, but he can't dance like Jean-Claude.

It is in the scenes that really matter – the fights – that Van Damme excels. Oiled and semi-naked, every one of the muscles from Brussels is shown off, along with the trademark splits and quick-fire kicks. The development from Western punk to White Warrior is fairly convincing. Choreographing all the action, Van Damme ensured that he could show off his kickboxing skills, and doesn't disappoint. The Belgian isn't a bad choice for the lead in a Hollywood martial arts film, having the massive advantage of being a trained kickboxer and student of karate. He had already proved his prowess in the surprise hit *Bloodsport* and his moves are convincing because he really knows how to hurt people.

The same can be said of Dennis Alexio, who plays brother Eric. This is the second of the only two films he has ever made, so he can perhaps be forgiven for his appalling acting, 80s perm and battered face. All of these facts are easier to overlook in the light of his pedigree as a kickboxing champion. Michel Qissi, credited in the film as Tong Po, is trained in the art of muay thai, and it shows. He really is shinning that pillar.

The true star of the show is Dennis Chan, who sparkles as Kurt's reluctant instructor. A malicious version of the Mr Miyagi character, he has faster moves and gets more comic lines. Encouraging other people to hurt his student, he also has a go himself, gleefully turning the screw on the side-stretch machine. Since the 80s Chan has appeared in a number of Chinese films, including several Hong Kong kung fu comedy efforts such as *Police Story 2* with Jackie Chan and *The Inspector Wears Skirts*, starring Cynthia Rothrock.

MARTIAL ARTS: Western kickboxing, with its fixed rules and regulated moves, is sharply contrasted with traditional muay thai, and there are no prizes for guessing which comes off worse. The superiority of the Asian way is underlined when Tong Po spits, 'Must train different in America – your defence stinks!' Unlike some US productions, there is plenty of fighting to be seen, and the story is never allowed to get in the way of the action. Of course, this is Hollywood, so the viewer is expected to believe that Kurt has mastered the secrets of muay thai in a matter of months, enabling him to beat a champion who appears to be seven foot tall (or is it just that Jean-Claude is so short?) and has been inured to the sport since birth.

With so many experienced fighters on set some quality action is to be expected, and *Kickboxer* delivers. They all play it up for the camera, exaggerating each movement. Getting the action right was very important to Van Damme in his role as fight choreographer: he pulled out of the title role in *Predator* because the rubber suit he was made to wear restricted his movement too much and prevented him doing his thing.

Despite Van Damme's roots in real fighting, he occasionally allows the ridiculous to overcome his sense of what makes for a good brawl. Foot-slapping Freddy Li repeatedly in the face is going a bit far, as is the moment when brother Eric manages to fell two evil henchmen while sitting in his wheelchair. Xian's half-hearted attempts to teach that muay thai is rooted in the ways of the ancestors and is all about spiritual peace and Zen philosophy are lifted straight out of *The Karate Kid*, and sit uneasily with the violence of the film: there are no repentant school kids here, just a lot of blood and snapped spines.

STUNTS AND SPECIAL EFFECTS: It seems to be a tradition, continued into the twenty-first century with *Ong-Bak*, that martial arts films featuring muay thai are all about keeping it real. No wires or special effects are in evidence, just the awe-inspiring sight of highly trained human bodies throwing themselves at each other. Jean-Claude Van Damme really did snap that palm tree in half with his leg. 'I was really hurt, but I wanted to show something on the camera that was different,' he says. 'I want to show things that are almost real. I choreograph all my fights and I edit all the fight scenes.'

DIRECTORS: Two directors had a go at this film, which probably didn't do the final product any favours. Co-writer Mark DiSalle also produced the movie, which was his first attempt at directing. His second, *The Perfect Weapon*, was also his last to date. As well as writing, directing and producing, DiSalle appears in the film as a US reporter; it is possible that he took on too much. His acting career was more prolific than his directing one. He played a boxer in the early Van Damme vehicle *Bloodsport* and has featured in every film he has produced. It can at least be said that he knows how to map out a martial arts movie, even if he did have to hand the directing reins to David Worth.

Worth also worked on *Bloodsport*, as a cinematographer, a role with which he was far more familiar than that of director. His artist's eye is clearly visible in his evocative use of Thai locations: the streets of Bangkok have a filthy realism; the lush jungle stretches on forever; the smoke-filled fight arenas almost reek of sweat and smog. Both men were sensible enough to let Van Damme get on with the fight choreography while they focused on the rest of the story, and this goes some way to saving the film.

PRODUCTION: Overall, the production on *Kickboxer* benefited from a Hollywood budget, albeit a small one, being spent on location in Thailand. Despite a number of continuity errors, the film doesn't look cheap and is relatively polished compared to some of the Hong Kong offerings of the time – indeed, the fighters are so polished they gleam. The exotic locations also add to the quality of the piece. The one thing that lets down the convincingly athletic fighting, if you ignore all the baby oil, is the ridiculous soundtrack. Almost cartoonish in their volume, the exaggerated slaps and thuds that resound off flesh every time it comes into contact with an opponent's fists or feet are ludicrous, and totally unnecessary.

TRIVIA: Michel Qissi, AKA Tong Po, was working as a technical advisor and choreographer when he heard that the producers were looking for a tall south-east Asian who was trained in muay thai. He stepped up and was given the role of Tong Po, throughout which he scowls masterfully. Dennis Alexio, who plays the American kickboxing champion who gets a short sharp lesson in how they do things in Thailand, was the 2001 IKF Full Contact Heavyweight Kickboxing Champion. In real life he fights under the moniker 'The Terminator' and is a lot scarier than Arnold Schwarzenegger. In *Kickboxer* he demonstrates amazing skills by managing to wax his chest halfway through his fight with Tong Po, and to pull his legs into the van to avoid the doors after he has just been paralysed.

THEMES: *Kickboxer* has been compared to *The Karate Kid*, and well it might be, released just five years later and sharing many of the earlier film's themes and plot devices, for all that the misfit characters are transplanted to Thailand instead of the exotic world of LA. But to draw the line there would be to ignore the fact that the film uses a template laid out in kick flicks stretching back to *Enter the Dragon* and *One-Armed Swordsman*. All the major threads that typify the gung-fu pian can be traced through it.

The underdog pledges his loyalty to the eccentric master, in order to learn the mystical martial art which will allow him to revenge the harm done to his brother. The plot begins with a tournament and ends with the climactic fight in which the bad guy gets his comeuppance. There is romance, in the form of local girl Mylee, and added complications introduced by the promoters who are determined to fix the fight at any cost. Above all, our hero remains righteous, a well-brought-up lad who only turns to violence when he discovers that there is no other option in a brutal world. In the end, however, even the ever-upright young Kurt benefits from cheating: in the fight with Tong Po, Taylor prevents the timekeeper from ringing his bell to end the round, allowing the hero to finish off his enemy. If the characters are somewhat over-egged, and there is a disturbing amount of racial stereotyping, at least the Americans come off as badly as the Thais. And although the villains really are ridiculously malicious, it only serves to make the audience all the more jubilant when they meet their bloody ends. *Kickboxer* is transparent, but it works.

PLACE WITHIN THE GENRE: As a showcase for Jean-Claude Van Damme, *Kickboxer* allowed the big little guy to show what he could really do. It also proved that Hollywood was capable of making a real martial arts film with real martial artists, in the traditional Asian mould. If the movie is not the best acted or best produced in the world, it still holds its own as an authentic kick flick and deserves its place in this book and the genre as a whole for bringing the art of muay thai to the fans of *Rambo*. As a product of the 80s it draws on contemporary Hollywood action films, including *Rocky*, but manages to cling to the spiritual side of martial arts as well, with Kurt contacting the spirits of dead Siamese warriors on the ancient training ground. It also harks back to more hallowed films, with the grimy locations reminiscent of Bruce Lee's *The Big Boss*. As one reviewer remarked, 'It's all pure comic strip, with many intentional laughs, deathless dialogue, cardboard acting and brutal high kicking action.' In other words, the classic wu da pian, produced in America for Americans.

Heroic Ones: Jean-Claude Van Damme

- **AKA:** Jean-Claude Vandam, J. Claude van Damme.
- **Birth name:** Jean-Claude Camille François Van Varenburg.
- **Nickname:** The Muscles from Brussels.
- **Not to be confused with:** Steven Seagal, Dolph Lundgren, Jean Reno.
- **Martial style:** Kickboxing and karate, enhanced with 360-degree spinning kicks and his oft-evidenced ability to do the splits. While dancing.
- **Born:** 18 October 1960 in Brussels, Belgium.
- **Biography:** A shy retiring child, interested in drawing and sport, obsessed with comic-book heroes, Jean-Claude was taken by his father at the age of 12 to karate instructor Claude Goetz. Though he was not a natural in the style, hours of body building, stretching and training resulted in a European Middleweight Championship in karate. While still a teenager, he set up the California Gym in Brussels, but his real goal was the movies. Moving to the US in 1982, speaking no English, he delivered pizzas, taught dancing and sparred with Chuck Norris, who got him a bit part in *Missing in Action*. Determined to

do better, Van Damme accosted producer Menaham Golan outside a restaurant, demonstrating his martial moves, and won the lead in *Bloodsport*, a low-budget film which became a surprise success. A series of action flicks followed, characterised by wooden acting, incredible kicking and extreme violence.

- Best kick flicks: *Bloodsport* (1988), *Kickboxer* (1989), *Streetfighter: The Ultimate Battle* (1994).
- Trivia: Van Damme's kickboxing career record in the ring is 12-1 with 12 knockouts. He has been married five times, twice to Gladys Portugues. He studied classical ballet for four years and learned to speak English by watching *The Flintstones*.
- Where are they now: Working on *Kumite*, due for release in 2006, written, directed by and starring Jean-Claude Van Damme, in which he reprises his role from *Bloodsport*. There have been rumours that the project could be shelved.

Kill Bill Volumes 1 & 2

USA, 2003 and 2004, 106 minutes and 131 minutes

Production company: Band Apart
Presented by: Miramax Films
Director: Quentin Tarantino
Martial arts advisor: Yuen Woo-Ping
Martial arts co-ordinator: Dee Dee Ku Huen Chiu
Samurai sword advisor: Sonny Chiba
Executive producers: Harvey Weinstein, Bob Weinstein,
Erica Steinberg, Bennett E Walsh
Producers: Lawrence Bender, Quentin Tarantino
Written by: Quentin Tarantino
Director of photography: Robert Richardson

CAST: Uma Thurman (*Beatrix Kiddo AKA The Bride AKA Black Mamba*), David Carradine (*Bill AKA Snake Charmer*), Lucy Liu (*O-Ren Ishii AKA Cottonmouth*), Daryl Hannah (*Elle Driver AKA California Mountain Snake*), Vivica A Fox (*Vernita Green AKA Copperhead*), Michael Madsen (*Budd AKA Sidewinder*), Julie Dreyfus (*Sofie Fatale*), Sonny Chiba (*Hattori Hanzo*), Kenji Oba (*Bald Guy*), Gordon Liu (*Johnny Mo/Pai Mei*), Chiaki Kuriyama (*Gogo Yubari*), Michael Parks (*Earl McGraw/Esteban Vihaio*), Perla Haney-Jardine (*BB*), Michael Bowen (*Buck*), Jun

Kunimura (*Boss Tanaka*), Akaji Maro (*Boss Ozawah*), Goro
Daimon (*Boss Honda*), Zhang Jin Zhan (*Boss Orgami*), Sakichi
Sato (*Charlie Brown*), Kazuki Kitamura, Tetsuro Shimaguchi,
Yoji Boba Tananka, Issei Takahashi, So Yamanaka, Juri Manase,
Hu Xiaohui, Chao Ren (*The Crazy 88's*), Sachiko Fujii, Yoshiko
Yamaguchi, Ronnie Yoshiko Fujiyama (*The 5, 6, 7, 8's*)

PLOT: Although it was released as two independent movies, *Kill
Bill* was written and filmed as a single story until it neared the end
of production, and for the purposes of this book, it is convenient
to address it as such. The plot is split into chapters, which made it
easy to divide in two, and even easier to synopsise. The film is not
chronological, but it all makes sense in the end. And it's easier to
follow than *Pulp Fiction*. The credit sequence reveals The Bride
being shot in the head by Bill, apparently during her wedding, at
the moment she reveals that she is pregnant with his baby. She is
left for dead, but then revealed to the audience lying comatose in a
hospital.

Chapter 1: '2' The Bride arrives at the house of Vernita Green,
former member of the Deadly Viper Assassination Squad
(DiVAS), intent upon exacting revenge for the attempted murder
of herself and the death, she thinks, of her unborn child four and a
half years before. Vernita, once known as Copperhead, can see
why she's angry and agrees to fight her, but not in front of her
own daughter: she is now an all-American mom. They arrange to
fight that night at the Little League baseball diamond where she
coaches. Then Vernita tries to shoot The Bride through the
bottom of a cereal box and it's game on. She gets a knife in her
stomach, observed by her daughter, to whom The Bride
apologises and promises she'll be waiting if the kid comes for
revenge. The Bride crosses off Vernita, number '2' on her hit list,
which already has a strike through O-Ren Ishii.

Chapter 2: The Blood Spattered Bride Track back to the
massacre in the Texas chapel. The local sheriff is just mourning
the murder of such a fine-looking woman when she spits blood in
his face, revealing that she has survived. Cut to a hospital scene.
The DiVAS also know she has survived, and Elle Driver, AKA
California Mountain Snake, has come to finish the job. Just as she
is about to inject the deadly venom, Bill calls the whole thing off,
thinking it dishonourable to kill The Bride in her sleep, much to

the annoyance of Elle. Unfortunately for them, four years later The Bride wakes up. In quick succession she discovers that her baby is gone, her unconscious body has been pimped out by the hospital orderly and her legs don't work. She kills a potential rapist and Buck the orderly anyway, and steals his car, the Pussy Wagon. It takes her thirteen hours to make her legs work again, during which she ruminates on the bastards who put her there.

Chapter 3: The Origins of O-Ren An anime sequence reveals how the Japanese-Chinese-American army brat O-Ren Ishii watched her parents being murdered by a yakuza boss, devoted her young life to taking her revenge, then became a top assassin before joining the DiVAS. She went on to beat the hell out of The Bride, for which she is going to pay. The Bride heads for Okinawa.

Chapter 4: The Man from Okinawa The Bride hunts down master sword-maker and Bill's former instructor Hattori Hanzo and convinces him to make her a sword with which to kill his wayward student.

Chapter 5: Showdown at the House of Blue Leaves While The Bride was lying in her hospital bed, O-Ren Ishii has established herself as the head of the Tokyo yakuza clans. Backed up by her personal bodyguard, psychotic schoolgirl Gogo Yubari, her lawyer Sofie Fatale and the Crazy 88s, a fighting squad led by Johnny Mo, she destroys anyone who stands in her way, usually in bloody style. Taking their ease in the House of Blue Leaves, the Ishii gang comes up against an enemy that just won't lie down. The Bride lops off Sofie's arm, dispatches Gogo and the Crazy 88s and sets up a duel with O-Ren. Her Hanzo sword wins out, and O-Ren loses her head. Sophie is separated from some more limbs, but is left alive to tell Bill that The Bride is coming for him. The Bride makes her death list, and crosses O-Ren off.

Volume 2

Chapter 6: Massacre at Blue Pines Back to the start, and the audience gets a bit more information about The Bride's past. It was her wedding rehearsal, not the happy day itself, that was so rudely cut short. Bill arrives to pay his respects, and she introduces him to her new beau as her father. All seems cosy until the rest of the DiVAS, including Bill's brother Budd, AKA Sidewinder, arrive to kill everyone. Cut to Budd in his present-day incarnation, when Bill comes to his trailer-home to tell him that The Bride is on a bloody rampage. Budd thinks that she deserves her revenge, and that they all deserve to die.

Chapter 7: The Lonely Grave of Paula Schultz Of course, that doesn't mean that Budd's just going to lie down and take it. He waits for The Bride to arrive, shoots her full of rock salt, and sells her Hanzo sword to Elle Driver. Then he buries The Bride, bound hand and foot, in the grave of Paula Schultz.

Chapter 8: The Cruel Tutelage of Pai Mei Around a campfire, Bill plays his flute and tells Beatrix Kiddo, AKA Black Mamba, AKA The Bride, the story of his sifu, Pai Mei, who once slaughtered an entire Shaolin Temple because a monk failed to acknowledge his bow. Cue the traditional training sequence in which Beatrix tries to show what she knows, gets set down, then learns everything her master has to teach – although she consistently fails to put her fist through a board no matter how hard she tries. Stuck in a coffin, six feet underground, however, she finds new motivation and punches her way out.

Chapter 9: Elle and I Elle Driver comes to Budd's trailer for the Hanzo sword and surprises him with a black mamba, the finer points of which she regales him with as he dies. Much to her consternation, The Bride arrives, coated in dirt and looking for blood. She is less than happy to discover that Elle killed their sifu Pai Mei by poisoning his fish heads after he plucked out one of her eyeballs. The Bride gets her revenge, however, removing the other eyeball, and leaves Elle thrashing on the floor of the trailer, blind and in the company of a black mamba.

Last Chapter: Face to Face Gaining information on Bill's whereabouts from his mentor and pimp supremo Esteban Vihaio, Beatrix the Bride comes to get him. She is somewhat confounded to discover Bill with her daughter BB. An atypical domestic scene follows, and a bedtime story, before Bill and Beatrix are left alone. Beatrix reveals that she left the business because she found out she was pregnant with BB, and Bill reveals that he doesn't give a damn. The last laugh is on him, however, when it turns out that the only person Pai Mei ever taught the Five Point Palm Exploding Heart technique to was Beatrix. He dies, and she gets the girl.

CASTING: Rather than finding actors to fill the parts he had created, Quentin Tarantino wrote or altered many of the roles specifically for actors he wanted to cast in the films. In many cases, they were the stars of the movies that influenced *Kill Bill*. The director wanted three actors of different nationalities to represent their countries, and got them with Sonny Chiba, Gordon Liu and David Carradine, his three favourite stars of 70s kung fu films and TV series, which are among his chief influences.

'Gordon Liu representing Hong Kong, Sonny Chiba representing Japan, and David Carradine representing America. That's a triple header, a triple crown. If Bruce Lee was alive, he'd be in it,' claims Tarantino.

The part of Bill was originally offered to Warren Beatty, when it was intended to be more of an evil James Bond character. After he had turned it down, Beatty suggested David Carradine, former star of the TV series *Kung Fu*, whose inclusion changed the nature of the film to include more martial arts. Bizarrely, Kevin Costner was also considered for the part, but chose to make *Open Range* instead. David Carradine clearly feels he had a strong influence on the growth of Bill's character: 'I think it may have been when [Quentin Tarantino] started using me as the character that he started thinking about samurai swords and the various genres that go along with that.' Carradine brings with him a certain element of the Old West to combine with the Eastern influences of the films.

Sonny Chiba reprises his role as Hattori Hanzo from the Japanese series *Hattori Hanzô: Kage no Gundan* (*Shadow Warriors*), in which he appears in each successive film as the next generation Hanzo. His portrayal in *Kill Bill* as a master katana maker, Tarantino claims, is the hundredth incarnation of the character, transported into the world of *Kill Bill Volume 1*. The actor makes the weapons in real life, and acted as the samurai sword advisor for the cast.

Gordon Liu has matured from the attentive student in his 1970s Shaolin monk films to become the white-browed teacher in *Kill Bill Volume 2*. Pai Mei was initially going to be played by Yuen Woo-Ping, but he was too busy with the martial arts direction. His replacement is far from second-best. The actor's voice only just made it on to the final cut, however. Tarantino was originally planning to have him speaking Cantonese and then badly dubbed in English – doing the voice-over himself – to look like a US release of a 70s kung fu film.

None of the other main characters in the films is played by a trained martial artist. Uma Thurman had the hardest task of any of the actors, having to master a range of martial arts as well as Japanese, although Japanese reviewers have remarked that her accent could use some work. The Bride's unwavering desire for revenge and caustic humour are more convincingly carried off. As Thurman had been discussing the development of the role with Tarantino since they worked together on *Pulp Fiction* almost a decade before, it is only to be expected that she should become The Bride in every way.

O-Ren Ishii was originally conceived as Japanese, but when Tarantino saw Lucy Liu in *Shanghai Noon* he rewrote the part for her, turning O-Ren into a Chinese-Japanese-American. She too had to learn Japanese for the part, telling Tarantino it would be more convincing for her character to speak the language. Apparently she makes a better job of it than Thurman. As the only character whose background and motivations are explored, she is the villain who inspires the most sympathy: just a poor little orphan girl trying to carve a place for herself in the Tokyo underworld, with 24 inches of katana.

Chiaki Kuriyama was cast as O-Ren's deadly sidekick Gogo following her performance in *Battle Royale*, epitomising in Tarantino's mind the schoolgirl assassin. Among the many cameos in the film are Samuel L Jackson appearing as the organ player at the wedding rehearsal and Bo Svenson as the preacher. Kenji Ohba reprises his role as the Bald Guy, Hattori Hanzo's sidekick from *Kage no Gundan*.

MARTIAL ARTS: The deadly technique, known only to a few and against which there is no defence, which appears in martial arts films from *The Story of Wong Fei Hung, Part 1* to *The Karate Kid*, can also be found in *Kill Bill Volume 2*. The Five Point Palm Exploding Heart technique is the trademark of Pai Mei, and no one else knows it – except The Bride, who uses it to finally kill Bill. Her other talents include the exquisite art of the samurai sword. Although The Bride commissions Hattori Hanzo to make her the finest katana ever created, far from being the most deadly weapon ever fashioned, The Bride's 'Japanese steel' is in fact the samurai sword used by Bruce Willis in *Pulp Fiction* to fight his way out of the Gimp's lair.

Says Tarantino of Uma Thurman's martial studies: 'It was essential that I get Sonny Chiba and Yuen Woo-Ping to put her through some really intense training. Yuen would show her the kung fu animal styles, and Sonny how to use a samurai sword.' The actors worked for three months with Yuen Woo-Ping and personal trainers in order to be convincing in their roles, eight hours a day, five days a week. They concentrated on wushu as well as bushido, to combine their performance of martial arts with an element of Eastern acrobatics.

The influence of both styles can be seen in the *Kill Bill* films. The beauty and athleticism of the combat in the House of Blue Leaves, with its elegant Hong Kong choreography, is harshly contrasted with the bloody grit of the duel between The Bride and Elle Driver, confined within Budd's trailer. 'It's a messy, gruesome, gross brawl, two cats in a bag,' says Daryl Hannah of the modern bushido battle. Though both are skilled in the way of the samurai, The Bride ends the fight with a kung fu technique.

STUNTS AND SPECIAL EFFECTS: As with everything else in the *Kill Bill* films, the stunts are done in Hong Kong style. David Carradine points out the difference between American stunts, where the actors hit as hard as they can but make sure they miss, and the Chinese methods, which are founded in traditional martial arts. 'In wushu, you move very softly, and you make contact . . . You make very light contact, and you make an impression of force by using the rest of your body to give that sense of power.' As in any good Hong Kong movie, the *Kill Bill* actors performed many of their own stunts. Vivica A Fox, who plays Vernita Green, claims that she and Uma Thurman were in on the action for 95 per cent of their single fight scene. 'There was one part that I didn't do, and that was when I go crashing through the glass table. That wasn't going to happen. We pretty much did everything else.' Fox trained for four months to prepare for the ten-minute sequence.

True to the early heritage of the genre, Tarantino refused to use any modern special effects, and stayed old-school, employing the technology available to Chang Cheh and Co. Cheap condoms filled with fake blood and tubes running beneath actors' clothes were used to spurt streams of gore. The gushing sound effects are hugely exaggerated and come straight out of B-movie slaughter-fests. Other 'authentic' Asian movie effects include the miniature model of Tokyo over which The Bride's plane flies on her way to meet O-Ren Ishii: it was originally made for the latest Japanese Godzilla film, *Gojira, Mosura, Kingu Gidora: Daikaijû Soukougeki*.

The wire-work used in the *Kill Bill* films is less flamboyant than the style usually associated with Yuen Woo-Ping, being more down to earth, so to speak, and only occasionally interrupting the flow of action. These are not the gravity-defying displays of **Crouching Tiger, Hidden Dragon**, but are more reminiscent of Jackie Chan at his most acrobatic. Tarantino claims that the use of CGI to create effects he has seen actually performed in the flesh leaves him cold. 'That's what's so great about those old Hong Kong films and the great wire-work. You knew some poor old stuntman was doing all that crazy stuff and that his body was really getting thwacked around.'

The weapons have that real edge as well. When Hattori Hanzo throws his baseball at The Bride, it was actually cut in half with a katana by Zoë Bell, Thurman's stunt double. The mace-on-a-chain used by Chiaki Kuriyama as Gogo was created for the film and is not based on a traditional weapon. It took the actress three months to become proficient with it, and she hadn't quite mastered it by the time filming began: she managed to thump Tarantino in the head as he stood by the camera. He wasn't the only one to receive some unexpected bruises. Daryl Hannah improvised the scene in which Elle Driver freaks after having her second eye plucked out, because she thought it would make the director laugh. He laughed and kept the scene, and she hurt herself smashing up real props.

DIRECTOR: Known for making cult films that have grown into international hits, Quentin Tarantino chose to channel his talent into making the ultimate tribute to grindhouse cinema. In the *Kill Bill* films he wheels out references to a huge store of 70s productions that have influenced his work, including a wealth of Hong Kong and Japanese action films. Tarantino's love of martial movies has been public since he wrote the screenplay for *True Romance*, in which Christian Slater's character tries to chat up a girl by offering to take her to three Sonny Chiba films. Despite this passion, *Kill Bill Volume 1* was the director's first attempt at shooting kick flick action. Like other Hollywood directors who have approached the genre, he had no experience of filming martial arts. The fight scene between The Bride and Gogo was the first Tarantino had ever shot. 'That was how I learned to do it, on that one. And I think that may be, so far, my favourite thing I've ever shot . . . I think that might be the best thing I've done.'

Although there are myriad nods to other films – as well as blatant rip-offs – the *Kill Bill* movies don't just draw on outside influences. They involve many of the director's trademark techniques, including incredibly long takes, such as The Bride and Sofie Fatale's journey through the House of Blue Leaves to the bathroom. Shooting from the perspective of someone trapped in a car boot is another common device; in *Kill Bill* it is seen from the point of view of Fatale, lacking several limbs. Tarantino's penchant for bare feet also surfaces; the band in the House of Blue Leaves, O-Ren as she kills Boss Tanaka and The Bride after she has escaped from the grave all appear shoeless.

But there is one Tarantino speciality missing. Unusually, the director refrains from making a cameo appearance in either *Kill Bill* movie, although at one point he was intending to perform the role of iron-hard kung fu master Pai Mei, which would perhaps have required more CGI than the director could have stomached. He is still there, however, albeit unrecognisably, as one of the slaughtered, masked Crazy 88s lying at The Bride's feet after the massacre in the House of Blue Leaves.

PRODUCTION: The look of *Kill Bill Volumes 1 & 2* is based on the kung fu films of the 1970s, and director of photography Robert Richardson was required to digest a huge number of Shaw Brothers films before shooting began, in order to understand the visual tone of the genre. So firmly did Tarantino feel the pull of films of this ilk that he went as far as getting permission to shoot at Shaw Brothers Studios. His choice of shots mimics the work of the Godfather of kung fu films 'Any time we put the camera way up in the air and pointed it straight down . . . we called that our "Chang Cheh POV shot",' he recalls.

It is possible to spot a number of continuity and technical 'errors' in the films, but there is a strong sense that these are largely deliberate and are included as a pastiche of 70s action B-movies. Along with these subtle-yet-obvious blips, the monotone photography of the wedding massacre harks back to gung-fu pian, and for the same reasons. Originally, no black and white scenes were planned (in the Japanese cut of the film, there are none), but the US censors required that less blood spatter the chapel. Just as distributors did to make martial arts films acceptable for US release in the 70s, Tarantino removed the colour from the film, turning the blood black.

Not to leave any martial sub-genre untouched, having covered kung fu kick flicks and Japanese heroic bloodshed, Tarantino includes a nine-minute anime sequence in *Kill Bill Volume 1*, created by Production LG, the company that made the seminal anime productions *Ghost in the Shell* and *Blood of the Last Vampire*.

There were initial teething troubles with the production processes on the film, due to the very different work habits employed by the Chinese and American crews. Producer Lawrence Bender explains how the orderly, precise, American way of working contrasted noticeably with that of their new colleagues. 'The Chinese way is to have twenty people making a ton of noise, and all working to get it done. They use a lot more crew, and they get things done very quickly.' By the end, the two production styles had married into an effective unit.

The biggest dilemma in the making of *Kill Bill* then became the decision to cut the film into two volumes. Where a Hong Kong film would have shoved it all in, cutting to achieve the right length no matter what the loss of continuity or how confusing it became to the audience, the Hollywood take was that there was just too much story to fit into one film. Rather than lose any of it, they divided it in two. Double the fun, double the profit.

TRIVIA: The Japanese symbols on the movie posters read 'kirubiru', the phonetic spelling for *Kill Bill*, while the characters that run down the side of the screen in the opening scenes proclaim 'The Bride is coming' over and over again. Vernita Green's codename started off as 'Cobra' before it became 'Copperhead', and all of the codenames are also enemies of Captain America.

In the closing credits, the line 'Based on the character of "The Bride" created by Q and U' refers to the development of the central character by Quentin Tarantino and Uma Thurman over the course of the decade between *Pulp Fiction* and *Kill Bill Volume 1*. Hattori Hanzo hides out in an Okinawan sushi bar because no one in their right mind would choose to eat sushi in Okinawa: it is reputedly the worst place in the world to sample the delicacy.

THEMES: From the moment it was conceived, the story of *Kill Bill* was that of a revenge movie. And The Bride has a lot to get even for. Almost murdered by her former lover, who succeeds in doing away with her fiancé and friends, her baby ripped from her comatose womb, subjected to rape by sleazy hospital orderlies: all this leaves her pretty angry. Her need for vengeance drives her to extreme lengths and even being buried alive doesn't stop her.

Family loyalty is a common theme in the martial arts genre, but in the *Kill Bill* films it is heavily entwined with betrayal. Bill is a father figure to his band of female assassins, each of whom he trains from a young age, but he perverts this role by becoming Beatrix's lover. Their daughter is the product of her parents: named BB for the two of them as well as for a type of gun, she kills her goldfish to see what death is, and favours *Shogun Assassin* as a bedtime story. The sifu-student relationship is explored through Bill and his Vipers, and later with Pai Mei and his differing attitudes towards star student Beatrix and rebellious Elle Driver, who eventually poisons him. Hattori Hanzo provides another twist in the relationships between students and teachers when he agrees to make a katana for The Bride after she reveals that it will be used to slay his former pupil. Tarantino has said that when Bill turned to evil, Hanzo was charged with his assassination but could not bring himself to do it, fleeing to Okinawa instead.

Prejudice associated with nationality is another of the genre's themes explored in the *Kill Bill* films, despite Tarantino's proclaimed aim to bring together the cult martial heroes of Hong Kong, Japan and the US. Pai Mei hates Americans, and Beatrix must convince him to teach her in spite of her origins. O-Ren slaughters the yakuza boss who calls her half-Chinese heritage a perversion of their proud tradition, and designates the subject taboo. She does not deny it completely, however: her elite fighting squad, the Crazy 88s, are made up of 44 Japanese and 44 Chinese masked assassins.

Although his previous films all have a very limited number of (admittedly powerful) female roles, in *Kill Bill* Tarantino has stayed true to the origins of the wuxia pian and made nearly all his central characters deadly women warriors. Raised by a tough single mother, the director has great affection for strong females, and in The Bride he has created a paragon. The 'deadliest woman in the world' never loses her female identity: when she discovers she is pregnant, she decides to give up her life of killing. But she is not above using her newly discovered maternal status to dissuade a hit-woman from killing her in turn.

The black and white characterisations of the main players are classic chopsocky fodder. Even when the DiVAS have turned from a life of assassination to become mothers or yakuza bosses, they are incapable of remorse. Of her character, the despicable Elle Driver, Daryl Hannah gushes: 'There is nothing whatsoever that is likeable about her other than she's so bad . . . My character is just bad all the way through.' As the villains are truly bad, so the heroine conducts her killing spree with absolute honour. Each opponent is challenged to a duel, following 'Viper rules of honour', on their turf, with their weapon of choice (which is nearly always the samurai sword). The Bride always offers them the upper hand before cutting it off.

Kill Bill creates its own world, one in which katana are not only acceptable carry-on luggage but have their own holders on airline seats. Just like the jianghu of the early wuxia films, the *Kill Bill* films invent a universe where justice is delivered on the blade of a sword. The predictability of events is also classic wuxia pian: the viewer knows O-Ren will die because her name is crossed off the death list before she is even introduced. The difference, of course, lies in the contemporary setting, reflecting the extreme mix of influences exerting themselves on Tarantino: the films cannot decide if they are wuxia, gung-fu or wu da pian. The director goes his own way with the ending however: no bloody death or heartbreak for the heroine. Beatrix gets her revenge and her daughter, her enemies are dead, and they can drive off to a motel together. This is Hollywood, after all.

PLACE WITHIN THE GENRE: Are these the most referential films ever made? If not, then they must surely come close. Spaghetti Westerns, Hong Kong kick flicks, and samurai and yakuza films are all drawn upon for their dominant themes. Rather than advancing the development of the martial arts genre, the place of *Kill Bill Volumes 1 & 2* is to pay homage to what has gone before. From Chang Cheh's **One-Armed Swordsman** films to the comedy kung fu movies of the 1980s, via a healthy dose of 90s epic wuxia, the *Kill Bill* films explore the full gamut of the martial genre. It would take an entire chapter to cover every filmic reference in the two movies, and the complete list probably only exists in Quentin Tarantino's subconscious. These, then, are just the ones that relate to martial arts films.

Kill Bill never tries to deny its nature as a tribute film. Tarantino even gained permission to use the classic 'Filmed in Shawscope' logo in the opening credits, leaving a knowledgeable audience in no doubt about the roots the films grow from. The credits dedicate the film to the memory of Kinji Fukasaku, the director of Japanese gangster classics who died shortly before the film's release. Scenes from Tarantino's favourite trash movies are also recreated, notably the bloody climax of *Kill Bill Volume 1*, which is a re-enactment from *Shogun Assassin*, Kenji Misumi's 1972 masterpiece (and BB's favourite bedtime film), with a flavour of Takashi Miike's *Ichi the Killer*. The single hero facing off against a hundred enemies is a common occurrence in kung fu films, but Tarantino specifically cites *Chinese Boxer*, the 1969 Jimmy Wang Yu movie, as his inspiration.

Although Tarantino could not cast Bruce Lee in *Kill Bill*, there are several references to the martial arts superstar. The Crazy 88s all wear masks modelled on that sported by Lee as Kato in the 60s TV series **The Green Hornet**. When the yakuza gang comes up against The Bride, she is clad in a yellow tracksuit with a black stripe down the side, a retro reference to the outfit worn by Lee in his unfinished swan song *Game of Death*. Even Uma Thurman's hair had a part to play in Tarantino's endless cross-referencing. 'He wouldn't let me mess with my hair because he loved the way the woman's hair in *The Killer* would fly in slow motion; he said "You're not going to take that hair from me",' reveals Thurman.

Other iconic actors were still available for the film. Sonny Chiba is the living embodiment of Japanese bushido films, actually reprising his character from *Kage no Gundan* in *Kill Bill Volume 1*, as well as bringing to mind his days as *The Street Fighter*. Gordon Liu, who plays both yakuza Johnny Mo and Beatrix's sifu Pai Mei, was the young punk monk in **36th Chamber of Shaolin**.

His opening training sequence in the film that made him famous is referenced in his scene with Uma Thurman when the two perform stylised kung fu in front of a coloured background – a device used in many 70s and 80s kung fu training films.

The character of Pai Mei is taken directly from the 1977 film *Executioners of Shaolin*. He was a real-life character who defected from Shaolin to Wudan and helped the Qing government to destroy the temples, and was played in the original film by Lo Lieh. Lucy Liu's O-Ren Ishii is a direct development of *Lady Snowblood* in the 70s vengeance film of that name, while David Carradine brings with him the flavour of *Kung Fu*. Even Vivica A Fox gets in on the old-school action. 'Chang Cheh's *Golden Swallow*, and those two other Chang Cheh films: *Vengeance* and *Duel of Iron*,' states Tarantino. 'Those were the films I had in mind when Vivica Fox has her confrontation with Uma in *Kill Bill*.'

When Bill and The Bride are catching up in the final scene, Beatrix says she would have 'jumped a motorbike onto a speeding train', an obvious reference to Michelle Yeoh's famous stunt in *Police Story 3: Super Cop*. Telling the story of Pai Mei, Bill begins: 'Once upon a time in China . . .' Most memorably, Sonny Chiba declaims 'Even if god gets in your way, kill him!', a quote from the Fukasaku series *The Yakuza Family Conspiracy*.

The props and sets are also drawn from Tarantino's host of favourites. The House of Blue Leaves carnage reflects the China Palace battle from 1985's *Year of the Dragon*, directed by Michael Cimino. The wooden flute played by Bill in the cosy fireside scene is the one that David Carradine carried in *The Silent Flute*. Carradine turned up to rehearsals with the instrument, and the director couldn't resist putting it in the film.

Much of the music used in the *Kill Bill* films is taken from the movies and television series that Tarantino absorbed during his formative years. Every time The Bride gets a rage on, the soundtrack cuts into the theme from *Ironside* by Quincy Jones. Of course, fans of the genre will know this better as the music that was (illegally) featured in *5 Fingers of Death* or *King Boxer*, America's first exposure to the genre. As the heroine arrives in Tokyo, the theme from *The Green Hornet* plays, and when O-Ren Ishii leaves The Bride fighting the Crazy 88s, she is accompanied by the music from the *Zatôichi* movies. Other memorable soundtrack moments include the cue from Jimmy Wang Yu's *Master of the Flying Guillotine*.

As with all the great martial arts movies, *Kill Bill*, as well as being a mini-series in its own right, has left the door open for spin-offs and sequels. Tarantino has hinted at an anime film of the Deadly Viper Assassination Squad, as well as a movie in which Vernita Green's daughter Nikki sets off for revenge against The Bride, who, to be fair, invites her to do so after she kills her mother in front of her.

Heroic Ones: David Carradine

- Birth name: John Arthur Carradine.
- Not to be confused with: Bruce Lee, whose part he was given in the series *Kung Fu*.
- Martial style: Carradine only started training in martial arts after being awarded the lead role in *Kung Fu*. After that he did: kung fu.
- Born: 8 December 1936 in Hollywood, California, USA.
- Biography: The eldest son of Hollywood actor John Carradine, David Carradine had brief careers in the Army, on Broadway, in the TV series *Shane* and in a Hollywood film before he was cast in the lead role in *Kung Fu*. Despite having no martial arts experience, Carradine was chosen to play the American-Chinese Shaolin monk Kwai Chang Caine over Bruce Lee – who had originally been singled out for the role, but was considered by Warner Brothers to be too Asian to play an Asian lead. Carradine twice reprised the role, in the made-for-TV *Kung Fu: The Movie* in 1986 and in the series *Kung Fu: the Legend Continues* (1993). Having played the sifu character in *Circle of Iron*, he sank into the world of straight-to-video, which included various martial arts workout tapes, until Quentin Tarantino revived his career by re-writing the part of Bill for him in *Kill Bill Volumes 1 & 2*.
- Best kick flicks: *Kung Fu* (1972, TV series), *Circle of Iron* (1978), *Kill Bill Volume 2* (2004).
- Trivia: Carradine claims to have had a lifelong fascination with Eastern culture, which led him to write a book about the philosophy of kung fu. Despite these principles, he was arrested in 1989 for drink driving and spent 48 hours in gaol. He has been married five times.
- Where are they now: Working on *Beyond Legend Johnny Kakota*, due for release in 2006.

Summary

It would be easy to mock Hollywood's efforts when it comes to making home-grown martial arts films. The requirements of the great US blockbuster do not, on the surface, appear to be met by the attributes of the average kick flick, and trying to shape the genre into something more recognisable to Western audiences should be a recipe for its destruction. But somehow, against the odds, Hollywood has managed it. Of course, there have been failures along the way, but it is undeniable that movies have been produced in the studios of California that owe their origins to, and fit snugly alongside, martial arts films with more recognisable pedigrees.

The Karate Kid turns cheesiness into a virtue, and defies accusations of triteness and comparisons with *Rocky* to take its place as a classic of the genre, pushing all the right buttons. Rarely will you find a more well developed student-sensei relationship in a martial arts film, or a more unlikely hero than the gawky Daniel-san. The karate may lack skill, but it has enough spirit and fire to carry the film to its predictable, inevitable and deeply satisfying conclusion.

While *Kickboxer* does not elicit the same levels of affection, or even appreciation, as *The Karate Kid* and is, frankly, a terrible film in many ways, it sticks strictly to the formula. Jean-Claude's success in the muay thai ring reflects Hollywood's success in producing a passable product in an alien arena.

Kill Bill Volumes 1 & 2 are two halves of a much more complicated beast. These films are both a part of the genre as a whole, serving to bring the joys of 1970s chopsocky to a wider audience, and a critique of its many foibles. By highlighting the idiosyncrasies of martial arts movies, the *Kill Bill* films put themselves in a position to undermine them. Fortunately for their own success as much as their effect on the genre, Tarantino never forces the point that far, and the movies stand as the ultimate tribute to all breeds of kick flick.

Snake in the Eagle's Shadow:
The Rest of the World

Just as China does not have a monopoly on Oriental martial arts, so Hong Kong and Mainland films do not make up the entirety of the martial arts back catalogue. Japan has been producing samurai films for decades, and their bloody, no-nonsense sword fighting has influenced kick flicks from *One-Armed Swordsman* to the *Kill Bill* films. The Japanese tradition of geyser-inspired blood-letting, performed by masterless ronin travelling the land and doing good deeds for oppressed minorities, is best illustrated by the long-running *Lone Wolf and Cub* and *Zatôichi* series, and in the work of directors such as Kinji Fukasaku and Takashi Miike.

The Thai film industry has always been aware of the screen potential of muay thai, its home-grown martial art, both for its dramatically physical violence and for the ability of its protagonists to carry on fighting after taking brutal beatings. (When a samurai cuts down an enemy, they stay down, which is impressive but can be a trifle limiting.) Unfortunately, the rest of the world has been slow to join the Thais in the appreciation of this ancient art; perhaps it has something to do with the music. Muay thai has generally been limited to a role as the combat style of choice for tournament thugs, despite the best efforts of Monsieur Van Damme. Minuscule budgets and the consequent appalling production values of many Thai films have denied the industry international recognition and funding, Until recently, that is.

Lack of technology stunted South Korean martial arts movies for a long time, but now the home of tae kwon do has brand-new studios, the ability to create some blinding special effects and a new generation of actors ready to burst on to the world stage. This relative youngster of the kick flick family has all the energy, kookiness and bleached-blonde arrogance of a teenager ready to take on the oldsters at their own game.

This chapter encompasses iconic films from countries other than China and America that have made significant contributions to the martial arts film genre: movies ranging from the longstanding traditions of Japan to the film that finally put Thailand on the international map and South Korea's first successful attempt at a CGI-loaded chopsocky fest.

Zatôichi the Outlaw

(aka *Zatôichi Rooyaburi, Zatôichi Rôyaburi, Zatôichi Breaks Jail, The Blind Swordsman's Rescue, Zatôichi Escapes From Jail*)

Japan, 1967, 95 minutes

Production companies: Katsu Productions, Daiei Studios
Director: Satsuo Yamamoto
Fight choreography: Kasumoto Eiichi
Executive producer: Masachi Nagata
Written by: Takehiro Nakajima, Koji Matsumoto, Kiyokata Saruwaka
Based on the story by: Kan Shimozawa
Cinematographer: Kazuo Miyagawa
Music: Sei Ikeno

CAST: Shintarô Katsu (Zatôichi), Rentaro Mikuni (Asagoro), Kô Nishimura (Uneshiro Suga), Yuko Hamada (O-Shino), Toshiyuki Hosokawa (Nisaburo), Takuya Fujioka (Zatô Sanji), Kenjiro Ishiyama (Tatsugoro): Utako Kyo, Tatsuo Endo

PLOT: The film opens with blind masseur and master swordsman Ichi taunting a man at an archery bar for not being able to hit a rather large, close target. Challenged to see if he can do better, Ichi requests a smaller target and, having got the barmaid to tap it for him, neatly puts an arrow in the middle of it, showing that you should never underestimate scruffy blind men. Back on his travels, Ichi is wandering through Hagata when he comes upon a village where the farmers sing about how they have virtuously given up gambling and whoring. Ichi meets the man behind their reform, Sensei Shusui Ohara, a former samurai trying to combat vice in the region by teaching people better farming techniques and the principles of working together. He gives Ichi a lecture on not soaking the earth with blood, and how violence doesn't solve anything. Sadly, he is soon to be proved wrong.

Ohara's antics have greatly displeased the local gambling bosses, who prefer the peasants to get depressed over bad harvests and then gamble away what remains of their money and land, rather than engaging in the communal rural idyll espoused by the former samurai. Gambling is a big problem in the area; most of the men are addicted to it, leaving the women penniless. One such foolish young man is Nisaburo, whose girlfriend O-Shino is desperate for him to give up his habit, in case he turns out like her wastrel father. Gambling in the local casinos is particularly unprofitable, as the bosses fix the games. Ichi exposes their wicked ways and nearly gets thrown out of the casino before Boss Tamizo realises who he is and invites him to stay as his honoured guest, proving that it can be extremely useful to have the reputation of a deadly swordsman.

In return for Tamizo's hospitality, Ichi agrees to deliver a message to another gambling boss, Asagoro, who pays off the debts of two of the villagers, arguing that if they are bankrupt, they can't gamble in his casino either. Ichi is impressed by his largesse, commenting how rare it is for a big man to help the little people these days. Tamizo's men attack Ichi on his way out of town, and he accidentally kills O-Shino's brother and chops off her boyfriend Nisaburo's arm at the same time. She is understandably upset and slaps Ichi repeatedly for his heartlessness, while he stands there and takes it. With Tamizo dead by Ichi's hand, Asagoro is free to take over all the gambling operations in the area and invites Ichi to return in a year when he is better set up. The blind swordsman leaves, content in the knowledge that an honourable man will be organising the gambling from now on, and the peasants will not lose their land.

Unfortunately, it was all an act. Asagoro gets promoted to a government position and begins to squeeze the peasants. Anyone who can't pay their casino debts is evicted, and Asagoro becomes rich on their misery. Ichi, who has taken up residence in a nearby town, working as a masseur, has no idea how bad things have become until he is attacked by Nisaburo. Nisa blames Ichi for the devastation of the village, and tells him about Asagoro's behaviour, which Ichi refuses to believe. He is forced to, however, when he discovers O-Shino in a brothel. She had been given by

Asagoro to Uneshiro Suga, his government boss, who in turn sold her to the whorehouse when she did not please him. O-Shino also blames Ichi for everything that has gone wrong.

Ichi charges back to the villages and meets with Asagoro, complimenting him on the quality of his brand-new floor mats and remarking on his new-found wealth. Meanwhile, Ohara has been arrested by Suga for raising insurrection, and is accused of trying to incite the peasants to overthrow the government. He refuses to confess or retaliate, and it is left to his peasant followers to break him out of gaol. Ichi gives the casino boss the most threatening massage in history and gets him to confess that he has been a bad man. He gives Ichi the key to Ohara's cell and tells him to go off and rescue the ronin, but follows him with the intent to kill him. Tricking Asagoro into thinking he is dead, Ichi returns 'from Hell' and kills the boss and his henchmen, before being swept up by the peasants who heard he was in the area and want him to rescue Ohara. This he duly does, in bloody style, and Ohara is forced to admit that swords can be useful sometimes. Ichi points out that Ohara's freedom will help the world more than the lives of the scum he has just killed, then limps off into the distance.

CASTING: The star of the entire *Zatôichi* series, Shintarô Katsu was synonymous with the role of the blind masseur with a taste for blood and justice. His shabby appearance, shambling gait and sweaty countenance came to personify the jovial killer who is underestimated by everybody. Katsu plays the part with great humour and charm. Known for his love of cigarettes and alcohol, he was a far cry from the clean-living idols of Chinese kick flicks, who honed their bodies to deadly perfection. His appeal was undeniable, however, and he was held in great affection by Japanese audiences: when he died of throat cancer at the age of 65, more than 5,000 people attended his funeral. Having produced *Zatôichi the Outlaw*, he went on to produce the *Lone Wolf and Cub* ronin films and star in the *Hanzo the Razor* series, which is so bloody that none of the movies has ever been granted a certificate in the UK.

Unusually for a film in the *Zatôichi* series, the supporting cast is given very little to go on: there are too many of them and they appear and vanish so quickly that their place in the film is never entirely clear. Even the character of Ohara is not explored, and when O-Shino kills herself, only the excessively sentimental will give a damn.

MARTIAL ARTS: He's hardly what you'd expect in the hero of what is essentially a samurai film, and Ichi the masseur doesn't really fight like one either. In fact, he isn't a samurai at all. Tired of being picked on by the sighted, he taught himself to become deadly with the sword concealed inside his cane, and his unusual style reflects its far from traditional development. While other men hold their katana straight in front of them, gripped with two hands, Ichi clutches his as he would a knife, pointing down from the hilt and slashing with a backhand motion. It is no less effective, judging by the amount of blood he manages to spill, but it does shorten his range somewhat. Given that he can't see, however, this can only be a good thing. The fighting is brief and vicious, emphasising Ichi's skill and the inability of anyone else to match it.

There is no elegant swordsmanship and testing of opponents, just an implacable killer doing his job. Ichi's style is known as Iai, from Iaijutsu, the art of drawing a sword and striking in a single motion, which renders drawn-out battles pointless, not to mention unlikely. The nature of the samurai warrior is covered briefly when Ohara, the swordless ronin, insists that he doesn't need a sword to fight and would eschew one anyway, as he no longer wishes to spill blood. *Zatôichi the Outlaw* generally lacks the action and extreme bloodletting for which the series is famed, focusing instead on the idea that fighting is not the only solution. Fortunately, all the rest are as gory as anyone could wish.

STUNTS AND SPECIAL EFFECTS: Like any good samurai flick, *Zatôichi the Outlaw* has plenty of bright red blood spurting from severed arteries and pasting Ichi as he mows his way through his opponents. Amputated limbs and heads abound. The most impressive effects, achieved largely through quick-fire if sometimes sloppy editing, are when Ichi demonstrates his speed and skill. Actions such as spearing a moth with a toothpick and slicing dice in half without anyone noticing occur in the blink of an eye. This is slightly frustrating, however: what is the point of a movie hero whose skills are too fast for the audience to see? A more satisfying display is when Ichi plays a stringed shamisen with a gold coin that is thrown at him, then uses the instrument to deflect the rest.

DIRECTOR: This was the only *Zatôichi* film to be directed by Satsuo Yamamoto. Indeed, the famous series passed from one director to another, Kenji Misumi holding the record with six *Zatôichi* movies to his name. Each director brought their own flavour to the action and, in the case of Yamamoto, also his social leanings. Yamamoto was selected by Shintarô Katsu to direct the film because the star liked the director's work on the *Ninja: Band of Assassins* films. Having begun his career as an actor in the theatre, Yamamoto started directing films in 1937. He became well respected for his literary adaptations, and in the 50s began making independent films that were decidedly left of centre. His most famous is *Storm Clouds Over Mount Hakone*. In *Zatôichi the Outlaw* his socialist political views are reflected in Ohara's assertion that the villagers' strength lies in their numbers, and that they should work together to produce a better harvest for all.

PRODUCTION: *Zatôichi the Outlaw* was the first of the series to be produced by Shintarô Katsu's own company, Katsu Productions. The star was keen to have control over the vehicle that had made him famous, and wanted to ensure that the films retained their fresh edge and that life would never become too easy for the blind hero. He achieved his aim with *Zatôichi the Outlaw*, which has a far more complex plot than many of the other films. This episode was also the first *Zatôichi* production to be made in the Toho studios, where the *Godzilla* movies were filmed.

One of the more experimental moments is the montage of the evil being enacted on the villagers by Boss Asagoro. As his black and white image strides smugly across the screen, in the background villagers are evicted, robbed and beaten. When Ichi is on his travels, the passing of time is simple but effectively represented by the weather changing with the seasons.

The only significant flaw in the production, besides the sometimes careless editing, is the music, which is strangely dramatic and brash at inappropriate moments and fails to reflect the mood of the action. The audience is treated, however, to the sound of Shintarô Katsu singing mournfully on the soundtrack as Ichi wanders aimlessly through the world.

TRIVIA: The character of Zatôichi has an entire fictional background, developed in the earlier films and referenced throughout the series. The story goes that a seven-year-old Ichi lost his father at a festival and never saw him again. In film after film the blind masseur encounters various men who he thinks might be his father. His family troubles did not stop there, however, as he became blind a year later and was eventually rejected by the woman he fell in love with because of his disability. She ran off with his brother (played by Katsu's actual brother Tomisaburo Wakayama), leaving Ichi to become a masseur. Tired of being taunted for his blindness, he studied with swordmaster Yajuro Banno and headed off into the world to right wrongs. In *Zatôichi the Outlaw* Ichi refers to his training while talking to the former samurai Ohara.

Zatôichi literally means 'Masseur Ichi', zatô being the lowest of the four official ranks within the Kyoto guild for the blind, established in the fifteenth century.

THEMES: *Zatôichi the Outlaw* is a classic samurai film, depicting the disreputable hero carving his way through villains who stand in the way of justice. Vice must be rooted out, in this case gambling and the thugs who run it, along with the corrupt government officials who benefit from the peasants' misery. Ichi is an unlikely hero, an automatic underdog, being both blind and working in a servile position as a masseur. He injects a humour into the film that is more in keeping with Hong Kong slapstick than with Japanese chambara cinema.

Ichi is betrayed by Asagoro, who he thought was his friend and a decent man. He returns to the village to seek vengeance both for the peasants who are being oppressed and for his own honour after being tricked. He realises, however, that ridding the world of one wicked man will not rid it of wickedness. Honour is a theme central to the story of O-Shino, who, unable to accept her shame at becoming a prostitute, throws herself off a cliff. The tradition of committing ritual suicide after honour is lost is also touched upon by the government officials early in the film, when they discuss the potential price of their failure.

The film ties itself into Japanese history with the inclusion of Ohara, modelled on the real-life figure of Yagaku Ohara, a reforming agriculturalist and philosopher who revolutionised farming in the eighteenth century. The benefits of a pure rural life over the vices of gambling and debt are made abundantly clear, and Ohara's dutiful followers are shown to be far happier, and cleaner, than their debauched brethren. This theme is unique to *Zatôichi the Outlaw*: in every other film in the series, Ichi is seen winning at dice, so he clearly doesn't think gambling is all that bad.

PLACE WITHIN THE GENRE: The fifteenth film in the *Zatôichi* series, this movie keeps it alive by examining its hero's emotions and motivations at a level that had not been attempted before. It marks the point at which Katsu took control of the production side of the filmmaking process, and with its unusually complex plot can be viewed as a turning point in the series. Featuring in some 26 films and more than a hundred TV episodes, Zatôichi is one of the most enduring heroes in Japan.

The *Zatôichi* films are a great introduction to Japanese martial cinema: to see one is to become addicted. In their themes and plot, samurai films have a lot in common with traditional Chinese wuxia, which draws heavily upon them. The Japanese equivalent of a Western, they focus on the homeless hero, roaming from place to place, guided by his code of honour. *Zatôichi the Outlaw* is no exception, although the series as a whole is less grim than many samurai films, with its happy-go-lucky hero. They are pulp fiction, and not meant to be taken seriously, but still managed to create a cultural icon in the 60s and 70s. Katsu returned to make a *Zatôichi* tribute in 1989, and his mantle was assumed after his death by Takeshi 'Beat' Kitano, who revived the character in 2003's *Zatoichi*.

The meeting between Ichi and Ohara presaged the blind masseur's later meetings with other heroes, including Yojimbo, star of a contemporary samurai series, and Jimmy Wang Yu's One-Armed Swordsman. The great shambling blind man with his lightning draw remains one of the most memorable characters in chambara cinema.

Heroic Ones: Shintarô Katsu

- AKA: Katsumaru Kineya, Sing San Iaai Long, Sheng Xin lai Lang.
- Birth name: Toshio Okumura.
- Nickname: Katsu-Shin.
- Not to be confused with: Wakayama Tomisaburo, star of the *Lone Wolf and Cub* films, to whom he bears a striking resemblance. Which is not really surprising, as the two are brothers.
- Martial style: Blind bushido.
- Born: 29 November 1931 in Fukagawa, Tokyo, Japan.
- Died: 21 June 1997 in Kashiwa, Chiba Prefecture, Japan, of throat cancer.
- Biography: In Japan, and in the minds of many samurai film fans, Shintarô Katsu and Zatôichi are one and the same. Despite appearing in some 107 films before his death, having starred in 26 as the fictional blind masseur and deadly swordsman over the course of 28 years, Katsu will always be synonymous with the role. His emotional treatment of the deadly massage artist reflected his deep understanding of human nature, making the character all the more believable. The son of a famed kabuki performer and master of the nagauta style of singing, and younger brother of the implacable star of the *Lone Wolf and Cub* films, Katsu was destined for a performer's life. As well as the hero of the popular swordplay films, he was also a singer, releasing several CDs during his career. His fame spread throughout south-east Asia, and he was the role model for many aspiring actors. Little is known about the personal life of this deeply private man, other than his marriage to a Japanese actress. Takeshi 'Beat' Kitano has recently had a hit with his performance as Ichi the Masseur in the 2003 remake *Zatoichi*, but he will never replace Katsu, who, when it comes to carving up people he can't see with a razor-sharp cane sword, is the original and best.
- Best kick flicks: *Zatôichi: The Life and Opinion of Masseur Ichi* (1962), *Blind Swordsman: Fight, Zatôichi, Fight* (1964), *Zatôichi the Outlaw* (1967), *Zatôichi in Desperation* (1972).
- Trivia: Coming from such a renowned family of performers, it is perhaps no surprise that Katsu's son is also an actor: Ryuutarô Gan. Katsu courted the famous geisha Mineko Iwasaki for three years before she succumbed to his charms. After five years she ended the affair, acknowledging that she would never come before his wife.
- Where are they now: Dead and mourned.

Volcano High

(aka *Whasango, Whasan High School*)

South Korea, 2001, 120 minutes

Production companies: Sidus Corporation, Cinema Service,
I Pictures, SBS, Shin Seung-soo Productions, Terasource
Venture Capital Co Ltd
Director: Kim Tae-gyun
Martial arts choreographer: Eung Jun Lee
Executive producers: Rob Edwards, Kang Woo-Suk
Producers: Kim Jae-won, Tcha Seung-jai, Kim Tae-gyun
Screenplay: Jung An-chul, Kim Tae-gyun, Park Hun-soo, Heo
Kyun
Based on the story by: Seo Dong-heon
Cinematography: Choi Yeong-taek
Music: Gary G-Wiz, Park Yeong, Amani K Smith

CAST: Jang Hyuk (*Kim Kyeong-su*), Shin Min-a (*Yu Chae-i*), Kim Su-ro (*Jang Ryang*), Kwon Sang-woo (*Song Hak-lim*), Kong Hyo-jin (*So Yo-seon*), Jeong Sang-hun (*Golbangi*), Kim Hyeong-jong (*Shim Ma*), Chae Shi-ah (*Yo-mi*), Heo Jun-ho (*Mr Ma*), Pete Sepenuk (*Dean*)

PLOT: It is the Year of the Volcano in a time that is neither past, present nor future, in a place where it rains a lot, and Kim Kyeong-su is battling to control his inner superman. Expelled from eight schools, the bleached-blonde teenager arrives at Volcano High, his ninth and last chance to make good. He has promised his father that he will not use the incredible chi abilities (gained during an accident involving a thunderstorm and a tank of electric eels) that have seen him kicked out of his other schools for, among other things, firing pieces of chalk at teachers. But things are not destined to run smoothly for our bleached hero: Volcano High is no ordinary school.

Since the Massacre of the Scholars seventeen years ago, the school authorities have lost all power to control the students, who are at war with each other and their teachers. Showing allegiance only to their different sports clubs, the students vie to become the most powerful in the school. For it is written (somewhere) that whoever becomes the Number One will gain possession of the secret manuscript and from it learn the secrets of unlimited power, bringing order to the chaos.

Number One guy at the moment is Song Hak-lim (or Elegant Crane in Pine Forest as he poetically likes to be known). His chi power is grade ten, meaning he can control flying tealeaves, shut doors with his mind and beat up anyone he chooses. Except the new boy. Alerted to Kyeong-su's incredible chi levels by his window-rattling sneezes, Hak-lim challenges him to a battle that tears up the floorboards but leaves neither the victor.

No one really knows where the magic scroll is, except perhaps the Principal, and he isn't telling – largely because someone has poisoned his tea and put him in a coma. Top suspects include the Vice-Principal, Song Hak-lim and Jang Ryang, or Dark Ox, Captain of the weight-lifting team. Jang Ryang and the Vice-Principal team up to take over the school, while Hak-lim is falsely imprisoned for poisoning the Principal. The hero of the piece, meanwhile, is unheroically keeping his head down and trying not to get involved. This is impressive in the face of pleas from Yu Chae-i, Icy Jade, head of the all-girl kendo team, for whom he has fallen. She is disgusted by his lack of courage, and eventually agrees to become Jang Ryang's girl when he sets himself up as the school's Number One, having beaten all the other team captains, including the carrot-topped rugby-oaf Shim Ma, The Headhunting Master.

Unable to find the magic scroll or control the students, the Vice-Principal brings in a set of substitute teachers from the depths of every school kid's worst nightmares. Clad in *Matrix*-style leather coats, the 'Five Great Cleaners' are there to instil discipline and make sure everybody goes to gym class. Their leader, the excessively Brylcremed Mr Ma, and Kyeong-su have met before, and it is the teacher's persecution of him that finally causes the blonde one to act. Banding together, the students rebel against the new teachers, setting up a climactic battle between Ma and Kim Kyeong-su on the rugby field. Kyeong-su beats the bully, proves that you don't need a secret manuscript to be a tough guy and even gets a smile out of Icy Jade.

CASTING: 'Since it was a completely new kind of film, we wanted new actors,' says producer Kim Jae-won. Relative unknowns, his teenagers and teachers do not suffer from sending their reputations before them – unlike Kim Kyeong-su – and so more readily become the characters they are portraying. The film relies upon its concept rather than star power. Much like the twenty-something actors that populate American high-school soaps, Jang Hyuk and Shin Min-ah both came from TV drama backgrounds.

Aged 25 when the film was made, Jang Hyuk fits this mould perfectly. His only previous film experience was in the little-known *Zzang*, about a group of troubled high-school students, predictably. Since *Volcano High*, he has featured in the bizarrely named Hong Kong movie *Public Toilet* and the action comedy *Jungle Juice*.

Because of the incredible amount of CGI in the film, Jang, like his fellow cast members, needed little martial training: all he has to do is glower and hold out his hands and let the effects do the rest. And be prepared to do it naked, in the shower. Jang is well cast as the authority-shy teen determined to keep himself in check for the sake of his father. His combination of naïve goofiness and the assurance that comes with the acceptance of his powers is perfectly balanced: his character has been described as 'A timid, James Stewart-style cowboy who finally finds the backbone to strap on his six shooters and put the bad guys in their place'. Jang's sudden switch from rigid kung fu stance to two-fingered victory salute is one of the most engaging moments in the film.

Shin Min-ah, former star of the TV series *Beautiful Days* (the Korean version of *Young and Restless*), does well enough as the reluctant prom queen with her own agenda, who is equally willing to use her looks or her kendo staff to achieve her aims. Attempting to reconcile the boys to the idea of joining together, she abandons them to their fate when all they seem to care about is power and the secret manuscript, not saving the school. Despite a hardened attitude to her own self-preservation – unwanted suitors get a stick up the arse – she is still ultimately waiting for Kyeong-su to come to her rescue when the oafish Weightlifting Captain comes calling. As the Kendo Captain, she and Vice Captain Kong Hyo-jin are the only ones required to perform real martial arts. In the whirling action, it's hard to tell how good their technique is, but they thump the guys with gusto and the scene where Chae-i trains in traditional kendo dress plus Converse All-Stars makes up for any lack of skill.

Kim Soo-ro nearly steals the show as the cartoonish Jang Ryang. 'He does things with his face that are amazing,' says Kim Jae-won. 'He is like Jim Carrey.' Flexing his weightlifting muscles, Kim Soo-ro has little martial technique to perfect – he throws a few kicks but mostly concentrates on squeezing his victims into submission, and on polishing his evil laugh and jugular-popping grimaces. Somewhat older than the other cast members – Jang Ryang must have been held back a lot at school – Kim Soo-ro had more film experience, having begun his career in 1993 in the cop movie *Tukabsou*.

MARTIAL ARTS: In *Volcano High* the martial arts are all about chi, the mystical energy that exists in all living things and can help you perform magic if only you can control it. Of course, this is true of most south-east Asian martial arts, but in this film the concept is taken to the extreme, characters throwing visible force-fields from their bodies and manipulating the elements around them. From the opening scene when Kim Kyeong-su stops a piece of chalk thrown by an irate teacher inches from his face before firing it back at his persecutor (and getting expelled for his trouble), the action places the film firmly between *The Matrix* and *X-Men*. All the fighting is deeply rooted in the comic-book style, with everyone walking (or limping) away from beatings that would cause anyone not protected by the laws of cartoon violence to die of internal haemorrhaging. The most they suffer is the odd nosebleed or string of bloody drool.

With the exception of the minimal bloodletting – which allowed the film to be shown to a juvenile audience – the action resembles nothing so much as manga. With capes and coats flying our behind them, the actors swoop through the stylised scenes like inked characters with the wind of their passing drawn in around them. They run leaning forward at extreme angles and launch themselves into the air spinning inside whirlwinds of special effects. The only disadvantage of this style is that the fight scenes, with the exception of the last battle, are far too short, almost as though they had been drawn in three manga frames.

The action relies largely on comedy rather then choreography, and the fight scenes remain essentially simple to give the actors room for posturing, pouting and oozing blood. The only serious martial moment is when Song Hak-lim, in Morpheus mode, tries to explain the principles of chi sharing. On the plus side, an enormous number of ideas are stirred into the mix, judo, swordplay, telekinetic powers, weightlifting and waterworks all adding to the fun. Adrenalin takes over from authenticity, and the pace of the fighting carries the audience along with little regard for accuracy. The last half-hour of the film is all combat, and it makes for a wild ride.

STUNTS AND SPECIAL EFFECTS: *Volcano High* is all about image: being cool and looking really cool. The overall feel is of the special effects team from *The Matrix* going on a school trip and seeing just what they can get away with when the teacher's back is turned. They scrawl graffiti across the screen, throw food around and bend the borders of reality. The special effects make the film, and its producers had to wait until technology had caught up with their ideas enough to allow them to complete it. It was a struggle to achieve the right look and feel. 'We knew that if they came off looking cheap or amateurish, the film would be a failure,' says producer Kim Jae-won. But hard work and a crew that was quick to learn won in the end. 'When we finally made an effect work we thought, "Hey, we can do this too".'

Unfortunately, the filmmakers get carried away with their new toys at times, and the effects become more important than the action. This is a trend too often seen in Asian martial arts films: because they can do it, they do. Since the Chinese first learned how to swing actors about on wires, and suddenly everybody could fly, special effects have been in danger of going over the top. A classic example is Tsui Hark's *Zu: Warriors from the Magic Mountain*, where the fantasy elements unforgivably upstage Yuen Biao and Co.

In spite of this, many of the set pieces work extremely well, and are comparable to *The Storm Riders*, that shining example of how to effectively represent chi power on screen. One of the most visually intriguing sequences is the shower scene, in which Kim Kyeong-su manipulates the water around him into Korean characters and spiralling tornadoes before dashing it against the walls.

DIRECTOR: Before *Volcano High*, Kim Kae-gyun had only had two mid-level hits with *The Adventures of Mrs Park* and *First*

Kiss. Like his cast, he was relatively new to the industry, although he had produced *As You Please* in 1992. He began developing the idea for the high-school kick flick after it was given to him at a pitching competition in 1994. 'No one else on the jury liked it, but I thought it was amazing,' he recalls. Fortunately, he also managed to convince Tcha Seung-jai, CEO of production company Sidus and one of the most powerful men in the South Korean movie industry of its potential.

The ultimate achievement of Kim Kae-gyun is in refusing to take his material too seriously. Unlike other CGI-infused action films (picture Keanu Reeves glowering in *The Matrix* or Hugh Jackman growling in *X-Men*), *Volcano High* keeps its tongue firmly pressed into its cheek. Every time the actors are allowed their moment of supreme cool, they are cut down again by the proverbial – and in some cases literal – bucket of water falling from the top of the door. As much as imitating the Hollywood films, Kim parodies them. Every time Kyeong-su gets something right, he ruins the moment by grinning goofily at his girl.

PRODUCTION: This film simply could not be made until the technology in South Korea caught up with the concept behind it. In 1997, the opening of a state-of-the-art studio near Seoul and the development of sophisticated production techniques by large movie companies such as the Sidus Corporation allowed home-grown filmmakers to begin exploring the possibilities of new genres, including sci-fi and fantasy martial arts.

After *Volcano High* had been completed and shown to the home audience, an improved version was created in 2002. During production, Kim Jae-won had managed to secure an agreement that before an international release they would have the opportunity to fine-tune the special effects.

In spite of the advances in technology, *Volcano High* was an ambitious project for a type of Korean filmmaking still in its infancy. With a budget of $1 million, its producers set out to find a location but failed to discover anything suitable. A large portion of the original budget was therefore spent building the old-fashioned high school from hell featured in the movie. This set the pattern for the rest of the project, as the shoot spiralled out of control. 'We originally planned for 100 days of shooting,' says Kim Jae-won. 'After 40 days, however, we had only completed 20

percent of the film.' By the end of the shoot, costs had risen to
$3.7million. Six months of post-production followed, the
filmmakers rushing to finish the movie so it could be released
ahead of *Harry Potter and the Sorcerer's Stone*. Despite the speed
at which they were working, each frame was digitally
colour-corrected, a first for the South Korean film industry.
Almost all of the colour has been leached out of the film, leaving a
stark, monotone world in which the only flashes of colour come
from the protagonists' dyed hair. Minute details are thrown into
sharp relief by the extreme contrast.

Kim Kae-gyun uses every trick in his book to keep the
audience's attention, flicking between extreme close-ups, using
slow motion to punctuate break-neck action, employing odd
angles and encouraging his cast to caricature their roles. The
camera is never still, swinging from the actors' feet to overhead
shots, while freeze-frames are used to introduce the protagonists
and break up the flow of the film. The black and white old-school
memory montage, in which the hero reviews his troubled youth, is
a stroke of comic genius, borrowed by Quentin Tarantino for The
Bride's narrative in *Kill Bill Volume 2*. The electric soundtrack
and cracking sound effects add to the sense that this is martial arts
for the MTV generation.

TRIVIA: When MTV screened a version of *Volcano High* in
America, the characters were dubbed into English using the voices
of famous rappers, with Snoop Dogg as Song Hak-lim and
Method Man as Mr Ma. *The Karate Kid*'s Pat Morita also makes
a vocal appearance.

THEMES: This might be the movie for the next generation of
martial arts fans, but it still weaves in many of the traditional
strands of storytelling that define the genre, even if some of them
are subverted and twisted. Set in an alternative universe in an
undefined time with its own rules of physics and social propriety,
Volcano High creates its own version of the world of martial arts,
reducing it to the size of a high school. Other than in Kyeong-su's
recollections, the action never leaves the school, neither do the
students: what they do when they're not beating each other in the
playground or tormenting their teachers is a mystery. The sports
clubs are allowed to rule the school, and corporal punishment

takes on a new meaning – the institution has its own prison and teachers are allowed to throw students off roofs.

Each character's martial abilities are defined by the sports club they belong to – they have their own styles, and nicknames to match. Jang Ryang calls his new move Supreme Power Lift, drawing on his weightlifting skills, while Chae-i won't fight without her kendo stick. Kyeong-su acquired his skills during an accident in a lightning storm, giving him an almost superhuman control of chi, while Song Hak-lim has apparently just practised really hard (which must be somewhat galling for him). You don't see anyone really training, although Kyeong-su does get a bit of coaching through a mystical vision. Nearly all of them are in search of the secret manuscript that will enhance their powers: a classic device, pulled straight from the reels of *The Dragon Chronicles: Maidens of Heavenly Mountain*. Everyone wants to be Number One, except the only one who can be, and there is a lot of 'My kung fu is better than your kung fu' posturing.

Filial loyalty is a binding force in Kim Kyeong-su's world, causing him to pull his punches and appear a wimp and a coward in front of his schoolmates. Tormented by the powers that have forced his parents to move from one region to the next as he is expelled from school after school, he forces himself to practise the restraint his father preaches. If he restrains himself three times, the paternal advice goes, he will manage not to kill anybody. Meanwhile, the student-teacher relationship is utterly perverted, with the kids battling their instructors for power and the Vice-Principal trying to brainwash his charges' minds. The School Five, masters of discipline, are less interested in teaching than in subduing their pupils.

The reluctant hero comes good, saves the day and wins the girl. He is initially presented as a rebel with shades of Bruce Lee in *Fist of Fury*, but is tempered with a healthy dose of Jackie Chan's trademark underdog comedy.

PLACE WITHIN THE GENRE: Aimed at an audience raised on high-octane video games and the disposable culture of music promos, *Volcano High* takes the genre in a new direction. Producer Kim Jae-won describes it as a 'contemporary martial arts film with a comic-book sensibility', while its director is in no doubt about his target viewers. 'This film will appeal to the

web-surfing generation . . . The younger generation is very
comfortable with rapid changes in style and tone.' In a
light-hearted way, the film also serves as a social comment on the
cruelties which go on in schools everywhere, bullying and
victimisation of students by their fellows and teachers. Its
conclusion will leave anyone who was ever picked on in school
smugly satisfied that justice has been done.

Predictably for a film that embraces the commercial world so
closely, the franchise was expanded with a novel, a prequel comic
and a computer game, continuing the trend for turning martial
arts action into PlayStation fodder. It attacked and flooded the
market with a ferocity unusual for the genre – how many people
have rushed out to buy the wuxia novels of Wang Du-Lu, on
which *Crouching Tiger, Hidden Dragon* is based?

A huge success in South Korea on its opening weekend,
Volcano High also took advantage of its potential appeal to an
international audience. An overseas release was edited to remove
references that were considered too local, losing almost twenty
minutes of running time, arguably at the expense of plot
coherence. Unsurprisingly, it did well in Japan, its appeal
stemming from the fact that it is essentially manga on film.
Although too extreme to become mainstream, this exhausting film
has become a cult favourite.

Volcano High borrows unashamedly from sci-fi and superhero
films, most notably *The Matrix* in its use of CGI and a plot-line
which sets up a reluctant hero who will not accept that he is
destined to be 'The One' who will bring order to chaos. And in the
long black coats. Hong Kong wuxia pian never made a big impact
on Korea, and this film has essentially absorbed the themes and
styles of the originals by way of Hollywood imitations. The grim,
fantastical landscape against which it is shot is reminiscent of the
French film *The City of Lost Children* by way of *Dark City*, while
the digitally enhanced frames are more like the *Final Fantasy*
video-game-cum-film. To complete its tour of genre, the
crumbling high school seems to have grown directly out of the
foundations laid by seminal anime *Akira*. Despite all these
influences, *Volcano High* has a style of its own, refusing to be as
dark, depressing, apocalyptic, philosophical or moralistic as its
role models, never forgetting that what it is all about is
entertainment.

Volcano High is important not just in reinventing kick flicks but also in reanimating the Korean movie industry, fighting back against the big fish in the international pond like a celluloid version of Kim Kyeong-su. Apparently, when Jackie Chan was filming his Bruce Lee copycat movies with Lo Wei in Korea in the 70s, the crew would mock the pathetic attempts of the Koreans to create their own productions. Until the twenty-first century, Korean films remained in relative obscurity, largely due to lack of cash for production and distribution. *Volcano High* has helped to turn the tide, encouraging worldwide audiences to enjoy the unique quirkiness of the Korean imagination while gaining an insight into its diverse martial arts traditions. It might not be what anyone would have expected, but it works. Closely following in its wake came *The Warrior*, an epic martial arts film starring none other than Zhang Ziyi, and with more than a passing reference to *Crouching Tiger, Hidden Dragon*. With *Volcano High* director Kim Sung-su announced that South Korean filmmaking should be taken seriously, as well as appreciated for its unique humour.

Heroic Ones: Shinichi Chiba

- **AKA: Sadao Maeda, Shinichi Chiba, Shin'ichi Chiba, Shin-Ichi Chiba, Shinichi 'Sonny' Chiba, Sonny JJ Chiba, Chiba Shin-Ichi.**
- **Birthname: Sadao Maeda.**
- **Nickname: Sonny.**
- **Not to be confused with: Gozilla, that other huge Japanese movie star.**
- **Martial style: Karate, judo, kempo. Ripping out throats and administering the x-ray punch.**
- **Born: 23 January 1939 in Fukuoka, Kyushu, Japan.**
- **Biography: Were it not for a back injury, Sonny Chiba might now be living in obscurity, his only claim to fame being part of the 1964 Japanese Olympic team. Instead, forced to quit the team while at university, he began to study karate under Masatatsu Oyama, his first step on the path to becoming the greatest action hero Japan has ever produced. Born the son of a fighter pilot, he was discovered by Toei Studios, renamed Shinichi Chiba and cast in a series of television and film action roles, including the fabulously weird *Invasion of the Neptune Men*. In 1969 he set up the Japan Action Club to train actors in martial arts and stunts, and he is still involved in developing young**

stars today. His defining part was as the fists-for-hire mercenary Terry Tsurugi in *The Street Fighter*, a brilliantly brutal film in which he punches people so hard their eyeballs pop out. The film and its three sequels rode the wave of enthusiasm for martial arts films created by Bruce Lee in the early 70s. They are among the most watched cult action movies in the world, prime examples of the chopsocky genre. Chiba was due to work on a project with Lee, but the Chinese star died before filming could begin. Although his later films received less attention outside Japan, he has appeared in several successful Hong Kong movies. Since playing the morose sword-smith Hattori Hanzo in *Kill Bill Volume 1*, it can only be hoped that Chiba will begin to receive the recognition he deserves in the West.

- Best kick flicks: *The Street Fighter* (1974), *The Executioner* (1974), *The Storm Riders* (1998).
- Trivia: Chiba is the student of Choi Bae-Dai, the founder of kyokushin style karate. He has a fourth degree karate black belt and is also highly skilled in the Japanese arts of judo, ninjitsu, kendo and kempo. The nickname 'Sonny' came from his association with an ad campaign for the Toyota Sunny-S.
- Where are they now: Although appearing in far fewer films these days – his prolific career has already spanned three decades – Chiba is still called upon to play the hard man of few words, most recently in 2004's *Explosive City*. He continues to work with the Japan Action Club.

Heroic Ones: Takeshi Kaneshiro

- AKA: Kaneshiro Takeshi, Wu Jincheng, Jin Cheng Wu, Jin Chengwu, Gum Sing Mo, Gam Shing Miu.
- Birth name: Takeshi Kaneshiro.
- Nickname: Aniki.
- Not to be confused with: Takeshi 'Beat' Kitano, star of 2003's *Zatoichi*.
- Martial style: High kicks and sword play.
- Born: 11 October 1973 in Taipei, Taiwan.
- Biography: Half Taiwanese, half Japanese, Kaneshiro is one of the few actors in Asia who can span the various national film industries, thanks to his looks and the fact that he speaks Mandarin, Cantonese, Japanese and English. Growing up in Taiwan, his mixed background led to bullying, but he has more than got his own back now. His screen presence was first noticed when he worked on commercials while at school. In 1992 he began a singing career in Mandarin and Cantonese, and then, as is the norm for Asian pop stars, was offered parts in films, initially in comedies. His penchant for darker roles soon became clear, and he worked with director Wong Kar Wai on the acclaimed *Chungking Express* in 1994. A role in the Japanese series *God Please Give*

Me More Time, in which he played the lover of a girl with HIV, launched a Japanese film career. The result was *Returner*, the futuristic gun-fu flick in which he broods magnificently. His appearance in Zhang Yimou's *House of Flying Daggers* has cemented Kaneshiro's place within the martial arts genre, as well as exposing him to a wider international audience.

- Best kick flicks: *Don't Give a Damn* (1995), *Returner* (2002), *House of Flying Daggers* (2003).
- Trivia: Due to his good looks and popularity, Kaneshiro is one of the most sought-after spokesmodels in Asia, representing Prada and Mitsubishi among other brands. The character of Samanosuke in the video game *Onimusha: Warlords* is modelled on him.
- Where are they now: Working on the completely non-martial *Perhaps Love*. Beyond work, no one really knows what the elusive star does with his time.

Ong-Bak

(aka *Ong-Bak: Muay Thai Warrior, Ong-Bak: The Thai Warrior, Daredevil*)

Thailand, 2003, 108 minutes

Production companies: Ram-Baa-Ewe, Sahamongkol Film Co.
Director: Prachya Pinkaew
Martial arts choreographers: Panna Rittikrai, Tony Jaa
Executive producer: Somsak Techaratanaprasert
Producers: Prachya Pinkaew, Sukanya Vongsthapat
Written by: Suphachai Sittiaumponpan
Story by: Panna Rittikrai, Prachya Pinkaew
Director of photography: Nuttawut Kittikun
Music: Atomix Clubbing

CAST: Tony Jaa (*Ting*), Mum Jokemok (*Humlae/George*), Pumwaree Yodkamol (*Muay Lek*), Suchoa Pongvilai (*Komtuan*), Chatthapong Pantanaunkul (*Saming*), Wannakit Siriput (*Don*), Chetwut Wacharakun (*Peng*), Rungrawee Borrijindakul (*Ngek*), Pornpimol Chookanthong (*Mae Waan*), Chumporn Teppitak (*Uncle Mao*)

PLOT: The village of Nong Pradu is a poor and simple but happy place, where the young men like to daub themselves in clay and race each other up trees. The people are blessed by the benevolence of Ong-Bak, their local Buddha, who is honoured at an annual festival when the fastest tree climber gets to dress him in ceremonial robes. This year that honour goes to Ting, the most athletic boy in the village, trained in the ancient art of muay thai and, unfortunately for the local girls, destined to be a monk. His teacher has warned him never to use the deadly fighting form against people, which is a shame, as he is very good at it.

One night, the Buddha's head is stolen by Don, a con-man from Bangkok, and the villagers fear that without it the rains will not fall and the crops will die. Ting offers to go to the wicked city to retrieve the relic and sets off determined to bring them the head of Ong-Bak. He aims to meet up with Humlae, the son of the village headman. Humlae is in Bangkok studying to become a monk – or so his father believes.

In fact Humlae, or George as he prefers to be known, is now a small-time hustler who makes money peddling drugs and scamming gamblers, and is none too pleased to see the rustic Ting, fresh from the country and wet behind the ears. He steals his money and heads off to an underground fight club to gamble it. Honest Ting is outraged and follows George and his street urchin sidekick Muay Lek to the club, where he is accidentally involved in a fight and ends it very suddenly with a blow from his knee. George realises Ting could be useful after all and tries to make him fight for money and protect him from the drug dealers whose wrong side he is permanently on.

Against his better judgement, Ting defeats all the fighters in the club after they show what nasty people they are by attacking women and skinny Thai men. This makes him most unpopular with Komtuan, the local crime boss, who speaks through an artificial voice box, smokes through a tracheotomy hole in his throat and loses a great deal of money when Ting beats his fighters. He also does a profitable line in flogging Thai artefacts to foreign dealers. Ting discovers his unpatriotic business dealings and Komtuan orchestrates various attempts to kill the country boy before setting him up in a traditional muay thai fight, which Ting agrees to throw in return for Ong-Bak.

Naturally, the arch villain double-crosses him and kidnaps Ting and his friends, leaving a henchman to execute them. A classic error: Ting fights his way out with elbows and knees flying, then chases the bad guys into the mountains where they are busy cutting off the head of a giant Buddha. Ting kills everyone but fails to save George, who has finally come to the rescue of his village's honour but is crushed by a falling Buddha. Ting returns to his drought-stricken village with Ong-Bak, brings the rains and becomes a monk.

CASTING: Tony Jaa is a muay thai machine. Originally a stuntman, he performs all his own death-defying feats without batting an eyelid. At the age of 15, inspired by the work of Bruce Lee and Jackie Chan, he sought out the Thai action star Phanna Rithikrai, after seeing his film *Born to Fight*. The actor took him on as his protégé and oversaw his training in tae kwon do, swordplay and gymnastics. Despite his lack of acting experience (and some might say ability), Jaa makes a passable job of his first starring role, and looks set to become the next Asian action hero. He has a brooding presence reminiscent of a young Sonny Chiba, and benefits greatly from the minimal dialogue required of him – he has fewer lines than Arnold Schwarzenegger in *The Terminator* – allowing his body to do the talking. This is probably just as well, as he has an inappropriately squeaky voice. In his willingness to perform his own stunts and fling himself through rolls of barbed wire, Jaa is comparable to Jackie Chan at his physical peak, but without the comedy. This is a shame: the film could have done with some light relief from Jaa, as Ting is so righteously upstanding as to be almost boring.

Mum Jokemok (also known as Petchtai Wongkalamao) is a popular Thai television entertainer who provides the much-needed comedy, bouncing jokes off Tony Jaa's very straight straight-man. The least convincing novice monk or muay thai fighter imaginable, Jokemok performs slapstick routines that hark back to the Jackie Chan of the early 80s. The film sees his character gradually reform from an unsuccessful con-man to become the man his father thinks he is (although there is rather too much brooding on the roof overlooking Bangkok). Shame he dies before he gets a chance to return home.

Pumwaree Yodkamol does her best with a very limited part as the hard-boiled tomboy Muay Lek. A fresh talent, she is very natural in the role. In the original Thai version of the film she has a sub-plot of her own about her sister's drug problem, but this is missing from the international cut. All that remains is the opportunity for her to follow George around wailing about how he hasn't given her a share of their ill-gotten gains and how expensive college is. She doesn't even get to be the muscled hero's love interest: he's off to be a monk, so women are right out of the question.

Suchoa Pongvilai's mafia villain is impressively sinister. Surrounded by fawning females, he refuses to let a little thing like throat cancer stop him smoking, or a little man like Ting come between him and his profits. His gurgling threats are all the more sinister for being delivered in the artificial tones of his handheld voice box, making him sound like a Thai Darth Vader. He even gets to do a bit of fighting from his wheelchair, having at Ting with a hammer before dying in a particularly unpleasant way.

At this point, a special mention should be made of all the stuntmen who appear in the film as fodder for Tony Jaa's flying elbows. It must have hurt a great deal.

MARTIAL ARTS: *Ong-Bak* is a showcase for traditional Thai fighting. Few movies have featured muay thai as their central style, but this film is an unashamed celebration of it. Chang Cheh may have included muay thai in *Duel of Fists* and Jimmy Wang Yu experimented with it in the *Chinese Boxer*, but never has it been shown in its unadulterated form, performed by such a diligent student. As well as the formalised fighting in the ring, complete with rope-bound fists, the audience is treated to a wealth of moves never before seen on screen.

Jaa's mentor Phanna Rithikrai is credited with the fight choreography, and as the veteran of more than fifty action movies he knows what he is doing. Each sequence was painstakingly rehearsed, and the resulting effect is a smoothness that makes the action flow even if it does lack spontaneity. Rithikrai benefitted greatly from the budget of the film, which was far larger than he was used to, and the result is more polished. Jaa himself also had a great deal of input. The two travelled the country searching out masters of the ancient strain of muay boran, a more elegant variant of the brutal martial art, and resurrected some hundred moves that had long been discarded in the more popular form. 'Muay thai boran hadn't really been seen before in Thai film,' explains Jaa. 'It's an ancient form of muay thai that's used in wartime. It's a novelty for the audience to see.' Muay boran bears some resemblance to kung fu and is said to be the original fighting art of the Siamese warriors. Although it is more stylish than muay thai, it is no less vicious, proving that the Thais really do know a thing or two about using the body as an offensive weapon. In the underground fight club, Jaa faces off against opponents using a variety of fighting styles, and defeats them with ease. The message is clear: muay thai is the best, and deserves a prominent place in the genre.

The film is a vehicle for getting Tony Jaa into one fight after another, and from the first time he fells an irritating opponent with a single knee strike, it launches into an action reel showcasing the very best of muay thai. 'We just wanted people in Thailand to be able to see muay thai boxing and to see it as a part of our tradition and culture . . . to bring Thai culture and muay thai for the world to see,' says Jaa. Its direct approach and lightning feints give the style a unique character. The only disappointment is that none of Ting's opponents even comes close to Jaa's skill, or at least they are not allowed to demonstrate it, so the fights are too one-sided. Even the nemesis who beats him in the ring is seen to gain his strength from PCP or steroids rather than training and talent.

STUNTS AND SPECIAL EFFECTS: There is no CGI in the fight scenes. That's it. That's the reason why *Ong-Bak* is a must-see film for anyone who loves martial arts – it shows what can really be achieved with the human body. 'We wanted people to see that these were their real talents and real abilities,' says Jaa. And they manage to carry it off – the lack of wire-work doesn't prevent the action from flying, or Tony Jaa from running up walls. From the opening scenes, where men fall several stories out of a huge tree, the stunt work is immaculate, and the fighting gains a raw edge from the fact that the blows are really landing. No one slides or flies gracefully out of the way in slow-motion. They stand and take a pounding. This is partly because the team practised so hard together for so long, and mostly because they were prepared to do extreme things to their bodies in the name of film history. This attitude is reminiscent of the early days in Hong Kong, when stuntmen put themselves on the line and everyone involved could really do all the moves, before wires, CGI and insurance companies took over.

There are a number of classic action sequences, from the tree moment to the chase through the streets in which Tony Jaa cartwheels between panes of glass, vaults a car, does sliding splits under a truck and jack-knifes his body through a roll of barbed wire. The motorised chase is pure Thailand, taking place on tuk-tuks rather than in cars, and ends with some great explosions. The final fight in the cave gives Jaa a chance to demonstrate some less than traditional weapons, and the fine art of snapping leg bones (this moment is so stomach-turning, it has been removed from some edits). There are also moments of individual brilliance, such as Jaa's flying kick with legs ablaze, the splitting of a motorcycle helmet with his knee and of course that opening knee strike, which left cinema audiences in stunned silence.

DIRECTOR: With *Ong-Bak*, director Prachya Pinkaew decided to raise the profile of muay thai in the martial arts genre and thus bring added validity both to the Thai culture it stems from and the Thai film industry which should, by rights, be the conduit bringing it to the world. He has said that he always wanted to make a Thai action movie, and he got his chance when the martial arts maniac Phanom Yeerum (as Jaa was formerly known) pitched him the idea for a muay thai hero. So excited was he by the project that he left his habitual producer's chair to take over the directing reins for the first time in eight years.

After introducing the basic plot in the first 25 minutes, Pinkaew lets his action star have his head. His direction (and writing) is fast and fun, keeping the film bowling along and not bothering with unnecessary devices such as romance. He manages to strike a great balance between the dusty purity of rural village life and the hot, dark seediness of Bangkok.

PRODUCTION: Almost as though he cannot believe Jaa's abilities himself, director Pinkaew returns again and again to the slow motion re-runs of his craziest stunts, inviting the audience to share in his wide-eyed astonishment. This revisiting of action moments is straight out of the reels of *Project A*, but occurs far more often. Seeing each move from different angles in this way should be tedious, but they are all worth watching over and over again. Fast cuts and slow motion make up most of the rest of the camera effects, as well as an elliptical depiction of a poker game, shot in close-up.

The film is very atmospheric, with muted colours to emphasise the simplicity of country life, and gritty filth which graphically depicts the underside of Bangkok. Sweat glistens, smoke swirls and the whole thing practically stinks. An understated Thai soundtrack, largely orchestral with catchy percussion, doesn't distract from the action, and underscores the director's nationalistic leanings.

In the international cut, the handiwork of Luc Besson is obvious. No stranger to the genre, having directed Jet Li in *Kiss of the Dragon* and *Unleashed*, Besson has not interfered with the action, but he couldn't keep his hands off the story-line. In addition to cutting a sub-plot, he introduced a techno soundtrack that includes an incongruously large amount of French hip-hop for a Thai film.

TRIVIA: *Ong-Bak* is peppered with not-so-subliminal messages to Hollywood directors. In the tuk-tuk chase, the wall that one of the taxis crashes into is daubed with the message 'Hi Luc Besson we are waiting for you'. The French director took heed, buying the international distribution rights and re-editing the film for worldwide release. Steven Spielberg also gets a shout, with the invitation 'Hi Spielberg, let [sic] do it together' graffiti-ed on the wall of an alleyway. This was added to the Asian DVD release in post-production. Despite the realism of the stunts, some protection was used: when Jaa leaps from the truck to split open his opponent's motorcycle helmet, it is apparent that he is wearing kneepads.

THEMES: There is much that is new and fresh about *Ong-Bak*, not least Tony Jaa, but in many ways it is also a return to the simple brilliance of kick flicks from the 60s and 70s. This is reflected in its basic, textbook themes. The first muay thai sequence is a midnight training session, during which Ting names each of the deadly moves he performs with their esoteric titles, watched over by the (incredibly frail-looking) monk who has apparently taught him everything he knows. The only thing he still has to learn, the monk explains, is that muay thai is for control of the body and mind, not for killing people. Having waxed lyrical on the spiritual side of this brutal fighting art, he extracts a promise from Ting that he will not use it without just cause.

And a just cause is exactly what he finds. Ting is the knight-errant, using his special skills to defend Bangkok waitresses and save his village. Although not an outlaw, he is definitely an outsider in the big city, not least because he is the only righteous character in the entire place. Good battles evil, and evil has a heart as black as pitch and a set of accomplices straight out of the James Bond guide to really bad guys. The nationalistic theme is explored through Ting's outrage that Thais are destroying their own heritage for profit, selling their Buddhas to crass overseas collectors. Ting is an old-fashioned hero in the mould of Wong Fei Hung, never doubting his moral superiority and not bothering with the self-doubt made popular by Jimmy Wang Yu. Good and evil are also represented by the contrast between the pure joys of rural life and the corruption endemic in the city.

Betrayal gets a brief airing, as does filial duty, with George desperately trying to ignore his responsibility to his father back home. He is redeemed in the end, although he is never really presented as a villain, just a lost and confused ex-novice monk. With the real bad guys, the only solution is to split their skulls. Another genre box is ticked with the underground club brawls and the ring fighting. Forced to throw his fight, Ting gets his own back in the final scene. *Kickboxer*, anyone?

PLACE WITHIN THE GENRE: A welcome return to the purity of early action films, of which there has recently been something of a drought, brought on by too much wuxia, *Ong-Bak* could be the film that wins Tony Jaa the well-worn mantle of the next Bruce Lee. He has the hardened body and martial skills to carry it off. Whether he can match the dead icon's acting ability remains in doubt, however. The film itself is poised between the stern rigidity of Lee's films and the slapstick of Jackie Chan's.

Ironically, it may just give the kiss of death to the Hong Kong industry that produced these heroes, by doing the action better than anything that has come out of the home of kick flicks for years, up to and including *Kung Fu Hustle*. This is what Hong Kong movies were like before Hollywood's overpowering influence washed over them.

Ong-Bak eschews the sweeping grandeur of *Crouching Tiger, Hidden Dragon*, which gentrified the genre, and instead takes it back to its foundations. There is nothing genteel or epic about this film. It has the direct, old-school approach of *The Street Fighter*, and its plot also places *Ong-Bak* deep in the heartland of martial movies. The rural innocent abroad in the city mimics Bruce Lee's character in *Way of the Dragon*, while the opening of the cave battle draws on both *Project A* and *Enter the Dragon*.

This approach threatens to limit the appeal of the film to the movie-going public, but perhaps it doesn't care. It is aimed at a very specific demographic, and has even been described as 'martial arts porn'. If you're looking for beautiful landscapes and equally beautiful fight scenes, this is not the film for you. If you love watching people who are really good at being violent hit each other, you will watch it again and again. This film has the potential to raise the bar on what knowledgeable audiences look for in martial arts action, and do for muay thai what *Swordsman 2* did for wuxia, *Police Story* did for stunts and *The Killer* did for gun-fu.

A huge hit in its own country, the film has rewarded Prachya Pinkaew for his attempts to make a popular film about Thai culture. He has redressed the balance that previously hung heavily in favour of imported kung fu films, instead of supporting home-grown talent. *Ong-Bak* has been steadily gathering a fan base across the world, spearheaded by Luc Besson. Its reputation preceded it and ripped-off VCDs were circulating for two years before it finally got a UK cinema release. Muay thai is set to conquer the world, a refreshing blast of reality to combat an overdose of CGI.

Heroic Ones: Tony Jaa

- **AKA:** Tony Ja, Panom Yeerum.
- **Birth name:** Panom Worawit.
- **Nickname:** Jaa.
- **Not to be confused with:** Jean-Claude Van Damme. As if.
- **Martial style:** Muay thai. No stunt doubles, no special effects, no wires. It's all in the elbows and the knees.
- **Born:** 5 February 1976 in Surin Province, Thailand.
- **Biography:** The son of rice-farming elephant herders, Jaa – whose real name is Panom Yeerum, changed from his birth name Panom Worawit – grew up watching martial arts movies. After seeing the Thai film *Born to Fight*, he began to train under the film's director Panna Rithikrai, learning martial arts and stunt work. At university he majored in practically every fighting style from judo to tae kwon do, and his first film work was doubling for Robin Shou and James Remar in *Mortal Kombat: Annihilation* in 1997. He came to the attention of director Prachya Pinkaew, who wrote the part of Ting in *Ong-Bak* for him. Starring in this film, he changed his name for the second time, to Tony Jaa, in order to gain international recognition. And anyone who doesn't give due recognition to a man who can break open a motorcycle helmet with his elbow is either blind or mad.
- **Best kick flicks:** *Ong-Bak* (2003), *The Bodyguard* (2004), *Tom Yum Goong* (2005).
- **Trivia:** His main inspirations are Jackie Chan and Bruce Lee: it was watching their movies that encouraged him to become a stuntman. Jaa grew up with two elephants, on to whose backs he used to jump. As the elephants grew, so did his leap.
- **Where are they now:** Working on the sequel to *Ong-Bak*.

Summary

It would be impossible in a single chapter to convey the essence of martial cinema from the world outside Mainland China, Hong Kong and Hollywood: the genre is too huge and diverse. But these films offer a flavour of three very different cultures and the martial movies that have sprung from them. The samurai film is deeply rooted in the culture of Japan, and has as illustrious a history as Chinese wuxia. Within it, the *Zatôichi* series holds a very special place, combining grim death with a light-heartedness that makes the films appealing and accessible to Western audiences not raised with the history of samurai culture. The bloodletting is extreme enough to make up for the speed of the swordplay: from a martial arts point of view, it's all about aftermath. *Zatôichi the Outlaw* was my first introduction to Japanese bushido cinema, and he film, along with its bear-like hero, will always retain a special place in my DVD collection,

The only resemblance between *Zatôichi the Outlaw* and *Volcano High* is that it rains a lot in both. The live-wire Korean fantasy and its punk schoolkids could be from another planet, with its drawn-out battle scenes and lack of gushing blood. Seeing it in the cinema was like being slapped in the face with an electric eel, and it is a film I have kept returning to ever since. It is not a classic in the mould of *Fist of Fury*, nor will it be as enduringly popular as *Project A*. But, for no good reason other than its youthful exuberance, this is one of my top kick flicks.

When it comes to real martial arts, however, you're going to have to go a long way to outclass *Ong-Bak*. Say what you like about its lack of plot and wooden acting, it is impossible to argue with Tony Jaa's fighting ability. And after seeing the film, you wouldn't want to. Even with the multiple repeats of amazing stunts, this is one for the rewind button, with action that rates watching again and again.

Little Godfather from Hong Kong: The Small Screen

When charting the development of the martial arts film genre, it is impossible to ignore its brash, rebellious, lurid little brother: the trash television made up of martial arts soap operas and cult TV shows on which many martial movie stars cut their teeth. Epic themes, mythical stories and characters straight out of legend populate worlds in which rocks are made of foam and the scenery is painted onto canvas. Badly. These series are cheap, poorly translated, contain some painfully slow fighting and are fantastically addictive. Marginalised, ignored or ushered into another room like an embarrassing relative, the shows were the diet on which many of today's martial arts filmmakers were raised. The time has come to bring them out into the light.

Long-running television serials featuring martial heroes have been popular in the East since TV started to compete with cinema for the viewing audience, and many have also been exported overseas, dubbed and released on the small screen in the West. Before kick flicks became a worldwide phenomenon, outside China and Japan many fans' introduction to martial arts as entertainment came from comic books and television. Famous for their low budgets and indecipherable dialogue, extended Asian martial TV serials proved tremendously popular. Some of the best known and most affectionately remembered are those which came out of Japan in the 1970s, such as *The Water Margin* and *Monkey*. As kung fu movies began to build up a cult following in art-house cinemas, the flying wuxia swordsmen of China and samurai warriors of Japan were already being beamed into homes around the world.

Responding to the popularity of Asian imports, American studios began to include martial arts in their own serials, spearheaded by the emergence of Bruce Lee and his unique talents. The actor got his first big break playing a superhero's deadly sidekick in *The Green Hornet*, a character culled from the *Batman* TV series. Lee also co-created *Kung Fu*, which starred David Carradine as a Shaolin monk on the run in the Wild West. Mixing a genre that was new to American audiences with the established, familiar cowboy brand, the near-immortal serial proved extremely popular and helped to spark a wave of interest in Shaolin martial arts. Eventually even cartoon animals got in on the act, with the 80s comic book *Teenage Mutant Ninja Turtles* being turned into an animated series and later a film starring four oversized terrapins skilled in Japanese martial arts. Their sensei was a rat, yes. Although less popular in the West today than they were in the 70s and 80s, martial arts on the small screen are still huge in Asia, and have long provided a training ground for actors and audiences alike.

The Green Hornet

USA, 1966–67, 26 30-minute episodes

Production companies: 20th Century Fox Television,
Greenway Production
Directors: William Beaudine, Norman Foster, Robert L
Friend, Murray Golden, Darrel Hallenbeck, James Komack,
Leslie H Martinson, Larry Peerce, Allen Reisner, Seymour
Robbie, George Waggner
Martial arts: Bruce Lee
Executive producer: William Dozier
Producers: Richard Bluel, Stanley Shpetner
Written by: Ken Pettus, Arthur Weingarten
Characters created by: George W Trendle
Original music: Billy May

CAST: Van Williams (*Britt Reid/The Green Hornet*), Bruce Lee (*Kato*), Wende Wagner (*Lenore 'Casey' Case*), Lloyd Gough (*Mike Axford*), Walter Brooke (*District Attorney Frank P Scanlon*), William Dozier (*Narrator*)

Episodes
1. The Silent Gun
2. Give 'Em Enough Rope
3. Programmed for Death
4. Crime Wave
5. The Frog Is a Deadly Weapon
6. Eat, Drink, and Be Dead
7. Beautiful Dreamer (1)

 8. Beautiful Dreamer (2)
 9. The Ray Is for Killing
10. The Preying Mantis
11. The Hunters and the Hunted
12. Deadline for Death
13. The Secret of the Sally Bell
14. Freeway to Death
15. May the Best Man Lose
16. The Hornet and the Firefly
17. Seek, Stalk and Destroy
18. Corpse of the Year (1)
19. Corpse of the Year (2)
20. Ace in the Hole
21. Bad Bet on a 459-Silent
22. Trouble for Prince Charming
23. Alias The Scarf
24. Hornet Save Thyself
25. Invasion from Outer Space (1)
26. Invasion from Outer Space (2)

PLOT: 'Another challenge for the Green Hornet, his aide Kato, and their rolling arsenal, the Black Beauty. On police records a wanted criminal, Green Hornet is really Britt Reid, owner-publisher of the *Daily Sentinel*, his dual identity known only to his secretary and to the District Attorney. And now, to protect the rights and lives of decent citizens, rides the Green Hornet!'

Britt Reid, media mogul, has a secret identity! Apparently an upstanding businessman, by night (and sometimes by day) he dons a trilby and impenetrable mask and becomes the Green Hornet. Ably assisted by his valet and kung fu kicking sidekick Kato, he battles crime with his sting gun from the backseat of the Black Beauty, a customised car with green headlights. He is wanted by the police and only a trusted few know who he really is. He must avoid arrest despite continually showing up at crime scenes in his battle against local gangsters, crazed scientists and invaders who appear to be from outer space.

CASTING: Bruce Lee once said that he got the part of Kato because he was the only Asian actor they could find who could pronounce the name 'Britt Reid'. Whether or not this is the case, his inclusion ensured that this standard 60s superhero series, which ran for only one season and lost ratings throughout its run, has secured a place in martial arts legend. It was the vehicle that launched Lee in the US, and when a feature-length version was released in Hong Kong it was entitled *The Kato Show*, recognising that his character was the one audiences wanted to watch. People did not tune in to this programme to see Van Williams stun people with his poison gas gun. They did it for the chance to see Bruce Lee do his thing.

Bruce Lee made the character of Kato his own. In the original radio series, Reid's valet was Filipino. He drove the car, kept watch for the police and occasionally helped with the fighting. Clearly this was not the role Lee signed up for. The American-born actor tried to raise the role above that of the obedient Oriental aide, and increasingly pushed for the chance to show off his skills. In a crossover episode of the 60s *Batman* series in which Batman and Robin believe the Hornet's bad press and attempt to apprehend him and his sidekick, Kato and Robin fight. As it was his show, Robin was scripted to win the confrontation, but Bruce Lee refused to film the scene until it was re-written as a stalemate. No one would want to be beaten by the tights-wearing Boy Wonder, and no one would believe that Kato could lose to him. Unfortunately for his character development, Lee gets few lines and is largely left to talk with his feet. And act as chauffeur. Most of his dialogue consists of asking Britt Reid searching questions like what now, where next and whodunit?

Van Williams has the misfortune to play a leading role that is utterly eclipsed by his sidekick. He isn't helped by the Green Hornet mask, which instantly ages his clean-cut American features by about a decade. Although the Green Hornet gets to use his fists as well as his gun, he is grossly upstaged by his valet in every fight scene. Following *The Green Hornet*, Williams' career never really took off, languishing in a series of small TV roles. Both Williams and Lee argued for an expansion of the franchise into hour-long rather than half-hour episodes, to allow greater development of their characters outside their superhero personas, and it is a shame this never happened: it might have boosted Williams' career, and the world would have seen a lot more of Bruce Lee a lot sooner.

MARTIAL ARTS: If you're looking for a kung fu spectacular, then look elsewhere. The martial arts in this series are severely limited, with brief fight scenes and a restricted array of moves. The main problem is that as no one is a match for Lee, no one tries to be. There is little suspense invoked as he fells opponents with his trademark jumping side-thrusting kick or occasionally, for variety, a roundhouse. There are some chops too: it seems likely that Mike Myers' fighting style in *Austin Powers: International Man of Mystery* was entirely based on Kato in *The Green Hornet*. The plucky valet does have one original technique: he flicks hornet darts at his enemies. These tend to land beside them rather than in them, as a warning shot, but are still just about the most exciting thing he gets to do. Lee was clearly fond of the dart-throwing technique: it reappeared in *Enter the Dragon* as one of the special talents of secret agent Mei-Ling.

The best episode from a martial arts point of view, and also in terms of plot, is *The Preying Mantis*, in which a group of Chinese thugs are running a protection racket and generally giving kung fu a bad name. Kato is taken by surprise and dumped in a trash can by the leader, Lo Sing. He returns to seek his revenge, leading to the only real fight in the series. Lo Sing, a proponent of the Preying Mantis style of kung fu (and owner of the most alarming red bodysuit), succeeds in drawing Kato's blood, but naturally the good guy wins out in the end.

Although unique and exciting for its time, the fight scenes in *The Green Hornet* now look staid and slow. The action is tame, and it is all over much too fast. It is interesting primarily as an examination of how restricted the talents of Bruce Lee were by the role, and as a comparison to the high-intensity fighting that characterised his subsequent film career – which in turn serves as a measure of the lack of sophistication of US TV audiences compared with those in Hong Kong cinemas.

STUNTS AND SPECIAL EFFECTS: Although there are eight stuntmen listed among the crew of *The Green Hornet*, and Van Williams even had his own stunt double, you would be hard pressed to say what they were employed for. Generally speaking, the worst that happens to a character in any episode is ending up on intimate terms with the business end of Kato's fist. They then fall dramatically to the ground, groaning.

In the episode *Invasion From Outer Space (1)*, the heroes are zapped by some 'alien' lightning, emanating from the fingertips of a shapely, gold-clad visitor, apparently from another planet. Along with some smoke and the Black Beauty's miscellany of gadgets, this is the sum total of the special effects on display. The Green Hornet and his faithful valet don't even get 'Pow!' and 'Sock!' graphics when they pummel their enemies – although it could be argued that the series is the better for it.

DIRECTORS: Among the directors of *The Green Hornet* are some of the most prolific ever to have worked in American TV. Most of them are also dead. The curse of *The Green Hornet* strikes again! Of course, several of them would be fairly old by now in any case. William Beaudine, the king of cheap productions, developed the ability to edit on camera, meaning he only shot as much as he needed and never wasted his budget. Norman Foster was a B-movie director who had previously been very successful with the *Charlie Chan* and *Mr Moto* films. Bruce Lee must have come as quite a surprise after those stereotypical Asian characters. Robert L Friend and Murray Golden both had histories with series set in the Wild West, including *Rawhide* and *Bonanza*, which must have made them very comfortable with their Lone Ranger type hero. Darrel Hallenbeck, however, was more into the spy game, directing *The Man from U.N.C.L.E.* and *One of Our Spies Is Missing*. Leslie H Martinson had done the superhero thing before with *Batman* and continued in kind with *Wonderwoman*. George Waggner and Larry Peerce also worked on *Batman*. The only one with any other experience directing martial arts is Allen Reisner, who went on to oversee David Carradine in *Kung Fu*. Perhaps *The Green Hornet* gave him a taste for it.

PRODUCTION: Filmed at the 20th Century Fox Studios in Los Angeles, *The Green Hornet* has the claustrophobic, artificial feel that affects so many of the television productions from the era. Because of the age of the series, the surviving prints appear grainy, with a noticeable amount of dirt on them. The picture is also very dark, which makes it hard to tell what is happening in night shots. This causes something of a problem: because of the Green Hornet's subversive double identity, and the natural habitat of the villains he comes up against, much of the action takes place in the dark. Combined with the black suits, black car and dark masks, this makes following the action in many of the scenes something of a guessing game. Just as well the dialogue is so lacking in subtlety.

A DVD release of four episodes of the original TV series cobbled together into a feature film attempted to improve the quality of the image (and cash in on Bruce Lee's posthumous fame). It didn't succeed. The colours are still faded, and much of the action is blurred. The darkness does match the gritty tone of the plots, however, and adds a sense of film noir that has made the series collectable rather than laughable.

The theme tune for *The Green Hornet*, is, appropriately, an arrangement of Nikolai Rimsky-Korsakov's *The Flight of the Bumblebee*, performed by Al Hirt, which gives the production a classy note, as well as referencing the insect theme. The incidental music also has a droning edge to it, presumably to create the same effect. There are few sound effects, and most of the audio is concentrated on the dialogue. And Bruce Lee's animal screams.

TRIVIA: The Green Hornet was created by the writers of *The Lone Ranger*, and Britt Reid was said to be the horseback hero's great-grand-nephew. In the upcoming Hollywood film about the crime-fighting journalist, written by *Clerks* director Kevin Smith, this family connection is not mentioned because Miramax does not own the rights to the original character. Unusually for a disguised superhero, Kato does not have an alias, and the Green Hornet repeatedly calls him by his name when they are meant to be incognito. Lucky he wears that mask.

Black Beauty, the Green Hornet's enormously conspicuous car, is a customised Chrysler Imperial modelled by specialist car-customiser Dean Jefferies at a cost of $50,000. The Black Beauty features a TV camera that can see up to four miles ahead, front and rear rockets, smoke jets, brushes to disguise the signs of its passing and the ability to spread ice over the road. Pretty high-tech stuff. The curse of *The Green Hornet* cannot be discounted: of its five leading actors, only Van Williams remains alive.

THEMES: *The Green Hornet* was not pitched as a kung fu series, but Bruce Lee and his unique skills were the reason why it aroused contemporary interest, and explain its continuing survival as a cult classic. As a standard 'good guys fighting crime on the outside of the law' comic-book story, many parallels can be drawn between the series and the themes that run through the martial arts genre. Branded criminals, Green Hornet and Kato are the classic outsiders, the ronin or knights-errant of 60s American superhero pulp fiction. Misunderstood, they assist the police in their work, but must flee before the officers arrive lest they be arrested themselves. Their hidden identities are typical of the heroes of traditional wuxia (although there is no cross-dressing), as is their undisclosed motivation. The concept of heroes who are taken for villains when in fact they are on the side of righteous ideals is a basic version of the characterisations that run through Zhang Yimou's *Hero*.

Despite the central characters' intentionally ambiguous position in the fight between good and evil, the audience is left in no doubt about which side they are on. Nor is the theory ever advanced that crime can be made to pay. The bad guys are for the most part a series of undeveloped, nondescript thugs who troop through the episodes waiting to be defeated by the heroic pair. Painted with the blackest brush, they are more thoroughly evil than Tong Po in *Kickboxer*, and elicit no sympathy (or interest) from the viewer. There are no returning nemeses: each evildoer is dealt with and dispatched, never to return, having presumably learnt their lesson or been terminally dispatched.

Britt Reid's decision to fight crime comes, in part, from a sense of family duty. Entrusted with *The Daily Sentinel* by his father, he must run the Reid family business, while also continuing the traditions of the Lone Ranger, his swashbuckling (masked, misunderstood) relative. Although Reid is neither Kato's relative nor his teacher, he is the focus of his unswerving loyalty. Kato's primary role is to save his employer's neck, and this he does with little thought for his own. As well as loyalty, Kato gets to demonstrate that other great kick flick emotion, the desire for vengeance, when he takes his revenge on Lo Sing for jumping him from behind in a classic set-piece confrontation.

PLACE WITHIN THE GENRE: Based on a popular radio series that ran every week from 1936 to 1952 in 30-minute slots, it is surprising in some ways that *The Green Hornet* only lasted for one season on TV. Despite being fêted as hot property when it launched, it never went the distance. There are several possible reasons for this: the increased sophistication of an audience which needed more than simple plots in which good endlessly triumphs over evil; trying to fit enough action into half-hour episodes to retain viewer interest; a failure to develop the main characters. All of these factors led to plummeting ratings that dissuaded 20th Century Fox from making another series. Where they really missed a trick, however, was in not making more of Bruce Lee. He was the man who could have saved *The Green Hornet* and brought success to the studio. Instead he went to Hong Kong and made some of the most memorable kung fu films of all time. Nonetheless, *The Green Hornet* deserves its place in this book, and in the history of the martial genre, for introducing the Little Dragon to the viewing public.

Lee refused to be typecast in the role, or to be merely a supporting character. He played Kato as an intelligent, competent Asian who spoke American-English and didn't fit the stereotypes of 60s television. His portrayal of Kato as the thinking man's sidekick opened the way for more varied roles for Oriental actors, and probably assisted the acceptance of *Enter the Dragon* when it was released in 1973. Not that it needed much help.

The legend of *The Green Hornet* retains a place in popular culture today. It is being remade as a movie, and it can only be assumed that Kato will have more opportunity to strut his stuff in the twenty-first century. The series has been referenced in *Kill Bill Volume 1* (but then, what isn't?), *Dogma* and Jackie Chan's *The Tuxedo*. Perhaps the winged one's legacy will never die.

Heroic Ones: Tony Leung Chiu-Wai

- **AKA: Tony Leung, Leung Chiu Wai, Liang Chao Wei.**
- **Not to be confused with: Tony Leung Ka-Fai, obviously.**
- **Martial style: Shaggy-haired anti-hero with the ability to do incredibly vicious things with a sword.**
- **Born: 27 June 1962 in Hong Kong.**
- **Biography: One of the biggest stars in the Hong Kong movie business, Leung has not limited himself to martial arts films, but that doesn't mean he hasn't made some classics. Most recognisable to Western audiences as Broken**

Sword in Zhang Yimou's *Hero*, he began his career in far less auspicious – and less brooding – roles hosting children's shows and in comedy television series. On the advice of friend Stephen Chow, director of 2005's *Kung Fu Hustle*, he trained with TVB and made a name for himself in the company's TV projects. In 1992 he got his first real film break in John Woo's *Hard Boiled*, having played only supporting roles until that point. He went on to work with director Wong Kar Wai, starring in five of his films, including *Ashes of Time*, in which he plays a wandering knight afflicted by growing blindness. In recent years he has had lead roles in *Infernal Affairs* and *Hero*, two of the highest grossing Hong Kong films in history.

- Best kick flicks: *Butterfly and Sword* (1993), *The Magic Crane* (1993), *Hero* (2002).
- Trivia: In addition to acting, Leung has a flourishing musical career, and is one of the most popular recording artists in Asia. As well as serious roles, he has a penchant for B-movie farce. He has won a record four Best Actor Hong Kong Film Awards.
- Where are they now: Leung has most recently finished work on *Seoul Raiders*.

The Water Margin

(aka *Outlaws of the Marsh*)

Japan/China, 1976–78, 26 50-minute episodes

Production company: China Central Television
Producers: Kensuke Ishino, Toshio Kato, Kazuo Morikawa, Norio Kato
Based on the story by: Shi Naian
Written by: Shi Naian, Koki Yokoyama
Music editor: Masuru Satô
English adaptation: David Weir

CAST: Atsuo Nakamura (*Lin Chung*), Sanae Tsuchida (*Hu San-Niang*), Kei Sato (*Kao Chiu*), Isamu Nagato (*Lu Ta*), Toru Abe (*Tseng Lung*), Teruhiko Aoi (*Shi Shin*), Hajime Hana (*Wu Sung*), Akio Hasegawa (*Chang Shun*), Yûnosuke Itô (*Lo Chen Yen*), Yoshiro Kitahara (*Wang Lun*), Toshio Kurosawa (*Tai Sung*), Toshi Matsuo (*Hsiao Lan*), Takeshi bayashi (*Sung Chiang*), Hitoshi Omae (*Li Kwei*), Sachio Sakai (*Ko Shou*), Tetsuro Tamba (*General Hu*), Takahiro Tamura (*Chai Chin*),

Minori Terada (*Kung Sun Sheng, the Sky Dragon*), Ryohei Uchida (*Chu Wu*), Go Wakabayashi (*Kuang Sheng*)

Episodes
1. Nine Dozen Heroes and One Wicked Man
2. None Ever Escape Alive
3. Both at Last Will Reach the Sea
4. Ever Busy Are the Gods of Love
5. A Treasure of Gold and Jade
6. Bandits Who Steal Are Executed
7. How Easy to Die, How Hard to Live
8. A Man's Only Happiness
9. A Dutiful Son and the Love of a Brother
10. Escape Is Not Freedom
11. The Girl Who Loved the Flower Priest
12. Kao Chiu Loses His Heart
13. When Liang Shan Po Robbed the Poor
14. A Death for Love, More Deaths from Greed
15. The Bravest Tiger Is First Killed
16. Heaven Aims the Master's Arrow
17. The Traps of Love and Hate
18. A Foolish Sage Who Got Involved
19. Mourn the Slaughter of So Many
20. The War to End All Wars
21. Death of a Great Man
23. A Concubine's Dowry
24. Liang Shan Po and the Millionaire
25. Knight of the Long Sword
26. The Dynasty of Kao

PLOT: 'The ancient sages said: "Do not despise the snake for having no horns, for who is to say it will not become a dragon?" So may one just man become an army. Nearly 1,000 years ago in ancient China, at the time of the Sung Dynasty, there was a cruel and corrupt government. These men riding are outlaws, heroes who have been driven to live in the water margins of Liang Shan Po, far to the south of the capital city. Each fights tyranny with a price on his head, in a world very different from our own. The story starts in legend even then, for our heroes, it was said, were perhaps the souls reborn of other, earlier knights.'

Based on the Chinese literary epic of the same name, *The Water Margin* tells the tale of nine dozen wandering knights in ancient China, unjustly outlawed by the Empire, who fight for the rights of the people against a corrupt government. Kao Chiu, the weak Emperor's tyrannical favourite, visits a monastery, demanding tribute. Seeing a barred door, he forces his way inside – much to the horror of the Abbot, who tells of a legend in which the souls of 108 rebels were sealed in a stone tablet and buried in the temple. Laughing off such superstition, Kao Chiu opens the chamber and is assailed by the trapped souls, which fly off into the world to inhabit new bodies and return as valiant heroes. He's going to regret doing that.

Every episode tells the story of how each of the nine dozen heroes is forced into the water margins of Liang Shan Po by the evil machinations of Kao Chiu, taking up outlawry in the Robin Hood mould and violently opposing the twisted official and his bumbling army. In the marshes they form a steadily growing force against Kao. Swordfights, subterfuge, multiple sub-plots and a healthy dose of 'ancient' Chinese philosophy follow, as the main characters are developed, brought together, and finally succeed in overthrowing their nemesis.

CASTING: One of the strangest things about the cast is that, despite playing heroes from ancient China, they are for the most part Japanese. The series was released in Mandarin, so there was either some very dubious dubbing or some extremely dubious accents in the original version.

First among the heroes is the swordsman Lin Chung, played by Atsuo Nakamura. His attitude throughout the series is one of suffering, and he rarely has the chance to crack a smile. Unpopular with Kao Chiu for refusing to let him sleep with his wife, Lin Chung was an imperial soldier before he was set up by Kao and imprisoned. Only when he realises that there is no justice to be found in the world does he escape from prison and start searching for his wife. Nakamura spends most of his time looking noble and pained, and refusing to lead the bandits. He is, however, the driving force in the series, the Robin Hood figure who puts his own life on the line to save the people. He also embodies the cult of *The Water Margin*: Nakamura's face has become the enduring symbol of the series, and he is the focal character.

His unfortunate wife, Hsiao Lan, played by Yoshiyo Matsuo, is raped by Kao and as a result keeps trying to kill herself. She succeeds just as Lin Chung finds her, early in the series, thus truncating her role in the show. Unusually for the wuxia tradition, of which *The Water Margin* is very much a part, this leading female character is weak, defenceless and spends a lot of time unnecessarily falling over. To her credit, she refuses to abandon her husband when he tries to divorce her (to save her life, naturally: he is the ever-noble Lin Chung, after all), fighting to have him freed through the courts and then travelling on foot through the wastes of China to find him. Matsuo is well cast as the wide-eyed wife who is constantly surprised by how evil the world is, although she overdoes her death scene just a touch.

A much stronger female character is the warrior Hu San-Niang. Kao also tries to rape her, but soon comes to regret it. Although bedecked in an unfortunate turban, Sanae Tsuchida never loses her pluck, tossing her head and laughing in the face of death like a Japanese Errol Flynn. Armed with matching curved short swords, she flings herself at her opponents, grinning with glee. Her character's only weak point is her love for the too-serious Lin Chung. The actor's only weak point is her inability to ride very well. As a martial arts star, she is a worthy small-screen successor to Cheng Pei-Pei.

On the side of evil, Kei Sato is fabulous as the emaciated, leering, rapacious Kao Chiu. Like an Asian portrait of Dorian Grey, he becomes more twisted and grotesque with every evil deed he performs. Starting as a small-time bully, he ends up with designs on the invisible Emperor's imperial throne. Sato takes on the role with gusto, lecherously drooling over the women and throwing bones to his fawning lackeys, while plotting the downfall of every upstanding citizen in the country.

The casting of Isamu Nagato as Lu Ta, the fake Flower Priest, provides comic relief and fulfils the Friar Tuck role. Disguised as a monk, he is anything but holy, an ex-soldier on the run for accidentally killing an extortionist, with an unapologetic taste for wine and women. Helping Lin Chung escape, he falls in with a horde of bandits who are also friends of the righteous outlaw and have sworn to help the Liang Shan Po outlaws. These include Shih Chin, the Tattooed Dragon. Once a nobleman, he had to flee after protecting Lin Chung and now rides with the rebels, although his delicate sensibilities are often at odds with their coarse ways. Teruhiko Aoi does a fine turn as the constantly offended swordsman, ripping his shirt off, Bruce Lee-style, every time he fights. It is a shame that he doesn't have the Chinese actor's physique.

The bandit leader, Chu Wu, played by Ryohei Uchida, is a Genghis Khan figure who fights first and asks questions later. He also has a great moustache. Other allies include Wu Sung, the Tiger Hunter, confusingly clad in leopard skin, who likes a drink and prefers not to think. Actor Hajime Huna competes with Isamu Nagato for the greatest slapstick performance of the series.

Toshio Kurosawa, who plays Tai Sung, and Tetsuro Tamba as General Hu are notable for their presence in the series, in which they take on completely different characters from those they played in Chang Cheh's film of *The Water Margin*, made just four years before the TV show.

MARTIAL ARTS: One of the reasons why *The Water Margin* is such a great addition to the martial arts genre is that each of its characters is defined by their fighting style. Just as they have differing personality traits, so they fight with different weapons and techniques, showcasing many of the classic Chinese martial arts. If the actors do not quite have the talent to match their legendary roles, and clever editing is used to disguise the lack of convincing combat, this is forgivable in the face of such a heroic attempt to arm each outlaw with a unique, authentic skill-set.

In doing so, the makers of the series stay true to the original text of the Chinese literary classic *The Water Margin*, which describes in detail how the heroes use various weapons, forms, free-hand techniques and overall battle strategies to defeat their enemies. Many of the legendary literary outlaws have nicknames relating to their special skills, such as Zhu Wu the Miraculous Strategist, Kuang Sheng the Big Sword and Hsu Ning the Spear Expert. The book itself is an important work partly because it records the use of traditional weapons and the training patterns employed to learn them. In Shandong Province, where the story is set, traditional wushu styles are practised whose history can be traced back to the Sung Dynasty described in *The Water Margin*.

Lin Chung is the master of the sword, matched in skill by few people in the country. Like Zatôichi, he sometimes uses a cane sword concealed in his walking stick – an oddly Japanese weapon for a Chinese hero. He is no slouch with a staff either. When he fights Yang Chih, another great swordsman, the pair face-off for two days and two nights, unmoving, waiting for an opportunity to strike. 'Only great masters know when they are evenly matched.' It is a device used by Zhang Yimou in *Hero* when Sky and Nameless fight their mental battle, and when Yang Chih finally strikes behind the cover of a dust storm it is already decided that Lin Chung will triumph.

Hu San Niang fights with damask blades, matched, lightweight, curved swords that are her one concession to femininity. Wu Sung hunts tigers with his bare hands, and has such strength that few men can stand against him in hand-to-hand combat. He carries a broadsword slung on his back, but rarely bothers to draw it, preferring to use his fists.

Yang Chih, Shih Chin and Chu Wu are all swordsmen, but from very different schools. The bandit king fights with a broadsword, swinging its mighty weight with all his strength. Shih Chin has a nobleman's straight sword while Yang Chih's is almost a samurai katana.

Tai Sung's special power is to be able to run faster than an arrow, striding across the land with lesser men stumbling in his wake. He rarely needs to fight, but when he does he uses forearm guards fitted with special blades to block and slash. The leader of the Liang Shan Po outlaws, Wang Lun, is a noble scholar who commands with philosophy, not with force.

STUNTS AND SPECIAL EFFECTS: The effects in *The Water Margin* are fairly crude and mainly consist of extreme editing techniques, used to suggest that the protagonists are endowed with superpowers. When Lin Chung leaps, he is shot in close-up from below, with no point of reference, and the shot is replayed several times to give the impression that he has jumped enormously high and is taking a really long time to come back to earth. Similarly, when Tai Sung demonstrates his faster-than-an-arrow running style, actor Toshio Kurosawa is seen taking ridiculously long strides across the countryside before the action cuts to him standing somewhere completely different.

When the souls of the nine dozen warriors are released by Kao Chiu, they are represented by fireworks being let off in the pit from which they escape, swirling up around the tyrant's head. Overall, though, effects are kept to a minimum, reminding the viewer that these heroes, though possessed of legendary skills, are still human. This is fitting for characters based, albeit very loosely, on historical figures.

PRODUCTION: On the surface *The Water Margin* is a sumptuous production, with a large cast of extras, custom-built sets, varied locations and impressive 'period' costumes (although it is unlikely that in ancient China even warrior women wore hotpants like those modelled by Hu San-Niang's sister). Unlike many serials, the characters are able to change their wardrobes throughout rather than remaining in the same set of clothes, although as outlaws it would be understandable if they had trouble getting to the tailor. From Kao Chiu's sumptuous robes of office to Wu Sung's mangy orange 'tiger' fur, each part is completed by its costume.

The action takes place in temples, on rivers, in the marsh and on barren mountainsides. The main let-down is the use of background shots of 'Chinese' scenery, which are clearly painted on to screens. The moon is a little dodgy as well, appearing as a perfect crescent of bright light outside a prison window, or flashing on and off above the battle between Lin Chung and Yang Chih. The fake moon is made up for, however, by plenty of authentic dust and dirt. The colours of the film are still excellent after 30 years, imperial yellow and blood red showing bright and vibrant.

Although it is usually preferable to watch the original language, subtitled versions of Asian martial arts films, in the case of *The Water Margin* the English language release is often all that is available to Western audiences. Unlike many dubbing attempts, is not a trial for the viewer, as David Weir's excellent adaptation is well crafted, almost perfectly lip-synched to the actors' speech. Although this creates some odd cadences and pauses at times, the effect adds to the entertainment, and the fake Oriental accents produced by Michael McClain, Miriam Margolyes *et al.* are not overly offensive. Burt Kwouk is almost iconic as the narrator on the English dub, and is probably responsible for every bad impersonation of an ancient sage spouting Chinese philosophy ever made.

TRIVIA: There are two versions of the original text of *The Water Margin*, one containing 70 chapters and one 120. The first 69 chapters are essentially identical, but in the shorter version the final chapter has the outlaws accepting an amnesty and giving up their bandit lifestyles. In the longer version they continue the fight for a further 50 chapters, and their ending is less happy. In the TV series, of course, the heroes succeed in overthrowing the evil Kao Chiu. Hurrah!

THEMES: Based as it is on an ancient Chinese text, the televised version of *The Water Margin* stays firmly within the traditions of Chinese wuxia. The action is set in the time of a weak and corrupt dynasty, where only those outside the law choose to fight for what is right, as the officials bleed the land dry for their own gain. There is an element of social comment in the series, as the landlords send gifts to Kao Chiu to ensure their personal advancement, and leave the peasants to starve.

Weaving historical figures into fictional plots is a common device in the genre. The North Sung Dynasty of the thirteenth century declined due to corruption and decadence (although not quite the 1,000 years ago that the series' introduction claims). There are traces in historical records of outlaws who challenged imperial authority and died under the executioner's blade for their rebellion: in the Sung Dynasty history, an account survives of a popular rebellion in the Liang Shan Po area of Shandong Province, the region where the wushu of *The Water Margin* is still practised.

Although it has a basis in history, there are minor fantasy elements in the show, creating a parallel with the mystical jianghu of the early wuxia pian. In the original text, 36 of the heroes are heavenly spirits, laying the foundations for an undeniably mythical element. The complex story recounts the trials of each hero, the majority of whom are first introduced as upright citizens, only later forced into rebellion, twisting multiple characters and sub-stories into the plot in the manner of an extended wuxia.

The usual suspects that populate the wuxia pian are also present in *The Water Margin*, such as the female warrior, disguised this time not as a boy but as a girl – a pretty gift sent to Kao Chiu that conceals a deadly trap. This theme is less well developed than in the early martial chivalry films, however: there is only one consistently strong female role – all the others either die or disappear in fairly short order – and she is prevented from joining the outlaws at Liang Shan Po because of her gender. Fully aware that she lives in a far from equal world, Hu San-Niang gazes from the window of her jail and sighs, 'Oh, to live in a world where a woman can be as free as a man!' She spends much of her time fighting off men intent on ravishing her, but at least she succeeds, which is more than can be said for most of the other female characters, who are routinely drugged, raped and killed.

The solitary figure of Lin Chung shares many of the attributes of the lone warriors of Chang Cheh's gung-fu pian. Disillusioned with the world, he has come to accept that killing is the only answer and travels through his homeland isolated from his fellows, trying to right injustice. Even the outlaws who call him brother are kept distant from Lin Chung, who suffers alone and refuses to endanger others because of their association with him.

No martial arts production is complete without a few laughs to grease the action, and typical comic relief is provided by the bumbling exploits of Wu Sung and Lu Ta. The womanising monk and the simple tiger hunter have the best of intentions but always seem to end up causing more trouble than they solve. They are solid companions in a fight, however, and no one can doubt their motives.

In addition to lust and lechery, romance also plays its part, with Hsiao Lan walking across China to find her husband, who for his part has attempted to divorce her in order to save her pain. Rather than join the outlaws at Liang Shan Po, Lin Chung continues to look for her, while she makes the ultimate sacrifice when she kills herself to save her husband. The course of true love never seems to run smooth. Shih Chin manages to get his sweetheart killed by coming to rescue her when she is kidnapped by soldiers, and Hu San-Niang spends all the time when she is not fighting swooning with unrequited affection for the enigmatic (and conveniently widowed) Lin Chung.

The spiritual sides of martial arts and Chinese society are explored to some extent. The leader of the outlaws, Wang Lun, is an intellectual, not a warrior, and Lin Chung prefers to reason rather than fight. The opening narrative on the possible development of the snake into a dragon introduces a pattern of pseudo-Confucian philosophising, while the themes of morality and anarchy run throughout each episode.

PLACE WITHIN THE GENRE: The tales of the Outlaws of the Marsh, as well as making up a classic of Chinese literature, are some of the most retold stories in martial arts film and television. The original text contains enough excitement, heroes, villains and, of course, fighting to provide material for myriad productions. The outlaws' popularity is reflected in the 1972 film *The Water Margin*, directed by Chang Cheh for Shaw Brothers, and the 1996 remake of the TV version. This had higher production values but lost the essence of the epic struggles of the outlaws of Liang Shan Po, overlooking several of the key characters and missing central details.

Chang's film was one of the most expensive ever made by Shaw Brothers, with a star-studded cast and fantastic sets. In telling an epic tale, the director wanted to make an epic film. The martial arts are superior to those in the later series, choreographed by Lau Kar-Wing and Chan Chuen and adapted directly from descriptions in the original text. *The Water Margin* ideally suited Chang's style of heroic bloodshed, and the success of the film may have contributed to the decision of China Central Television to make a series out of the lives of the Outlaws of the Marsh.

Although less true to the book than some of the other interpretations, the 1976 series managed to make the legendary characters more human by following them through their trials and battles over the course of 26 episodes. The series follows in the traditions of Chinese wuxia pian, while introducing elements of Japanese swordplay films. Its release in a well-dubbed version in the West gained it a cult following, allowing the tales of the 108 heroes to go beyond the realm of Chinese folklore.

Heroic Ones: Tony Leung Ka-Fai

- **AKA: Tony Leung Kar-Fai, Tony Ka Fai Leung, Tony Leung, Kar Fai Leung, Leung Ga Fai, Liang Gu Hui.**
- **Not to be confused with: Tony Leung Chiu-Wai, naturally.**

- Martial style: Trained as an actor rather than a fighter, Leung gives a creditable performance with both the jian straight sword in *New Dragon Gate Inn* and the less traditional 1920s pistol in *Gunmen*.
- Born: 1 February 1958 in Hong Kong.
- Biography: Raised in Hong Kong, after leaving college Leung attended a training course for actors at Shaw Brothers TVB Acting School. He never completed the programme, however, dropping out after nine months due to lack of funds and the need to start earning a living. In 1984 director Lee Hang-Sheng, who conveniently happened to be the father of his then girlfriend, cast him as the lead in his film *The Burning of the Imperial Palace*. Leung walked away with the first ever Hong Kong Film Award for Best Actor, and his success was assured. More of a straight actor than a martial arts performer, Leung has nonetheless appeared in several classic kick flicks, such as the almost comedic *Eagle Shooting Heroes*.
- Best kick flicks: *New Dragon Gate Inn* (1992), *All Men Are Brothers: Blood of the Leopard* (1993).
- Trivia: Leung is the proud father of twin daughters.
- Where are they now: Just completed filming *Election*.

Monkey

(aka *Saiyûki*, *Monkey Magic*)

Japan, 1978–80, two series, 52 54-minute episodes

Production companies: Nippon [Nihon] Television, Kokusai Hoei
Directors: Toshi Aoki, Jun Fukuda, Kazuo Ikehiro, Yusuke Watanabe, Daisuke Yamazaki
Producers: Teisho Arikawa, Tsuneo Hayakawa, Yoji Katori, Ken Kumagaya, Kazuo Morikawa, Tadahiro Nagatomi, Muneo Yamada
Screenplay by: Motomu Furuta, Hiroichi Fuse, Hirokazu Fuse, James Miki, Moto Nagai, Yooichi Onaka, Eizaburo Shiba, Yu Tagami, Kei Tasaka, Mutsuo Yamashita
Based on the novel by: Wu Ch'eng-En
Cinematographer: Yukio Yada
Music: Godiego, Micky Yoshino

CAST: Masaaki Sakai (*Monkey/Sun Wu-Kong*), Masako Natsume (*Tripitaka/Xuanzang Sanzang*), Toshiyuki Nishida

(*Pigsy/Zhu Ba-Jie, season one*), Tonpei Hidari (*Pigsy/Zhu Ba-Jie, season two*), Shirô Kishibe (*Sandy/Sha Wu-Jing*), Mieko Takamine (*Buddha*), Shunji Fujimura (*Yu-Lung, season two*)

Episodes
Season one
1. Monkey Goes Wild About Heaven
2. Monkey Turns Nursemaid
3. The Great Journey Begins
4. Monkey Swallows the Universe
5. The Power of Youth
6. Even Monsters Can Be People
7. The Beginning of Wisdom
8. Pigsy Woos a Widow
9. What Monkey Calls the Dog-Woman
10. Pigsy's in the Well
11. The Difference Between Night and Day
12. Pearls Before Swine
13. The Minx and the Slug
14. Catfish, Saint and the Shape-Changer
15. Monkey Meets the Demon Digger
16. The Most Monstrous Monster
17. Truth and the Grey Gloves Devil
18. Land for the Locusts
19. The Vampire Master
20. Outrageous Coincidences
21. Pigsy, King and God
22. Village of the Undead
23. Two Little Blessings
24. The Fires of Jealousy
25. The Country of Nightmares
26. The End of the Way

Season two
27. Pigsy's Ten Thousand Ladies
28. The Dogs of Death
29. You Win Some, You Lose Some
30. Pigsy Learns a Lesson
31. The Land with Two Suns
32. The House of the Evil Spirit
33. Am I Dreaming?

PLOT: 'In the worlds before Monkey, primal chaos reigned. Heaven sought order, but the phoenix can fly only when its feathers are grown. The four worlds formed again and yet again, as endless aeons wheeled and passed. Time and the pure essences of heaven, the moisture of the Earth, the powers of the sun and moon all worked upon a certain rock, old as creation. And it became magically fertile. That first egg was named Thought. Tathagata Buddha, the Father Buddha, said, "With our thoughts, we make the world." Elemental forces caused the egg to hatch. From it came a stone monkey. The nature of Monkey was – irrepressible!'

To the consternation of the high host in Heaven, the King of the Monkeys has gained intelligence, learned some magic and is referring to himself as the Great Sage, Equal of Heaven. They invite Monkey to Heaven to put him in his place, but he runs amok, eating the Peaches of Immortality, which only ripen once every 9,000 years, and continually challenging the celestial beings to fight. His antics cause two angels, both Marshals of the Heavenly Army, to be cast down to earth and there take on the forms of a water demon and a pig monster. Monkey himself is trapped beneath a mountain by Buddha, and left for 500 years to learn the art of patience.

To save the souls of mankind, Buddha creates the Great Scriptures and places them in a mountain temple in India. A holy mortal must journey from China to fetch them, thus helping to save mankind. The boy-monk Xuanzang Sanzang is chosen after he reveals his extreme piety by praying for the souls of his father's murderers, and is renamed Tripitaka. To help him on his way, he is assigned a rag-tag bunch of companions: the Monkey King, whom he frees from the mountain; Sandy, the water demon; greedy Pigsy, the pig demon; and Yu-Lung, the wicked dragon, who eats Tripitaka's horse and is forced to assume equine form and take its place. The companions set off on their journey to the West, 108,000 leagues, on which they encounter opposition from various devils who do not want mankind to be saved, and get into lots of fights.

CASTING: The son of a comedian, Masaaki Sakai was born to play the cheeky, irreverent Monkey, most troublesome of immortals. He made his first screen appearance at the age of six, and as a teenager joined the Japanese rock group The Spiders. He got the part in *Monkey* having made a number of comedies for Toho Studios and gained a reputation as a genius of slapstick. No martial artist, Sakai instead uses his acrobatic skills to make up for lack of training, and taught himself the basic kung fu moves he employs in the series. Short, with an enormous grin, even in dubbed versions of the series his physical acting portrays a childish petulance and exuberance that make him appear more monkey than man.

In the fine tradition of the martial arts genre, the main (human) male role is actually a woman. Or at least he is played by one. Masako Natsume became an icon in Japan after portraying the boy priest Tripitaka. Unfortunately, she also became an icon because she was very attractive and doesn't look anything like a boy. Everyone dutifully ignores this, of course, and it is never alluded to by the other characters.

Long-faced Shirô Kishibe is suitably fishy as the wet water demon Sandy, who prefers philosophising to fighting. Like Masaaki Sakai, he was a member of a formative Japanese rock band, The Tigers, and featured in a number of Toho comedies.

Although appearing to be the straight man, he has a wicked sense of the ridiculous and in *Monkey* spends most of his time insulting Pigsy in imaginative ways.

That worthy is played by two different actors over the course of the pilgrims' journey to the West. The first, Toshiyuki Nishida, dons the pointy plastic ears to portray a lustful, greedy character, ruled by his desires for women and food. He once won a prize for 'best dresser', but it certainly wasn't for the pom-pommed beret he sports in *Monkey*. The second Pigsy, Tonpei Hidari, brings a greater sense of the ridiculous to the part, making the pig monster a more cuddly, comic character. Bizarrely, he once played a Japanese version of Columbo.

MARTIAL ARTS: Monkey loves to fight, and repeatedly says so. He fights with his hands – pretty effectively too – using basic kung fu techniques until he forces the Dragon King of the Western Ocean to give him the magic wishing staff, which can shrink or expand to any size. Although it doesn't appear to have any special powers beyond that of a normal staff, apart from being devastating in the hands of the Monkey King, it can be conveniently stored behind his ear.

The other characters are assigned their own weapons too. Pigsy fights with the over-long muckraker allegedly forged for him by the philosopher Lao Tzu, the father of Taoism, which is harder than iron (but not Monkey's head). Sandy carries a chan, or monk's spade, the weapon immortalised by Gordon Liu in *36th Chamber of Shaolin*, which he wields with intent, if little skill.

Although a healthy dose of magic is mixed into the series, the actual combat tends to take place on a plane of relative reality. Stick and sword fighting are the order of the day, and our heroes usually get the best of their foes. Monkey shows his versatility by using everything from a broadsword to a skirt, pretending to be a girl and kicking Pigsy in the face after flashing his ankles.

STUNTS AND SPECIAL EFFECTS: The special effects in the fight scenes come straight out of *The Water Margin*, with the classic 'shot from below to make it look as if people are jumping really high' technique. The majority of special effects look utterly ridiculous by modern standards, though for its time *Monkey* was a big-budget production. Monkey himself flies around on a pink cloud, which is clearly a cartoon when it is up in the sky and badly superimposed when it is down on the ground. It looks a lot like candyfloss.

Another notable superimposition, which screams 'blue screen', is created when Monkey stands on Buddha's hand. Monkey's expanding staff is drawn rather than filmed, although some of his magic effects are better done, such as the creation of multiple Monkeys with mirrors, which looks as if it came straight out of *Enter the Dragon*. When volcanoes explode and rivers rise, they are clearly plasticine models. The dragon Yu-Lung is cute but very plastic, while the skulls on Sandy's necklace have a disconcerting habit of floating.

PRODUCTION: The locations used in *Monkey* are ambitious, drawn from north-west China and inner Mongolia, but as often as not any dusty desert would have done. The Forbidden Palace makes an appearance, but as there are no people present, and the aspect doesn't change, the suspicion has to be that a photograph is being displayed on screen. The rest of the action is shot in Japan – in a Tokyo studio, on the foothills of Mount Fuji and in the Yushima Confucian temple at the centre of the capital.

One of the key production techniques is the seemingly random insertion of modern references and anachronisms in the series, somewhat out of place even in mythical China. Disco music floods the sound track and vampires complete with opera-capes stalk across the screen. Mass appeal is the name of the game, and the only traditional Chinese influence appears to be on the characters' costumes and facial hair. At one point a set of machine guns emerges from Monkey's cloud. Most of the demons seem to come straight out of Japanese kabuki or opera styles rather than Chinese mythology, the result of a Japanese studio producing a Chinese classic, no doubt. They did somewhat better with *The Water Margin*.

When Nippon Television commissioned the series to celebrate its 25th anniversary, it did so partly on the understanding that the BBC would buy the series for UK television, as it had with *The Water Margin*. Similarly an English language version of *Monkey*, adapted by David Weir, was released. This is as well done as its predecessor, with excellent lip-synching, and some classic 'translations' and British colloquialisms, including the moment when Monkey tells Pigsy he is going to turn him into a pork pie. The only flaw in this version of the soundtrack is that the Oriental accents are utterly over the top. This has added to the programme's cult appeal, but it compares poorly with *The Water Margin*.

TRIVIA: *Monkey* was never actually called *Monkey Magic*: this was the title of the theme song, which proved to be the most memorable part of the production other than Monkey's sideburns. The song is sung entirely in English, even in the Japanese version of the series, and in 1980 the BBC released it as a single. When *Monkey* was shown in South Africa, it was dubbed into Xhosa. Although Masako Natsume died in 1985 before fully realising her potential as an actress, she is still a poster girl in Japan.

THEMES: A hearty helping of Chinese cod philosophy permeates the series, which detracts somewhat from the serious Buddhist message that it attempts to impart. Monkey apparently gained his powers through achieving 'partial' enlightenment, and the principles of the belief system are apparent throughout: Pigsy is punished for his lust and greed, Monkey for his brash impatience and Sandy for his lack of thoughtfulness. Charity, courage and honesty are lauded, while Tripitaka constantly preaches against violence, to the point of apathy, insisting that his companions do not fight and sounding a lot like Wong Fei Hung in *Once Upon a Time in China*. Luckily for the sake of the action, they are usually forced to ignore him.

Double identities are rife, as is the habit of gender bending. Deciding that a feminine approach is needed, Buddha appears to Monkey as a woman, causing him to exclaim (in the English version at least), 'I always thought you was a fella!' Monkey, who can turn himself into whatever he wants, frequently impersonates women. At one point he also turns Tripitaka into a girl, creating the unlikely scenario of a girl playing a boy playing a girl. The goddess of compassion, Kwan-yin, decides to get in on the act as well, and confuses everyone by turning up as a man.

The story is based firmly in Chinese legend, if not quite history, being drawn from the novel *Record of a Journey to the West* (sometimes known simply as *Journey to the West*) by Wu Ch'eng-en, written in the sixteenth century. This in turn is based on the semi-mythical journey of the priest Xuanzang, or Tripitaka. The story of Tripitaka and the irrepressible Monkey King is as well known in Japan and China as that of King Arthur in the West. Tripitaka is the holy innocent, wandering blind in the world.

Magic plays as large a part as Buddhism; mystical powers are taken for granted and Tripitaka controls Monkey through the 'headache sutra', which tightens a gold fillet around his temples every time he is disobedient. Being a polite monk, Tripitaka does at least apologise for putting it there. Monkey himself can pluck a hair from his chest and turn it into an army of replicas. And he's immortal.

Comedy is a staple of *Monkey*, as it is of many other entries in the genre. Pigsy and Monkey have the lion's share of the japes, but everyone else gets to join in at some point, with Tripitaka commenting 'It's an improvement' when Monkey transforms into a mouse. The classiest moment has to be when Monkey realises he has answered nature's call against Buddha's fingers.

The plot revolves around a quest, in the tradition of many martial arts productions, although in this case it is not for revenge but for knowledge. The characters never reach their destination and the second series finishes with them still on their journey to the west. This may, however, be due to NTV's plan to make a third series rather than a comment on the futility of human endeavour or the fact that these stories rarely have a happy ending.

PLACE WITHIN THE GENRE: More memorable even than *The Water Margin*, *Monkey* is a cult classic in the countries where it has been shown. In south-east Asia at least, this is partly due to the familiarity of the subject matter and the affection in which the Monkey King is held. The story works on so many levels, from action-adventure to spiritual insight, that it appeals to every generation. There have been many adaptations of Wu Ch'eng-en's text, which is regarded as one of the four greatest works of Chinese literature, alongside *Dream of the Red Chamber*, *Romance of the Three Kingdoms*, and *The Water Margin*. The most famous screen versions of the story are 1959's *Son Go Kû*, the 1960 animated classic *Saiyu-ki* and the TV series *Chai Tin Dai Sing Suen Ng Hung* from 2001. In 1994, NTV produced another version of the series to mark its 40th anniversary. It was hailed as a special effects masterpiece but lacked the appeal of the earlier series and was cancelled after one season.

Monkey is a series cast in the traditions of *The Samurai* and *The Water Margin*, with many of the same production techniques. Like the latter, it is a Japanese show based on a Chinese tradition, and as such has influences both from Chinese wuxia pian and Japanese swordsman classics. With its bolts of lightning and flying clouds, it is definitely in the fantasy mould, rather than following in the gory footsteps of the heroic bloodshed films.

Summary

Although they are not martial arts films themselves, it is easy to see the exchange of influences and ideas between these series and the movies in that genre. And although they often lack the budgets and production values of their big-screen counterparts, they have the advantage of being far longer and so able to cover their epic subject matter in greater detail, developing characters and rendering literary classics in more depth. In some ways they can be seen as a reflection in miniature of how the genre developed.

The Green Hornet is of interest to the martial arts fan only as the vehicle in which Bruce Lee found adult fame. It does, however, bear some interesting portents of how martial arts would come to be depicted by Hollywood and the West. Kato's skills are superior to any other fighter's, presaging a time when no modern hero or villain would be without an arsenal of Asian martial moves at their disposal, representing the ultimate battle skills.

The Water Margin and *Monkey* are two sides of the same coin, sharing many of the same themes. One, however, is an epic tale spiced with comedy, while the other is a hilarious romp through the teachings of Buddhism. As a martial arts classic, *The Water Margin* must surely triumph, based as it is on one of the fundamental martial texts. *Monkey*, however is undeniably more fun.

Conclusion: Century of the Dragon

At first glance, the films that make up the martial arts genre do not form a cohesive whole. They can be more easily classed as action, fantasy, sci-fi, comedy and even romance, all recognisable categories in their own right. The common focus on traditional, and not so traditional, Asian fighting styles makes for a very loose classification, which could be applied to a host of films from *The Manchurian Candidate* to *Charlie's Angels* by way of *The Matrix*. These are not, of course, martial arts films, as any fan knows. The main parts are played by actors with no real martial arts training. While they may use fight choreographers from Hong Kong, the combat is far from traditional and the action sequences are secondary to the plot, rather than being the driving force of the movies.

So how should true kick flicks be identified? It is obvious that *Young Master* is a martial arts film, but what about the Japanese sci-fi action adventure *Returner*, with its gun-fu/kung fu mix? They don't even all include kicking – Zatôichi might bare his legs, but he never deigns to lift them. Actors posing as martial artists, made-up styles of fighting and long periods without any action proliferate in *bona fide* martial arts movies, so what makes them different from films where the hero just happens to know some kung fu because it looks cool?

On closer examination this incredibly diverse genre is seen to grow from a single set of roots, just as karate is formed from the mastery of a few fundamental techniques. The comedies, tragedies and mindless action films are all woven into a broader pattern of shared influences and an almost incestuous degree of mutual referencing. Stunts are borrowed, developed, made more dangerous and then copied again elsewhere. The themes are often repeated. And all of the films are defined by the martial arts they employ.

The magic swordplay of the wuxia pian creates a fantasy world in which opponents run up walls and balance on bamboo branches. Life is lived by the rules of the martial world, and its mystical precepts are woven into the plot-lines of *Dragon Gate Inn* and *Crouching Tiger, Hidden Dragon*. In *One-Armed*

Swordsman, *Ong-Bak* and *Kickboxer* the brutal, realistic fighting is reflected in grittier stories, darker films and more violent action. Mysticism is replaced by the blood, sweat and tears of physical training. Both philosophies are embraced in *36th Chamber of Shaolin*, in which the combination of the Buddhist spirituality of the monks and the need for endless practise of fundamental skills takes up the majority of the film. In Japanese samurai films, such as *Zatôichi the Outlaw*, the heroes are restrained within the code of honour of the ancient fighting art of bushido. The wu da pian comedies of the 80s, epitomised by *Project A*, draw inspiration for their slapstick humour from the insane acrobatics of their opera-trained stars. The *Kill Bill* films, as absolute martial arts tribute movies, take all of these principles and twist them together. The Bride is rarely seen without her katana, relentless kung fu training helps her punch her way out of a coffin and she kills Bill with an ancient Chinese technique known to few and taught to fewer.

The fighting itself is more formalised than in other action genres. Beyond the obvious differences between wild gun battles, during which sprays of bullets rarely hit the impervious hero, and close-range hand-to-hand or traditional weapons combat, there are accepted forms that have developed over time and become a classifying staple of the martial arts genre. The heroes must battle their way through levels of adversaries, who become more skilled as the film goes on. Being ridiculously outnumbered and winning through superior skill is a guaranteed situation for any martial character. And it all culminates with the one-on-one showdown between hero and nemesis.

As well as being shaped by the philosophies they expound, the seminal, art-house and blockbusting films dissected in this book share a series of themes that define the genre beyond the fighting. These include common, popular storytelling devices, but there are several that are unique to the genre. It is the combination of these that makes a martial arts film. The outsider, a hero beyond the reach of the law who uses deadly skills to fight for righteous causes, is a familiar figure in any type of film. In some superhero movies, they can even fly. But if they're swinging a sword and wearing long, flowing robes while they do it, chances are it's a wuxia pian. The martial tournament has a parallel in the endless sports films churned out by Hollywood, but compresses the entire plot concept of this predictable pap into a small section of a kick flick. The heroes lose a lot, then win in the end.

Revenge is a popular motive for quests, but in kick flicks you can guarantee that vengeance is being sought on behalf of a wronged family member. Or, more outrageously, a murdered or dishonoured teacher. The unbreakable relationship between student and sifu, which only the most dastardly of villains (Elle Driver, Han) would betray, is unique to martial arts films. A cynical viewer might look with consternation upon the interdependent relationship between Daniel and Mr Miyagi, but anyone versed in the ways of the kick flick will recognise it as the devotion required to earn the right to be taught, and the respect to teach. *Kill Bill*, in true Tarantino style, emphasises the importance of this relationship in the genre by subverting it. The heroine has an affair with her teacher, upsetting the traditional balance of master and disciple. The consequences and ultimately the punishments for this blasphemy are Bill's betrayal of The Bride and, in turn, her assassination of him.

Martial arts films have a unique foundation in Asian belief systems, particularly Buddhism, Taoism and Confucianism, and in Eastern medicine, with its emphasis on chi, the life energy found in all things. This sets them apart from other types of film, including the various schools of Asian cinema, which more often focus on modern life or the historic epic. The expounding of various ancient philosophies, to greater or lesser levels of seriousness, is a necessary part of the genre, as is the acceptance that martial powers can be gained through meditation. Proponents draw on the chi present in every body and thing and manifest it in the ability to fly, move with superhuman speed, throw bolts of lightning and fall several stories before getting up and walking away.

These elements combine to create a genre with its own unique draw, which has been appealing to audiences for the better part of 75 years. Since the early tales of martial chivalry, kick flicks and heroic swordplay films have captured the imagination of viewers around the world. By constantly reinventing themselves, while retaining the successful facets of the formula, martial arts films have held audiences attention, experiencing a form of renaissance in each decade of their development. From tales firmly rooted in the classics of Chinese literature through blood-drenched sword-wielding warriors to action comedy, the genre has grown and taken its audience with it. No aspect of the original films has ever been left completely behind, as the successes of the modern wuxia reveal, but the genre has expanded into the international heartland of movieworld: Hollywood. Martial arts films have won a new generation of fans and finally appear to be leaping, kicking and screaming out of the cult arena into the mainstream. It may prove to be a fad, and perhaps in the future they will be overtaken by sci-fi tragedy or romantic bloodletting, but for the time being it is a situation to rejoice in, as it encourages both the production of new movies and the rerelease of genre classics.

After two decades of closure, the film lots of Shaw Brothers are open for business once again. The company has a new studio in Hong Kong and is launching itself back into kick flick production after years of concentrating on the small screen. Planned since 1998, the studio has been built at a cost of approximately $130 million. It includes five sound stages, a state-of-the-art post-production centre, a 400-seat auditorium which doubles as the largest dubbing final mix theatre in the world, and a colour lab that allows the creation of digital graphics. This enormous investment is a resounding response to the international demand for martial arts movies. Where better to make them than the spiritual home of chopsocky, which produced so many of the genre's defining films in the 60s, 70s and 80s: Hong Kong? And who better to helm the resurgence of the Kowloon kick flick than the next generation of Shaws?

Starring in the martial movies of the twenty-first century are a cast of actors who have served their time in cult classics and are now taking on the international box-office. Jet Li is spreading the word of wushu through the studios of America as well as China, in English as often as Mandarin. Jackie Chan, the undisputed king of the kick flick, is reaching the end of his action career, due to a much-battered body rather than any failure of will, but his experience and the innovative touch that has scored him an uninterrupted succession of hits since the late 70s remain. Michelle Yeoh has been polishing her skills for years, and now has a choice of roles in the type of film she was made to perform in. The likes of Tony Leung and Maggie Cheung are receiving the recognition they deserve, while a new generation of actors is lining up to take on the challenges of acting while fighting.

Some 30 years after the death of a martial icon, his name is still entwined in the ongoing growth of the genre. Among many other reverent epithets, Tony Jaa, iron-limbed star of *Ong-Bak*, is being called the next Bruce Lee. It is an easy comparison to make: both have made films that utilise real martial artists, and are actors of the brooding-looks-and-little-dialogue school. Their brand of brutal action, typified by martial arts in their purest form, barely tempered to suit the camera, is at the root of what makes kick flicks so successful. All the CGI in the world can't make up for the thrill of seeing on the big screen what the human body is capable of when trained in the ancient martial arts of Asia. That is why these films have continued to be made and replayed down the decades. As Ang Lee has said, 'This is a genre that will never die.'

Index of Quotations

59   'The most significant . . .', Pollard, Mark, *One-Armed Swordsman*, from www.kungfucinema.com

Rumble in Hong Kong: The Golden Age of Kick Flicks
75   'Stylistic shoddiness of . . .', Tarratt, Margaret, 'Enter the Dragon' in *Films & Filming*, March 1974
87   'At that time . . .', Gordon Liu from *The Art of Action: Martial Arts in the Movies*, Starrz Encore Entertainment LLC, 2002
87   'So what did . . .', Gordon Liu from *The Art of Action: Martial Arts in the Movies*, Starrz Encore Entertainment LLC, 2002
87   'I wanted to . . .', Liu Chia-Liang from *The Art of Action: Martial Arts in the Movies*, Starrz Encore Entertainment LLC, 2002
88   'The best kung . . .', Anonymous, 'The 36th Chamber of Shaolin' in *Variety*, 11 September 1978
95   'I rarely used . . .', Lee Hoi San from *Project A* Platinum Edition DVD, Hong Kong Legends, 2002
99   'I hate violence . . .', Jackie Chan from *The Art of Action: Martial Arts in the Movies*, Starrz Encore Entertainment LLC, 2002
108 'When you are . . .', Yam Sai-Kwoon from *Once Upon a Time in China*, Hong Kong Legends, 2000
109 'I'm a great . . .', Tsui Hark from Ange Hwang, 'The Irresistible: Hong Kong Movie Once Upon a Time in China Series – an Extensive Interview With Director/Producer Tsui Hark' in *Asian Cinema*, vol. 10, no. 1, Fall 1998
112 'It connects to . . .', Tsui Hark from Ange Hwang, 'The Irresistible: Hong Kong Movie Once Upon a Time in China Series – an Extensive Interview With Director/Producer Tsui Hark' in *Asian Cinema*, vol. 10, no. 1, Fall 1998
112 'You have this . . .', Tsui Hark from Ange Hwang, 'The Irresistible: Hong Kong Movie Once Upon a Time in China Series – an Extensive Interview With Director/Producer Tsui Hark' in Asian Cinema, vol. 10, no. 1, Fall 1998

Return of the Deadly Blade: Modern Asian Classics
127 'He'd maybe only . . .', Yuen Woo-Ping from Husband, Stuart, 'Come Fly with Me' in The *Guardian*, 21 December 2000

146 'Zhang lacked something . . .', Maggie Cheung from
   Macnab, Geoffrey, ' "I'm Not Interested in Politics",'
   interview with Zhang Yimou from *Guardian Unlimited*, 17
   December 2004

146 'My favourites are . . .', Zhang Yimou from Reid, Dr Craig,
   'A Cut Above' in *Cinefantastique*, vol. 36, no. 6,
   December/January 2004/5

146 'It seems to . . .', Zhang Yimou from Reid, Dr Craig, 'A Cut
   Above' in *Cinefantastique*, vol. 36, no. 6, December/January
   2004/5

155 'What I really . . .', Zhang Yimou from Reid, Dr Craig, 'A
   Cut Above' in *Cinefantastique*, vol. 36, no. 6,
   December/January 2004/5

155 'Bamboo forest fights . . .', Zhang Yimou from Reid, Dr
   Craig, 'A Cut Above' in *Cinefantastique*, vol. 36, no. 6,
   December/January 2004/5

155 'Those good chase . . .', Zhang Yimou from Reid, Dr Craig,
   'A Cut Above' in *Cinefantastique*, vol. 36, no. 6,
   December/January 2004/5

156 'Wires can easily . . .', Zhang Yimou from Macnab,
   Geoffrey, ' "I'm Not Interested in Politics",' interview with
   Zhang Yimou from *Guardian Unlimited*, 17 December 2004

156 'My goal is . . .', Zhang Yimou from Reid, Dr Craig, 'A Cut
   Above' in *Cinefantastique*, vol. 36, no. 6, December/January
   2004/5

157 'We burned incense . . .', Zhang Yimou from Reid, Dr Craig,
   'A Cut Above' in *Cinefantastique*, vol. 36, no. 6,
   December/January 2004/5

Exit the Dragon, Enter the Tiger: Hollywood

164 'American actors aren't . . .', Yuen Woo-Ping from Husband,
   Stuart, 'Come Fly with Me' in the *Guardian*, 21 December
   2000

164 'I wouldn't call . . .', Yuen Woo-Ping from Husband, Stuart,
   'Come Fly with Me' in the *Guardian*, 21 December 2000

178 'I was really . . .', Jean-Claude Van Damme from Morgan,
   Susan, 'Sensei ni Rei' in *Interview*, vol. 21, no. 3, March
   1991

180 'It's all pure . . .', Anonymous, 'Kickboxer' in *Screen
   International*, no. 718, 19 August 1989

Snake in the Eagle's Shadow: The Rest of the World

207 'Since it was . . .', Kim Jae-won from Paquet, Darcy, 'Case Study: Volcano High' in *Screen International*, no. 1359, 14 June 2002

208 'A timid, James . . .' Hunter, Allan, 'Manic Manga Mish-Mash Has Cult Potential' in *Screen International*, no, 1370, 30 August 2002

209 'He does things . . .', Kim Jae-won from Paquet, Darcy, 'Case Study: Volcano High' in *Screen International*, no. 1359, 14 June 2002

210 'We knew that . . .', Kim Jae-won from Paquet, Darcy, 'Case Study: Volcano High' in *Screen International*, no. 1359, 14 June 2002

211 'No-one else . . .', Kim Kae-gyun from Paquet, Darcy, 'Case Study: Volcano High' in *Screen International*, no. 1359, 14 June 2002

211 'We originally planned . . .', Kim Jae-won from Paquet, Darcy, 'Case Study: Volcano High' in *Screen International*, no. 1359, 14 June 2002

213 'Contemporary martial arts . . .', Kim Jae-won from Paquet, Darcy, 'Case Study: Volcano High' in *Screen International*, no. 1359, 14 June 2002

213 'This film will . . .', Kim Kae-gyun from Paquet, Darcy, 'Case Study: Volcano High' in *Screen International*, no. 1359, 14 June 2002

221 'Muay thai boran . . .', Tony Jaa from Anderson, Jason, 'Jaa Rules' in *Eye Weekly*, 10 February 2005

221 'We just wanted . . .', Tony Jaa from Anderson, Jason, 'Jaa Rules' in *Eye Weekly*, 10 February 2005

221 'We wanted people . . .', Tony Jaa from Anderson, Jason, 'Jaa Rules' in *Eye Weekly*, 10 February 2005

Conclusion

261 'This is a . . .', Ang Lee from *The Art of Action: Martial Arts in the Movies*, Starrz Encore Entertainment LLC, 2002

Bibliography

Adair, Gilbert, 'The Karate Kid' in *Monthly Film Bulletin*, vol. 51, no. 608, September 1984

Anderson, Jason, 'Jaa Rules' in *Eye Weekly*, 10 February 2005

Ange Hwang, 'The Irresistible: Hong Kong Movie Once Upon a Time in China Series – an Extensive Interview With Director/Producer Tsui Hark' in *Asian Cinema*, vol. 10, no. 1, Fall 1998

Anonymous, *Berlin Film Festival Catalogue*, 2003

Anonymous, 'Dragon Gate Inn' in *Monthly Film Bulletin*, vol. 44, no. 517, February 1977

Anonymous, *Green Hornet* from www.fiftiesweb.com

Anonymous, 'Kickboxer' in *Screen International*, no. 718, 19 August 1989

Anonymous, 'One-Armed Swordsman' in *DVD Times*, 2004

Anonymous, *One-Armed Swordsman* from www.hkfilm.net

Anonymous, 'Return of the One-Armed Swordsman' in *DVD Times*, 2004

Anonymous, 'The Karate Kid' in *Motion Picture Product Digest*, vol. 12, no. 1, 4 July 1984

Anonymous, 'The Karate Kid' in *Screen International*, no. 460, 25 August 1984

Anonymous, *The 36th Chamber of Shaolin* from www.lovehkfilm.com

Anonymous, 'The 36th Chamber of Shaolin' in *Variety*, 11 September 1978

Anonymous, *Water Margin* from www.chinapage.com

Anonymous, 'Zatoichi the Outlaw' in *DVD Times*, 5 December 2002

Auty, Daniel, *Ong-Bak* from www.thespinningimage.co.uk

Bordwell, David, *Planet Hong Kong: Popular Cinema and the Art of Entertainment*, Harvard University Press, 2000

Bradshaw, Peter, 'Crouching Tiger, Hidden Dragon' in the *Guardian*, 5 January 2001

Bradshaw, Peter, 'House of Flying Daggers' in the *Guardian*, 24 December 2004

Brooks, Xan, 'Crouching Tiger, Hidden Dragon' from *Guardian Unlimited*, 5 January 2001

Caro, Jason, 'Crouching Tiger, Hidden Dragon' in *Film Review*, no. 602, February 2001

Carutthers, Avril, *Ong-Bak*, from www.movie-vault.com, 14 February 2005

Chen, Pauline, 'Hero' in *Cineaste*, vol. 30, no. 1, Winter 2004

Chen Xihe, 'On the Father Figures in Zhang Yimou's Films From Red Sorghum to Hero' in *Asian Cinema*, vol. 15, no. 2, Fall/Winter 2004

Cheshire, Ellen, *Ang Lee*, Pocket Essentials Film, 2001

Chute, David, *Heroic Grace: The Chinese Martial Arts Film*, UCLA Film and Television Archive/Hong Kong Economic and Trade Office in San Francisco, 2003

Cole, Angie, 'Let Off the Leash' in the *Independent*, 7 August 2005

Day, Martin, *The Water Margin*, series notes

Ebert, Roger, 'The Karate Kid' in *Chicago Sun-Times*, 1 January 1984

Fainaru, Dan, 'Ong-Bak: Muay Thai Warrior' in *Screen International*, no. 1428, 7 November 2003

Foster, Dave 'Project A' in *DVD Times*, 2002

Flora, Mark, *Whasango* from www.kfccinema.com, 8 May 2002

French, Philip, 'I Get a Kick out of Kung Fu' in the *Guardian*, 7 January 2001

French, Philip, 'Well, Mao Would Have Liked It' from *Guardian Unlimited*, 26 September 2004

Gaetjens, Warwick, *Volcano High* from *www.dvdanswers.com*

Garcia, Roger, 'Alive and Kicking: The Kung Fu Film Is a Legend' in *Bright Lights Film Journal*, issue 13, 2001

Glaessner, Verina, 'Kickboxer' in *Monthly Film Bulletin*, vol. 56, no. 668, September 1989

Hicks, Chris, 'Kickboxer' in *Desert Morning News*, 14 September 1989

Hunt, Leon, *Kung Fu Cult Masters: From Bruce Lee to Crouching Tiger*, Wallflower Press, 2003

Hunter, Allan, 'Manic Manga Mish-Mash Has Cult Potential' in *Screen International*, no. 1370, 30 August 2002

Husband, Stuart, 'Come Fly with Me' in the *Guardian*, 21 December 2000

Jones, Carl, *King Boxer: The Story of the First International Kung Fu Movie Hit* from www.dragonsden.co.uk, 2001

Kenny, Simon B, *Bruce Lee*, Pocket Essentials Film, 2001

Kuo Wei Tehen, John, 'East Through the Looking Glass: A Discussion on Asian Americans in Hollywood' in *Cinevue*, September 1992

Kurland, H 'The Web of Tai Chi Chuan Parts 1 & 2' in *Karate/Kung Fu Illustrated*, July & August 1998

Le Blanc, Michelle and Odell, Colin, *Jackie Chan*, Pocket Essentials Film, 2003

Lee, Bruce, *Bruce Lee: Artist of Life*, edited by John Little, Tuttle Publishing, 2001

Lee, Susie J, 'Once Upon a Time in China' in *Asian Cinema*, vol. 15, no. 1, Spring/Summer 2004

Levie, Matthew, 'Crouching Tiger, Hidden Dragon: The Art Film Hidden Inside the Chop-Socky Flick' in *Bright Lights Film Journal*, issue 33, July 2001

Machiyama, Tomohiro, *Kill Everyone*, 2003

Machiyama, Tomohiro, 'The Japattack Interview: Quentin Tarantino' in *Eiga Hi-Ho [Movie Treasures]*, 2003

Malcolm, Paul, *Heroic Grace: The Chinese Martial Arts Film*, UCLA Film and Television Archive/Hong Kong Economic and Trade Office in San Francisco, 2003

Michaels, Phil, *The Karate Kid* from www.thespinningimage.co.uk

Mikhailov, Danil, *The Water Margin* from Wushu Scholar, www.kungfu-taichi.com

Minns, Adam, 'Foreign Language Films Take on the Popcorn Crowd' in *Screen International*, no. 1472, 15 October 2004

Morris, Gary, 'Beautiful Beast: Ang Lee's Crouching Tiger, Hidden Dragon' in *Bright Lights Film Journal*, issue 31, 2001

Morris, Gary, 'Tsui Hark's The Blade in *Bright Lights Film Journal*, issue 18, March 1997

Odham, Lisa and Hoover, Michael, *City on Fire: Hong Kong Cinema*, Verso, 1999

Pacquet, Darcy, 'Case Study: Volcano High' in *Screen International*, no. 1359, 14 June 2002

Pendleton, David, *Heroic Grace: The Chinese Martial Arts Film*, UCLA Film and Television Archive/Hong Kong Economic and Trade Office in San Francisco, 2003

Percy, James, *Zatôichi* from www.kungfucinema.com

Plath, James, 'The Karate Kid Collection' in *DVD Town*, 30 January 2005

Pollard, Mark, *Jet Li and the Essence of Hero*, from www.kungfucinema.com, 2004

Pollard, Mark, *One-Armed Swordsman* from www.kungfucinema.com

Pollard, Mark, *Ong-Bak* from www.kungfucinema.com

Pollard, Mark, *The 36th Chamber of Shaolin* from www.kungfucinema.com, 2004

Pollard, Mark, *The Water Margin* from www.kungfucinema.com

Pollard, Mark, *Wong Fei Hung: The Man and the Legend* from www.kungfucinema.com, 2001

Pollard, Mark, *Wuxia Pian Introduction* from www.kungfucinema.com

Pollard, Mark, *Zatoichi the Outlaw* from www.kungfucinema.com

Profancik, Eric, 'Kickboxer' in *DVD Verdict*, 26 January 2004

Pulver, Andrew, 'Tiger, Tiger Burning Bright' in the *Guardian*, 3 November 2000

Rayns, Tony, 'Enter the Dragon' in *Monthly Film Bulletin*, vol. 41, 1974

Rayns, Tony, 'Laying Foundations: Dragon Gate Inn' in *Cinemaya*, no. 39/40, Winter/Spring, 1997/8

Rayns, Tony, *Kung Fu Comedy: The Genre Deceased* from www.dragonsdenuk.com, 2001

Rayns, Tony *Wang Yu: The Agony and the Ecstasy* in *A Study of the Hong Kong Martial Arts Film*, 4th Hong Kong International Film Festival, 1980

Rayns, Tony, *Yuen Biao: Little Brother, Big Star* from www.dragonsdenuk.com, 2001

Reid, Dr Craig, 'A Cut Above' in *Cinefantastique*, vol. 36, no. 6, December/January 2004/5

Reid, Dr Craig, 'Hong Kong Calling' in *Cinefantastique*, October/November 2003

Rich, B Ruby, 'Day of the Woman' in *Sight & Sound*, June 2004

Richards, John, 'Once Upon a Time in China' in *Wasted Life*, 2002

Rose, Steve, 'Hero' in the *Guardian*, 24 September 2004

Rose, Steve, ' "The Film is so Slow – it's Like Grandma Telling Stories" ' from *Guardian Unlimited*, 13 February 2001

Russell, Jamie, 'Ong-Bak' in *Sight & Sound*, vol. 15, no. 5, May 2005

Rynning, Roald and Mottram, James, 'Ang Tough' in *Film Review*, no. 602, February 2001

Schuchardt, Richard, *The Green Hornet* from www.dvdanswers.com

Sek Kei, 'Achievement and Crisis: Hong Kong Cinema in the '80s' in *Bright Lights Film Journal*, Issue 13, 1994

Sloane, Judy, 'A Little Bit of Violence Does You Good, Kill Bill'/Vivica A Fox feature in *Film Review*, special edition, no. 50, Oscars Issue

Sloane, Judy, 'Eye for an Eye, Kill Bill'/Daryl Hannah feature in *Film Review*, special edition, no. 50, Oscars Issue

Sloane, Judy, 'Partner in Crime, Kill Bill'/Lawrence Bender feature in *Film Review*, special edition, no. 50, Oscars Issue

Sloane, Judy, 'The Bride Laid Bare, Kill Bill'/Uma Thurman feature in *Film Review*, special edition, no. 50, Oscars Issue

Smith, Adam, 'Hero' in *Radio Times*, 21–27 May 2005

Soh Yun-Huei, *Volcano High* from www.filmasia.net

Stephens, Chuck, 'The Whole She-Bang' in *Film Comment*, vol. 40, no. 4, July/August 2004

Tarratt, Margaret, 'Enter the Dragon' in *Films & Filming*, March 1974

Thomas, Brian, *Videohound's Dragon: Asian Action & Cult Flicks*, Visible Ink Press, 2003

Thomas, Brian, 'Zatôichi the Outlaw' in *Cinescape*, 11 March 2003

To, Tony, 'Thirty Years of Golden Harvest' in *Variety*, 26 June 2000

Valentin, Mel, *Volcano High* from www.movievault.com, 5 February 2005

Various, *The Making of Martial Arts Films – As Told by Filmmakers and Stars*, Hong Kong Provisional Urban Council, 1999

Watts, Jonathan, 'China Rubbishes its Oscar Favourite' in the *Guardian*, 18 December 2004

Watts, Jonathan, 'Snow White and the Seven Kung Fu Monks: Disney Sets Sights on China' in the *Guardian*, 5 July 2005

Wheadon, Robert, 'The Oldtime Radio Show The Green Hornet' in *Pagewise*, 2002

White, Nikki, 'Monkey Magic' in *Multiverse Fanzine*, no. 6, November 1981

Williams, Tony, 'Under "Western Eyes": The Personal Odyssey of Huang Fei-Hong in Once Upon a Time in China' in *Cinema Journal*, vol. 40, no. 1, Fall 2000

Wu, George, *Ong-Bak: The Thai Warrior* from www.culturevulture.net

Yin, Eric, *An Introduction to the Wuxia Genre*, 2001, from www.heroic-cinema.com

Yip Man, *History of Wing Chun* from the WingChunKuen Archives

Zigelstein, Jesse, *Heroic Grace: The Chinese Martial Arts Film*, UCLA Film and Television Archive/Hong Kong Economic and Trade Office in San Francisco, 2003

Interviews

Ang Lee, *The Art of Action: Martial Arts in the Movies*, Starrz Encore Entertainment LLC, 2002

Ang Lee and James Schamus, the *Guardian*/National Film Theatre, 7 November 2000

David Carradine, interviewed by Patrick Macias in *Eiga Hi-Ho [Movie Treasures]*, 2004

Dick Wei, *The Art of Action: Martial Arts in the Movies*, Starrz Encore Entertainment LLC, 2002

Gordon Liu, *The Art of Action: Martial Arts in the Movies*, Starrz Encore Entertainment LLC, 2002

Jackie Chan, *The Art of Action: Martial Arts in the Movies*, Starrz Encore Entertainment LLC, 2002

Jean-Claude Van Damme, interviewed by Susan Morgan in *Interview*, vol. 21, no. 3, March 1991

Lee Hoi-San, *Project A*, Platinum Edition DVD, Hong Kong Legends, 2002

Liu Chia-Liang, *The Art of Action: Martial Arts in the Movies*, Starrz Encore Entertainment LLC, 2002

Michael Lai, *The Art of Action: Martial Arts in the Movies*, Starrz Encore Entertainment LLC, 2002

Tsui Hark, interviewed by Ange Hwang in *Asian Cinema*, vol. 10, no. 1, Fall 1998

Yam Sai-Kwoon, *Once Upon a Time in China*, Hong Kong Legends, 2000

Zhang Yimou, interviewed by Geoffrey MacNab, from *Guardian Unlimited*, 17 December 2004

Index